ASE Guide to Research in Science Education

Edited by John Oversby

The **Association**
for **Science Education**

Promoting Excellence in Science Teaching and Learning

Published by:
The Association for Science Education, College Lane, Hatfield, Herts AL10 9AA

©The Association for Science Education 2012

ISBN: 978 0 86357 429 0

Design and layout by Commercial Campaigns

Printed by Ashford Colour Press, Gosport, Hampshire

Contents

Section 1 Thematic review of research in science education

Section 2 Doing research

About the authors

Amanda Berry is an Associate Professor in Science Education in the Faculty of Education at Monash University, Australia, and Associate Editor of *Research in Science Education* (RISE) journal. Amanda's research interests in teachers' professional learning, conceptual change and the development of pedagogical content knowledge (PCK) grew from her initial experiences as a high school science teacher, researching her classroom practice and her students' science learning. Amanda has authored numerous publications, including three Handbook chapters related to science teacher learning and PCK.

Paul Black is Professor Emeritus of Science Education at King's College London. He has made many contributions in both curriculum development and in assessment research. He has served on advisory groups of the USA National Research Council and as visiting professor at Stanford University. His work on formative assessment with colleagues at King's has had widespread impact.

Anna Cleaves was a science teacher for most of her career, in the last decade of which she became a researcher and teacher educator. She has worked in Kenya, Peru and Ghana. She is interested in many aspects of teaching and learning including the use of ICT, practical work, adaptations to new specifications, evolution and pupil choice.

Sibel Erduran is Professor of Science Education at University of Bristol where she has taught PGCE Science and coordinates the MSc Programme in Science and Education. She completed her higher education in the USA at Northwestern, Cornell and Vanderbilt Universities, and taught high school chemistry and middle school science in northern Cyprus. She is currently a Visiting Professor at Kristianstad University in Sweden. She has had guest editorship of *School Science Review* and is an editor for the *International Journal of Science Education*. Her research interests include the nature of scientific inquiry, discourse and argumentation.

Peter Fensham, the first professor of Science Education in Australia, led a large group of science educators at Monash University for 25 years, who worked extensively in developing countries and made many contributions to the development of research in Science Education. Now Emeritus Professor he has a position as Adjunct Professor at Queensland University of Technology. Served as an advisor to both TIMSS and PISA.

Wynne Harlen, OBE, has been a science educator and researcher and member of the ASE throughout her working life and its President for the year 2009. She was Sydney Jones Professor of Science Education at Liverpool University 1985–1990 and then Director of the Scottish Council for Research in Education until 1999. She now works from her home in Scotland as a consultant to various UK and international projects. Her research activity has focused on progress in learning science, student assessment and curriculum development and evaluation.

Chris Harrison taught in schools for 13 years before joining King's College London to run the Biology PGCE. She began working with Paul Black and Dylan Wiliam on the first long-term study of Assessment for Learning in UK schools following the publication of *Inside the Black Box*. She now leads the Assessment for Learning research group at King's as well as pursuing research interests in thinking skills and professional learning. Chris has an international reputation for the seamless way she manages to integrate research and classroom practice and this is because she still believes that teaching is at the heart of most good learning experiences.

Jane Johnston is a Reader in Education at Bishop Grosseteste University College, Lincoln, and Academic Coordinator for the MA in Education. She works extensively, both nationally and internationally, in three distinct areas: early childhood studies, primary science education and practitioner research. She passionately believes that effective research is that which impacts on practice and provision and this is reflected in her publications and the status of Chartered Science Teacher.

Virginia Kearton is a member of the ASE Research Committee. She was Head of Science for 14 years at Court Moor School, Fleet, Hampshire, a comprehensive secondary school for students from 11 to 16 years. She has taught in two sixth form colleges in Hampshire and been a tutor-counsellor for the Open University. She has completed two Best Practice Research scholarships for the DfE and is interested in practitioner research, working with the Palava group, based at the University of Reading.

Brenda Keogh started her career as a primary teacher. She also worked as a lab technician, advisory teacher and National Curriculum consultant. **Stuart Naylor** started his career as a secondary teacher. He also worked as a lab technician and advisory teacher and taught in the USA. Brenda and Stuart both have extensive experience in teacher education and as researchers, writers, publishers, consultants and INSET providers. Now working as Millgate House Education, they have a reputation for innovative publications, thought-provoking continuous professional development and creative ways of enhancing teaching, learning and assessment.

Vanessa Kind is currently Senior Lecturer in Education at Durham, working primarily in research on pedagogical content knowledge and subject matter knowledge for chemistry teaching. Vanessa trained originally as a chemistry teacher at the Insititute of Education, University of London. Her initial research was in chemistry misconceptions completing first an MA (Insititute of Education) and then a doctorate (University of York) probing these in secondary-aged students. Vanessa worked as Lecturer in Science Education at the Institute of Education from 1997–2002, including an appointment as the Royal Society of Chemistry's Teacher Fellow. She has taught in schools in London and Hull in the UK and was headteacher of an international school in Norway immediately prior to joining Durham's School of Education in 2005.

Debbie McGregor is a Professor at the University of Wolverhampton. She has been involved in education for over 20 years. She has led on a variety of science education research and professional development projects in both primary and secondary education during that time. Her current passions include exploring how learning theory can enhance practice, the development of thinking skills, helping teachers appreciate How Science Works and investigating effective science lessons from learners' perspectives.

John Oversby is a Lecturer in Science Education at the University of Reading, He was for most of his career a school teacher in Ghana and the UK. He is presently International Coordinator for the Changing with the Climate Comenius Network. His research interests include chemical education, modelling, teacher education, history and philosophy in science teaching, and climate change education.

Michael Reiss is Deputy Director and Professor of Science Education at the Institute of Education, University of London, Chief Executive of Science Learning Centre London, Director of the Salters-Nuffield Advanced Biology Project and an Academician of the Academy of Social Sciences. The former Director of Education at the Royal Society, he has written extensively about curricula, pedagogy and assessment in science education and has directed a very large number of research, evaluation and consultancy projects over the past 20 years funded by UK research councils, government departments, charities and international agencies.

Penny Robotham is Head of Science and Head of Chemistry at Alcester Grammar School. Her role includes linking with other schools as a Lead Teacher in pedagogy presentations. She has been active in research, especially through the Reading University's teacher researcher group, and as a member of the ASE Research Committee. She regularly makes presentations at regional and national meetings, and contributes to research articles for *Education in Science*.

Keith S Taber is Senior Lecturer in Science Education at the University of Cambridge, where he is part of the management team for the Masters Programme in Education and teaches research methods. He has previously taught sciences in secondary and further education, and was the Royal Society of Chemistry teacher fellow for 2000–2001. His research interests are mainly focused on aspects of student thinking and learning in science.

Rob Toplis taught science and chemistry in urban, rural and suburban secondary schools for over 25 years, with both departmental and whole school responsibilities. He is now Senior Lecturer in Secondary Science Education at Brunel University where he teaches and supervises on doctoral, masters and Postgraduate Certificate in Education (PGCert) courses. He has carried out research, both individually and collaboratively, in the main areas of: the science curriculum and curriculum change; conceptual understanding and modelling in chemistry education; initial teacher education including the use of ICT in science classrooms; and teaching evolution.

Introduction

The Research Committee of the Association for Science Education (ASE) commends the *ASE Guide to Research in Science Education* as a collaborative effort, including many outside the committee in the UK and beyond. Published at a time when the future of science education in higher education in the UK is uncertain, the book reflects our commitment to the invaluable contribution of research to teaching and learning at all levels, and in all places. Some may feel that the place of research in science education is self-evident, but our experience is that it is not. Research is central to that discipline taking its place alongside other academic studies. It aims to establish a body of theory that underpins a strong framework of causal and narrative explanation, confident prediction, and a professional language of discourse among researchers and practitioners. In short, research is an essential component of being an authoritative profession. In all professions, theory and research bind all committed members together in a learning community, where the outcomes of research may be useful and serve the function of a base for reflection. Research helps the community move from trial and error, in which the wheel is constantly being reinvented but the carriage stays still, to a progressive form. In this progressive form, trust in published rigorous and valid investigation enables us to 'sit on the shoulders of giants and see further'.

The editorial team, consisting of John Oversby as editor, Jane Johnston, Wynne Harlen, Deborah MacGregor, and Rob Toplis, has produced a consensus view of the substantial, robust, rigorous and valid empirical evidence across the wide range of science education research carried out in the world. As a team, we have gained tremendous insights into the quantity and quality of science education research that is available, and into the challenges of reviewing and interpreting this material for our readers. Writing a book, or part of a book, is not only for the readers, but for the writers as they faithfully reconstruct the evidence into a coherent story as well as they can. As we seek to recruit and rejuvenate the community of researchers, especially those conducting practitioner research in their own settings, we commend this writing experience as much a part of CPD as devising the research and collecting data.

The idea for the book came from the ASE Research Committee, most positively endorsed by Derek Bell, then ASE Chief Executive, and appropriately supported by funding from the Ros Driver Trust Fund, to whom we are most grateful. The idea was then taken forward most enthusiastically by the Research Committee, who chose to adopt an approach of a community of equals to design the book, convened by one who would be the editor.

The range of evidence we have called upon has highlighted for us the paucity of research in some fields. As an example, we have not been able to include much on teaching science to learners with visual and physical disabilities. Perhaps some researchers will take up the challenge of this topic. We have also had to make judgments about the rigour, validity and reliability of evidence. No doubt, in ten years time, future authors may make quite different decisions! The authors have, inevitably, used their expertise to stamp their personal values in their writing. Within the bounds of some coherence, we have encouraged independence but readers will be easily able to see that this is an edited volume, with the strengths and disadvantages that this brings.

Readers will also recognise that there are few clear-cut messages. Science education research can be regarded as a fuzzy discipline, where often the best we can say is that this kind of teaching usually works well in these circumstances and with these classes. This is inevitable in such a human endeavour as teaching, with such a wide range of teachers and contexts. We are sometimes much clearer in what does not work and we remain surprised that little notice is taken of this research. There are also some topics attracting attention at particular times in science teaching. A recent one is a strong focus on Science, Technology, Engineering and Mathematics (STEM), highly promoted by the learned scientific societies and by scientific industry. This research is then influenced by the needs of these interested bodies and sponsors, for example, such as whether interventions to increase the numbers choosing science as an option, rather than a more general motivation towards science irrespective of which career is chosen. As long as the researchers make clear the purposes of the research, and the influence of specific interested parties, as they usually do, then the research is legitimate. Being transparent about all aspects of the research is essential to ensuring validity.

Much has been written about the perceived gap between research and practice. A trawl through papers on this topic in the research literature shows that nursing education is the largest field of study concerning this gap! However, anecdotal evidence suggests that many teachers of science are also reporting this gap. Some research has obviously affected science education, although it is often very difficult to track back the links to provide clear evidence. As an example, the whole field of formative assessment has been strongly influenced by the writings and actions of colleagues at King's College London. They have carried out empirical research, and evaluated the whole range of research. Not only have they published the outcomes in peer-reviewed journals, but transformed these into professional articles, and conducted workshops and in-service training. Even so, some teachers will still claim that this work has had no effect, and they may well be correct for their own context.

It is important to know why a teaching method works, however imperfectly, so that we can rationalise from the patterns we discern. Such causal discoveries are central to implementing change that is embedded in the values of teachers. It is also important to test existing practices against claims that they do work.

The last third of the book is a guide to carrying out research by practising school teachers, and others, most impressively put together by Jane Johnston and strictly reviewed by the editorial team. We believe that this section makes the book unique among the many authoritative research guides that exist in the market. Practitioner research is being carried out by practising school teachers, showing concrete evidence of taking research seriously. By selecting topics pertinent to their own classrooms, designing their own research and acting on the outcomes, these practitioners are, inevitably, more engaged with existing research. Their work, if published, also contributes to the totality of research evidence available. It is for these reasons that the last third of this book is aimed at giving practical and theoretical support to this group of teachers, whether studying for a higher degree, or simply researching for their own delight. We also recognise that government policies over recent years advocate teaching as a research informed profession.

This book is a major innovation for the ASE. It sits alongside the guides to professional practice in primary and secondary published earlier. Our next tasks include dissemination in the UK and elsewhere. As researchers, we also need to explore how the book is used, its successes in supporting teachers, student teachers and researchers, and where it can be improved. We may be able to find out teachers' approaches to science education research as much from the use of it as anything else. We hope that readers will keep a journal, and some will share those journals with us so that we can learn more.

On a personal note, I express my deep gratitude to members of the Research Committee over many years, and particularly the editorial team who have taken me so far along the road of research and reflection.

John Oversby October 2011

Section 1

Thematic review of research in science education

Chapter 1

Science education research: a critical appraisal of its contribution to education

John Oversby

In *Improving Science Education* (Millar, Leach and Osborne, 2000, p. 1) the editors ask these two major questions:

1 'Why is the impact of science education research on practice apparently so slight?'
2 'Is there any sense that the field of science education research is making progress? (Do newer studies build on earlier ones? Is the effort *cumulative*? Are there any areas of agreement about theoretical frameworks and terminology, or about research approaches, procedures or tools, or even about areas of work that are more or less worthwhile? And are there findings that command general assent?)'

This chapter provides some positive answers to these questions, although the lack of documented evidence by some authors of how their ideas arose makes the historical trail patchy. Millar *et al.* (op. cit.) have provided a book that starts with a rather sceptical view but its structure demonstrates their attempt to deal with some overarching issues. Erikson (2000), in the same book, classifies research on student learning into three stages:

1 the Piagetian research programme
2 the constructivist research programme
3 the phenomenological research programme.

At the risk of oversimplification (the reader should read Erikson's claims in full), Erikson sees limitations in each approach as a driver for a new research programme, with Piagetians locked into a rigid and unchanging stage theory of learning, and constructivists focusing on individual mental constructions of knowledge, ignoring social working and the role of affect. The Piagetian school gave rise to notions of accelerated learning, such as those underlying the CASE project (*Thinking Science*), but research on this approach declined in the 1990s. The constructivist view adapted to the criticism that it ignored learners working collaboratively by including social constructivism. This view is dominant now in science education research. The phenomenological research programme starts from learners being able to see the world in different ways, according to Erikson's interpretation, in contrast to the constructivist theory comparing the learner's view with that of the scientist. The phenomenographers see science learning as enabling learners to see the world from different viewpoints, and to notice what is missing in each viewpoint when trying to make sense of the world. Unlike the two former research programmes, phenomenography has not yet been subjected to widespread scrutiny, and seems unlikely to be respected by most practising scientists with their dominant positivist and reductionist stance.

Gunstone and White (2000), also in the same book, comment on the methodologies adopted by science education researchers, drawing our attention to the strengths and weaknesses of qualitative versus quantitative data collection and analyses. Rather than taking one side or another, they point out that a new synthesis of methodologies is required in the light of teaching being such a complex activity, or set of activities.

Andrews, in his foreword to Bennett (2003, p. ix), draws immediate attention to *'the gap between research, policy and practice in public life'* as his starting point. He sees research evidence as *'inert'*, requiring transformation in the classroom if it is to be valuable to teachers. The implication here is that teachers must have sufficient knowledge about and commitment to the value of research in order to transform its processes and outcomes for their teaching. This is a massive requirement for those already dealing with a heavy workload, and with, perhaps, insufficient recognition among their peers for doing so.

Morris (2004) has explored what is meant by an evidence-based approach in education, in a discussion paper for the Higher Education Academy. She writes:

> *'Consider the following definition (Sackett* et al. *1996):*
>
> *"Evidence-based medicine is the conscientious, explicit, and judicious use of current best evidence in making decisions about the care of individual patients. The practice of evidence-based medicine means integrating individual clinical expertise with the best available external clinical evidence from systematic research."'*

If we substitute certain medically oriented phrases in this definition with the corresponding education-related terms, we obtain something along the following lines:

> *'Evidence-based teaching is the conscientious, explicit, and judicious use of current best evidence in making decisions about the learning and learning experience offered to students. The practice of evidence-based teaching means integrating individual academic and pedagogic expertise with the best available external evidence from systematic research.'*

This may be worth taking as a start in identifying what is meant by evidence-based teaching.

What counts as science education research?

Examples of science education research, categorised by the author, are as follows.

1 **Mega-scale projects**, such as:
- Children's Learning in Science Project (CLISP), concerned with exploring the ideas that children have about scientific concepts and processes
- Assessment of Performance Unit (APU), which worked on a sample-based assessment of scientific achievement in content and procedural knowledge
- Cognitive Acceleration in Science Education (CASE), devoted to faster learning through specially created tasks
- Assessment for Learning (AfL), taking evidence about learning in the classroom, giving constructive feedback to the learners with associated and focused targets for the next stage
- Relevance of Science Education (ROSE), an international survey in modern and traditional cultures to identify learner interest in science
- Programme for International Student Assessment (PISA), an international survey to characterise national achievement in reading, science and mathematics learning, including affective characteristics such as interest
- The Trends in International Mathematics and Science Survey (TIMSS), focused on assessing subject knowledge.

2 **Macro-scale projects** conceived and run by university staff, in education or psychology departments, often funded by research councils and charitable organisations and supported by researchers, research students and doctoral students.

3 **Micro-scale projects** individual teacher-based projects, subject to scrutiny within such groups as Local Authority meetings, by publication in professional journals such as *Primary Science* and *School Science Review,* or by dissemination at regional, national or international conferences.

4 **Action Research, Case Study Research** often supported by local authority staff or by tutors in higher education, and often published in the same way as micro-scale projects.

5 **Collaborative projects** for example, the Reading PALAVA Teacher Researcher Group (www.palava.wikispaces.com), subject to scrutiny within the group and at conferences.

Issues of tracking contributions of research

It is rare for the outcomes of science education research to be acknowledged or tracked for effectiveness.

How has research contributed to education?

Contributions at policy level

While there are some who consider that policy changes rarely occur in response to science education research, there are some signs that policy makers consider positive outcomes of such research in policy making. Identifying the impact of science education research outcomes is difficult since many policy documents fail to record or acknowledge their influence. However, some examples of research outcomes that have influenced policy making are outlined below.

1   Research into the role of assessment in both teaching and learning in science lead to the development of Assessment for Learning (see Chapters 15 and 17 in this book):

    'Purpose of assessment:

    Assessment, recording and reporting are important elements of teaching but they have to be manageable if the information they yield is to be useful. The best assessment has an immediate impact on both teaching and learning, enabling next steps to be identified and supported.

    Regular assessment:
    - *alerts you to the needs of pupils who are either out of step or exceeding expectations*
    - *helps you to maintain the pace of learning for all pupils by informing teaching plans in a continuous cycle of planning, teaching and assessment*
    - *helps pupils to identify how to improve their own work.'*

    The National Strategies, DCSF (2010)

2   Research into the role of misconceptions (alternative frameworks) (see Chapters 5 and 6) has informed policy making, as exemplified in The National Strategies: Secondary (The Framework for secondary science) on Intervention in Science:

    'Minor difficulties in learning can affect the rates of progress of a number of pupils. Some may have:
    - *misconceptions remaining from earlier work in science*
    - *difficulties in linking between the conceptual and contextual aspects.'*

    The National Strategies, DCSF (2010)

3   The role of modelling (see Chapter 14 in his book) has been identified as part of the toolkit of scientific explanation, especially for abstract concepts, concepts that are highly mathematical, and as a link to what learners are likely to know already. Explicit use of diagrams about particle models, together with a view about what is a 'good enough' model, have influenced teaching through the National Strategies programme (The National Strategies, DCSF, 2010), such as the use of particle diagrams of liquids with at least two thirds of the particles touching. This focus on models progression shows itself through the National Strategies materials.

Contributions at curriculum design level

Although it is difficult to point to a seminal piece of research, evidence from work on constructivist learning theory has had one of the most pervasive impacts on curriculum design in recent times (see http://en.wikipedia.org/wiki/Constructivism_(learning _theory) for example, and http://en.wikipedia.org/wiki/Constructivist_teaching_methods).

The How Should We Teach Science? team (howscience.wikidot.com/home) is attempting to write a curriculum based on the quantitative research evidence of Hattie and Marzano, among others (*Chapter 6* Petty, 2006 – see Hattie's table of effect sizes in Chapter 5, pages 61–70, and Marzano's theory-based meta-analysis in Chapter 6, pages 71–80).

Contributions at subject knowledge level

Abell and Lederman (2007), in their *Handbook of Research on Science Education*, devote a whole section of six chapters to review science teacher education, but only one of these is on science teacher knowledge, reviewing surveys on subject matter knowledge. This appears to be a relatively unreported area as far as effective intervention is concerned.

Contributions at pedagogic content knowledge level

Mulhall, Berry and Loughran (2003) have created a framework for representing the pedagogical content knowledge (PCK) of successful teachers, and this has been disseminated very widely. Heywood and Parker (2010), through case studies of topics in physics, have constructed a review of what they consider to be the main features of PCK in those domains.

Contributions at affective level

Research on affective components of science education, such as attitude, motivation and self-esteem, has been published for at least 30 years. Haladyna (1980) published his inventory assessment but the take up seems to have been unremarkable. The general principles seem to have resurfaced in the guise of preferred learning styles.

Contributions at continuing professional development level

Harrison *et al.* (2008) have explored evidence-based continuing professional development (CPD) in Israel and the UK to develop expertise in a particular topic in science teaching. The King's College London work on Assessment for Learning has spawned a plethora of CPD activities. An earlier project, CASE, similarly gave rise to a widespread CPD programme.

Parke and Coble (1997) explored the impact of continuing professional development (CPD), which was collaborative and sustained, on teachers' practice and students' attitudes and achievement in science. Their work highlighted the effective contribution to the CPD made by outside experts in the form of education staff from two universities, and also illustrates CPD which takes account of teachers' starting points.

Need for further research

Some successes have been noted here but these are perhaps all the more spectacular because they are not so common. In this sense, the value of science education research has yet to be fully realised in practice. Further work is needed, not least in linking researchers and teachers. This cannot just be a 'push' model, forcing information from researchers to teachers – there has to be some 'pull' from the teachers. Dissemination has to take note of contextual factors, and the values of the teachers. In their turn, researchers should engage critically with teachers in determining what kind of research is undertaken.

References

Abell, S.K. and Lederman, N.G. (eds) (2007) *Handbook of Research on Science Education.* Mahwah, NJ: Lawrence Erlbaum.

Bennett, J. (2003) *Teaching and Learning Science: a guide to recent research and its applications.* London: Continuum.

Erikson, G. (2000) Research programmes and the student science learning literature. In Millar, R., Leach, J. and Osborne, J. (eds) *Improving Science Education: the contribution of research.* Buckingham: Open University Press.

Gunstone, R. and White, R. (2000) Goals, methods and achievements of research in science education. In Millar, R., Leach, J. and Osborne, J. (eds) *Improving Science Education: the contribution of research.* Buckingham: Open University Press.

Haladyna, T. (1980) *Construct Validation of an Inventory of Affective Aspects of Schooling.* Paper presented at the Joint Annual Meetings of the American Educational Research Association and the National Council on Measurement in Education (Boston, MA, 7–11 April 1980).

Harrison, C., Hofstein, A., Eylon, B.S. and Simon, S. (2008) How can evidence-based CPD programmes improve the professional development of science teachers? *International Journal of Science Education* **30**(5) 57–59.

Heywood, D. and Parker, J. (2010) *The Pedagogy of Physical Science (Contemporary Trends and Issues in Science Education).* Dordrecht: Springer.

Millar, R., Leach, J. and Osborne, J. (eds) (2000) *Improving Science Education: the contribution of research.* Buckingham: Open University Press.

Morris, C. (2004) *Towards an Evidence-based Approach to Quality Enhancement – a modest proposal.* A discussion paper for the Higher Education Academy.

Mulhall, P., Berry, A. and Loughran, J. (2003) Frameworks for representing science teachers' pedagogical content knowledge. *Asia-Pacific Forum on Science Learning and Teaching* **4**(2) Article 2 (Dec 2003).

Parke, H.M. and Coble, C.R. (1997) Teachers designing curriculum as professional development: a model for transformational science teaching. *Journal of Research in Science Teaching* **34**, 773–789 (EPPI review study 366).

Petty, G. (2006) *Evidence-Based Teaching: a practical approach.* Cheltenham: Nelson Thornes.

Sackett, D.L., Rosenberg, W.M.C., Gray, J.A.M., Haynes, R.B. and Richardson, W.S. (1996) Evidence based medicine: what it is and what it isn't. *British Medical Journal* **312**, 71–72.

The National Strategies, DCSF (2010) Available online at:
http://www.teachingandlearningresources.org.uk

Chapter 2

International science education: what's in it for science teachers?

Peter J Fensham

In the last 15 years, large cross-national investigations of school science education have become established as regular sources of information. When the results of these investigations are released to the participating countries, it can be expected that they would exercise at least some influence in the educational systems of the countries that have paid considerable funds and human resources to participate. In some countries the findings also capture media attention but this attention inevitably focuses simplistically on the results as league tables of comparative achievement.

This chapter aims specifically to give science teachers information about the nature of some of these investigations, and to enable them to have a perspective on the general and particular value of their findings for their on-going work of teaching science.

The projects

Three projects will be used to illustrate the strengths and weaknesses of these large-scale investigations:

- the **Trends in International Mathematics and Science Study (TIMSS)**, initiated by the International Association for the Evaluation of Educational Achievement (IEA), an independent international cooperative of national research institutions and government agencies (Martin, Mullis and Foy, 2008)
- the **Programme for International Student Achievement (PISA)**, initiated by the Organisation for Economic Co-operation and Development (OECD) (Bybie, McRae and Laurie, 2009)
- the **Relevance of Science Education (ROSE)** project, based in Oslo, and initiated and led by Professor Svein Sjøberg (Schreiner and Sjøberg, 2004).

TIMSS science

The TIMSS project's primary purpose is to answer the question:

'How do countries vary in the intended learning goals for science (and mathematics) and what characteristics of educational systems, schools and students influence the development of these goals?'

(Robitaille and Gardner, 1996, p. 38)

TIMSS is thus concerned with the learning of the official *intended curriculum* content for science and mathematics. In practice, what students learn is more the result of the *enacted curriculum* in a nation's classrooms, a more complex reality not directly accessible to the project. The achievement tests in TIMSS are intended to provide some measure of the *attained curriculum*. The science content of the achievement questionnaire and the format of the items has to be meaningful to respondents in many countries where there are different educational traditions, science curricula and cultures of teaching and assessment. Achieving this common meaning in TIMSS meant identifying the science content that is common (or alleged to be common) in the intended grade level curricula across the participating countries – a lowest 'common' content. Accordingly, the set of science items in the TIMSS test excludes particular priorities that a given country may intend for its science education. For this reason, and those discussed above about methodology and the cross-national character of the project, TIMSS is limited in its capacity to answer its own question.

Two populations of students are studied – Population 1 comprises nine-year-olds (in the third and fourth grades), and Population 2 in made up of 13-year-olds (in the seventh and eighth grades). The project embraces both mathematics and science, but these are studied separately. The items in the science part of the achievement test consist mainly of isolated science topics. Initially, a framework for the science achievement test referred to eight content areas, but in practice, only four scaled scores for the traditional content areas – *Earth science*, *Life science*, *Physical science (physics and chemistry)*, and *Environmental science* – were possible, together with five scores reflecting different processes required in answering the items, such as *Understanding simple information*, *Understanding complex information*, *Theorising, analysing and solving problems*, *Using tools, routine procedures and science processes*, and *Investigating the natural world*.

In so far as the science topics behind the TIMSS items have been taught as part of the enacted curriculum, answering most of them involves only recall or low level transfer. The TIMSS test emphasises science as a store of stable knowledge to be recalled when asked for. Introductory science concepts, principles and process skills all take on the character of factual knowledge, the application of which is confined to contrived contexts, which are similar to those in science textbooks. This knowledge emphasis in science learning is still of major interest to the participating countries. It is an understanding of scientific literacy that Roberts (2007) described as Science Literacy, Vision 1 (*SL 1*), a view that is based in the established knowledge in the science disciplines.

In order to cover as many topics in this 'common' science content as possible, TIMSS uses simple multiple choice as its commonest form of item. The time and logistic efficiency of this form of item is to be set against the role of guessing, and the potential ambiguity of answers – wrong answer/right reason, right answer/wrong reason, for example.

National rankings are not the primary concern of science teachers, especially if their students were not part of the national sample. Nor are they interested in the framework for TIMSS, as it is already familiar as part of the curriculum they are teaching. Of more interest may be information that is provided in national reports about the spread of mean scores within the national sample, and particularly among socially defined groups of students, who may match, or seem to match, the students in a teacher's school or classrooms. Science teachers are interested, of course, in the content of the science test on which their nation's students have performed well or badly. The individual science items do invoke the curiosity response from teachers about how their own students would perform. Alas, the best that the TIMSS project offers in its international and national reports are the analyses of exemplary or released items, a small fraction of the whole test (see Endnote).

The relationships between the contextual variables and science achievement are also, in the main, disappointing for science teachers. Apart from some obvious associations between *time for science* and *time for science homework*, many of the other associations such as that between socio-economic background and achievement (quite variable across countries) are really outside the control of science teachers.

PISA science – a test for scientific literacy

The purpose the OECD chose for PISA is to answer the question:

How well prepared are 15-year-olds for the demands of 21st century life in the domains of Reading, Mathematics and Science?

This rather novel question was, and still is, of great interest to the member countries of the OECD and, as it has turned out, to many other countries as well. In many countries, 15-year-olds are near the end of compulsory schooling or at least compulsory science. They will also have had other avenues of learning over these years besides schooling as their major formal source. The PISA project is thus not confined to the curriculum of schooling. Indeed, its interest is forward to the application of science knowledge to the situations of 21st century life, rather than backwards to what has recently been learned.

In PISA the student achievement tests for science (as for reading and mathematics) were developed from a Framework that uses the general descriptor term *literacy* with the adjective for each domain – hence *scientific literacy*. For each of the literacies, a number of student competencies are clearly defined, and it is these that the PISA achievement tests set out to measure. Initially, the scientific competencies for PISA 2000 were defined in terms of five scientific processes (OECD, 2000):

1 recognising scientifically investigable questions
2 identifying evidence needed in a scientific investigation
3 drawing or evaluating conclusions
4 communicating valid conclusions
5 demonstrating understanding of scientific concepts.

The introductory verbs reflect the value PISA attaches to active learning that leads to students using their knowledge of science.

PISA sees the science learning behind its view of scientific literacy as encompassing both knowledge *of* and knowledge *about* science, and claims that scientific competencies always involve some specific science content.

After the minor science testings in 2000 and 2003, science was the major domain in 2006, and the project chose to provide measures of *Investigating scientific issues, Explaining phenomena scientifically,* and *Using scientific evidence* as the three cognitive components of its definition of scientific literacy, and measures of *Interest in science* and *Social worth of science* as the affective components (OECD, 2006).

PISA science chose five areas of application of science in everyday life as particularly important for students and citizens – *Health, Environment, Natural resources, Hazards* and *Frontiers of science and technology.* Each of these areas can present situations at the personal, societal and global levels, and it is just these real-life situations (often involving technology as well as science) that become the presenting contexts for the groups of questions in the PISA science test. For each authentic (real-life) situation, the students are asked a series of questions that relate to the competencies comprising the definition of scientific literacy. Because of this real-world emphasis on science and technology, the PISA test draws attention to certain topic areas of science in comparison with others that have had pride of place in school science curricula but impinge less obviously on real life. PISA's sense of scientific literacy is what Roberts (2007) calls Science Literacy, Vision II (*SL II*), a view based on the applications of science in the real lives of citizens.

The PISA science test also points to the tentative aspect of science through historical examples and through its greater acceptance of open-ended questions with more than one right answer. In PISA science, learning is valued when it can be applied to scientific situations of relevance in the students' worlds. Simple multiple choice items are still used, but there are also complex multiple choice items and free response items, both of which have greater capacity to provide clearer indications of active real learning.

The international rankings of countries on the PISA science test are again not of great interest to science teachers, but the Framework for the PISA science test is now of interest, because it outstrips the current sense of purpose for school science in most countries. In this way PISA science offers a real challenge to lively science teachers, who think about the role and purpose of their teaching. To learn that some country's students do better or worse than one's own country on an unusual science test is at least intriguing, and ought to encourage closer scrutiny of what else this project has to say. In addition, PISA's decision to use more varied forms of test item, the context-based nature of the test and the inclusion of affective questions alongside cognitive ones, extend the usual ways in which science learning is measured.

As in TIMSS, the spread of performance across the national sample is of interest, as is the relatively lower or higher performance of some subgroups. Apart from this, the associations between the educational context variables and science achievement add little of interest. The test questions and how their items are identified with the various dimensions in the PISA Framework have greatest interest to science teachers in the years of secondary schooling. The individual items and their clustering around a real-life context will be particularly interesting to teachers exploring context-based science teaching, and give examples of how flesh has been put on the novel skeletons that the PISA Frameworks outline – for many teachers, the range of ways in which students are required to respond will be a surprise. Sadly, again, only some of these clusters of items from each testing are released, but when the examples in the Frameworks are added to the released units in the reports for each testing (2000/2003/2006), there are now about 30 released PISA contextual units involving more than 100 items for teachers to try on their students. They are also very useful as starting points for discussing the question, *Why learn Science?*

ROSE – the issue of relevance

The ROSE project has been led by Svein Sjøberg and his team of collaborating scholars in more than 30 countries. It is an international project having as its focus affective factors that may be of importance to the learning of science and technology. Since 2000, disturbing evidence has been appearing in many developed countries indicating a loss of interest in science, for its own sake and for careers. The ROSE project was thus a timely complement to TIMSS and PISA, with their entirely and mainly cognitive emphases, respectively.

As for PISA, the target population of ROSE is 15-year-olds, near the end of compulsory secondary schooling. Although the inclusion of convenience sampling for some countries raises the issue of the comparability of these data sets, the analysed findings from countries that are commonly compared are sufficiently alike to give confidence to their validity.

The data are collected with a survey instrument containing a number of sets of mainly closed questions, to which the students are asked to respond by indicating a position on a four-point Likert scale that indicates *strength of agreement, frequency of occurrence, degree of interest, sense of importance*, and so on. The responses to the items in a set of questions are not intended to be scored as a scale. Each item is analysed individually, but together give a more comprehensive picture of the student's opinions, experiences, and so on. The sets of questions cover *Science topics I want to learn about, Future occupations, Statements about the environment, Views on school science, Statements about science and technology, Out-of-school experiences* and *If a scientist, what I would do and why?*

Overall, the ROSE questionnaires include 242 questions – a considerable demand on the student respondents and their teachers to maintain concentration and focus on the degrees of difference that the Likert-like items require.

The ROSE data do not include any related data from these students' actual participation in science at school, so that there are no direct checks in the project itself to confirm the importance of the factors analysed.

Much of the data are analysed for reporting as national means for single items so that the rigorous demands in cross-national scales are avoided. There remains, however, the problem of whether students, within a country and internationally, are responding to the Likert-type questions with more or less equivalent meaning of degree.

Many of the ROSE items pose interesting findings for science teachers (see Endnote). For example, Jenkins and Pell (2006) reporting the study in England found that:

- most students agree that science and technology are important for society
- there was a lower level of agreement that the benefits of science outweigh possible harmful effects
- most students do not like science compared with other subjects
- most do not agree that school science has made them more critical and sceptical and more appreciative of nature.

A great similarity has been found in the science topics that interest students in more developed countries and these contrast with the interests among students in less developed countries. The former are more interested in topics that rarely occur in school science, whereas the latter show more interest in traditional school topics. Less developed countries report higher personal interest in science and more value in science than is reported from many of the more developed countries.

The five most popular science topics for boys and girls in England are listed in Table 1 and the five least popular topics are shown in Table 2.

Table 1   The five science topics of high interest for boys and girls in England (Jenkins and Pell, 2006).

Boys	Girls
1 explosive chemicals 2 weightlessness in space 3 how an atom bomb functions 4 biological and chemical weapons and human bodies 5 black holes, supernovae in space	1 why we dream and the meanings of dreams 2 what we know about cancer, and its treatment 3 performing first aid 4 how exercise keeps the body fit 5 sexually transmitted disease and protection

Table 2   The five science topics of least interest to boys and girls in England (Jenkins and Pell, 2006).

Boys	Girls
1 alternative therapies 2 benefits and hazards of modern farming 3 famous scientists and their lives 4 organic and ecological farming 5 how plants grow and reproduce	1 benefits and hazards of modern farming 2 plants in my area 3 organic and ecological farming 4 treatment of wastes, garbage and sewage 5 atoms and molecules

General features of these projects

Interest in science and mathematics learning is high in many countries, but other important components of schooling have not been given the same international attention. Projects that focus on these two areas inevitably convey status and value to them (and to the modes of testing employed) that may be unwarranted in the overall task of educating a nation's young people.

The international projects are all restricted to survey methodology (questionnaires) for their data collection. There is a central set of questions directed at the primary interest of the project, but other sets of questions seek information about the students' contextual settings – personal aspects, their families, their schools, and so on – that may have an influence on achievement on the central set. Considerable care is taken during the development of all the questions to make them widely comprehensible and in a form that should lead to valid and reliable data. Expert panels for content and translation, participating national officers and field trials are regularly used to ensure this quality.

To obtain comparable data across countries, these projects seek to survey a representative sample of each country's students. TIMSS and PISA, which are government sponsored, are able to achieve this by randomly sampling schools. ROSE also aspires to this level of representation, but with its more limited resources has sometimes had to settle for convenience samples. Representative sampling does not, however, guarantee equal attention, across schools and across countries, to tests that have no personal significance.

TIMSS and PISA started as limited-cycle projects (1994/1999 and 2000/2003/2006 respectively), but both have now assumed on-going life, and this means the focus of countries' interest in them becomes the trends in performance over time rather than what they interpret contemporary science learning to be. This interest in trends constrains the degree to which the achievement items in the tests can be changed, and hence only a small number of these items (and not usually the better ones) are made public after each testing.

The paper-and-pencil format for data collection immediately sets a limit to the information that is collected. Important aspects of the students' science learning and of their educational contexts cannot be collected and are ignored by these projects. Science teachers will be aware of practical performance, oral communication of science, and the rich interchanges in science classrooms as examples of these omissions.

In TIMSS and PISA, the goals are scaled measures of student science achievement (and often also of the contextual variables). Scaled measures require a coherent set of questions (items) of sufficient number, again limiting the range of science knowledge and the contextual variables that can be asked of the responding students in a reasonable testing time. The raw scores of each country's students are statistically standardised to a common scaling and these national mean scores are listed in the international and national reports in rank order, even though the scores are also banded in groups within which there are no statistical differences. Country X may thus have a mean score that ranks it tenth, whereas, in fact, statistically its performance is only surpassed by four of the countries ranked above it, for example.

Conclusion

Science education in practice is always the consequence of interacting sets of values that operate at the systemic, the school and the classroom levels (Fensham, 2007). International comparative studies of student science achievement, such as the TIMSS, PISA and ROSE projects, are not immune from this interaction of values. They inevitably involve choices about science and science education and choices reflect value positions. These choices are first made by the initiating organisations in conjunction with the representatives of cooperating governments. Others choices are made by the project's managers on advice stemming from its group of science advisers. These influence the design of the project, the science content emphasised, and the practices that make up the implementing stages. Finally, what is presented as findings and the manner of their presentation are also value laden.

In a number of countries (for example, Norway, Japan and Germany), there have been claims that the publication of these projects' value-laden findings conflict with the national values that underpin current educational priorities and indeed the practice of science education itself. Science teachers have an important role in sorting out the limitations of these international studies from their positive features. They can then interpret which findings should be considered, in their efforts to keep science education up to date and of service to the interests of the wide spectrum of young people now experiencing more years of schooling than ever before.

Despite a brief gesture in its first testing, towards the scientific literacy of the final year population of secondary schooling, TIMSS has emphasised in its tests in the 1990s and 2000s an academically orientated science, rather than a wider 'science for all' that takes account of the demands for decision making about science and technology that contemporary life places on students and citizens. In this way, TIMSS has chosen to ignore the considerable concern in many of its participating countries that interest in science for careers or for life-long learning is waning alarmingly.

The proactive nature of the PISA project, on the other hand, has meant it has been free to include features that address some of these contemporary concerns. In doing so, it has publicised some quite novel goals for science education for the participating countries to consider. The OECD has directed its PISA project at young persons as current and future citizens, very much in line with the widespread international interest in the 1990s about public understanding of science. It has been very aware of the lack of interest in science, and the inclusion in 2006 of affective items in its achievement test affirms its belief that interest as well as knowledge should be a goal of school science education.

The ROSE project gives high value to individual young people's interests in science and technology, and this means it is less concerned with the national roles that science and technology education have to play. It opens windows to aspects of personal lives in 21st century society that are closed to TIMSS and PISA. Averaging individual responses to an extent mutes the individual voices, but nevertheless the windows are still open – just not so wide.

References

Bybie, R., McRae, B., and Laurie, R. (2009) PISA 2006: An assessment of scientific literacy. *Journal of Research in Science Teaching*, **46**(8) 865–883.

Fensham, P.J. (2007) Values in the measurement of students' science achievement in TIMSS and PISA. In Corrigan, D., Dillon J. and Gunstone, R. (eds) *The Re-emergence of Values in Science Education* (Chapter 15, pp. 215–230). Rotterdam: Sense Publications.

Jenkins, E. and Pell, R.G. (2006) *The Relevance of Science Education Project (ROSE) in England: A summary of findings.* Leeds: Centre for Science and Mathematics Education, University of Leeds.

Martin, M.O., Mullis, I.V.S. and Foy, P. (2008) *Findings from the IEA's Trends in International Mathematics and Science Study at the Fourth and Eighth Grades.* Chestnut Hill, MA: IEA TIMSS and PIRLS International Study Center.

OECD (2000) *Measuring Student Knowledge and Skills: the PISA 2000 assessment of reading, mathematical and scientific literacy.* Paris: OECD.

OECD (2006) *Assessing Scientific, Reading and Mathematical Literacy: A framework for PISA 2006.* Paris: OECD.

Roberts, D.A. (2007) Scientific literacy/science literacy. In Abell, S.K. and Lederman, N.G. (eds) *Handbook of Research in Science Education* (pp. 729–780). New York: Routledge.

Robitaille, D.F. and Gardner, R.A. (eds) (1996) *Research Questions and Study Design.* TIMSS Monograph No 2 (p. 50), Vancouver, BC: Pacific Educational Press.

Schreiner, C. and Sjøberg, S. (2004) *Sowing the Seeds of ROSE: Background, rationale, questionnaire development and data collection for ROSE (Relevance Of Science Education): A comparative study of students' views of science and science education.* (Acta Didacta 4/2004). Oslo: Department of Teacher education and school Development, University of Oslo. Available at: www.uv.uio.no/ils/english/research/projects/rose/actadidactica.pdf

Endnote

- The exemplary and released items from TIMSS and from PISA Science can be accessed via the following websites (follow the links to Frameworks):

  timssandpirls.bc.edu/timss2011/index.html
  www.pisa.oecd.org
- The questions in the ROSE Project can be accessed via: roseproject.no

Chapter 3

Teaching and learning about the nature of science

Keith S Taber

The nature of science as a focus of science education

It has been widely argued, by science educators working in various national contexts, that school science lessons should not *only* be about the products of science – the theories, laws and models that reflect current science knowledge – but should also emphasise the very nature of science (NOS) by which such products are constructed, debated and given status – provisionally, at least – as scientific knowledge. That is, that science lessons should be about *learning about science* as well as *learning some science* (Duschl, 2000; Osborne, 2002).

Science for all citizens

The arguments for teaching students about the NOS have been strongly linked to notions of teaching for scientific literacy, by considering what it is important for *all* young people to understand about science by the time they leave school (Millar and Osborne, 1998). As most school leavers will not study science further, nor enter employment that directly uses specific scientific knowledge, the focus has been on how an understanding of science is important for people who will be consumers – of commercial products (for example, in critiquing claims made in advertising), and of advice about such matters as medical treatment (for example, judging the pros and cons of particular medication or treatment, or of diagnostic techniques) – as well as being citizens in modern democracies (considering political stances towards such issues as action on climate change, the arguments for and against nuclear power and so on):

> '[14 to 16-year-olds] develop their ability to relate their understanding of science to their own and others' decisions about lifestyles, and to scientific and technological developments in society.'
>
> QCA (2007b, p. 221)

NOS aims for scientific literacy

For an individual to understand the NOS sufficiently to be considered scientifically literate in this way, he or she would need to be able to:

- appreciate why sometimes different scientists seem to disagree about scientific issues, despite both sides claiming they are supported by scientific evidence
- distinguish such on-going debates (where it is appropriate to consider the scientific jury to still be 'out') from issues where there is wide consensus but (inevitably) a minority view persists among a few scientists (for example, that the climate is not being changed by human activities; that HIV is not the major factor in AIDS; that the fossil record does not support evolution by natural selection)
- appreciate how on many major issues where the scientific evidence is clear, and is widely understood in a common way, different individuals and groups with distinct interests or perspectives may come to different value (not scientific) judgments despite being informed by the same science base (for example, nuclear power stations should/should not be built; using material from aborted foetuses or still-born babies in medical research is/is not acceptable)
- make sound judgments about when a claim should be considered to be scientifically supported (for example, appreciate why the uncertain knowledge offered by an astronomer is more worthy of being taken seriously than the uncertain 'knowledge' offered by an astrologer).

These, in turn, require an appreciation of both the logical rules applied in science (Taber, 2011), and of something of the community processes by which ideas are accepted (at least provisionally) into the canon of public scientific knowledge.

Attracting future scientists

While the potential needs of all citizens have been a major focus of much of the discussion, there are strong arguments for thinking that science education for future scientists can also be improved by providing a wider intellectual context, given that so many talented young people do not find school science to offer the basis of attractive options for further study (Cerini, Murray and Reiss, 2003).

It seems that for many students a broader vision of how science seeks to build a coherent understanding of the world is obscured by the piece-meal fashion in which learning about different ideas and concepts is often experienced. Unfortunately, for these students, science often seems a body of established, and largely disconnected, facts – rather than a dynamic and organic web of knowledge that they are invited to seek to contribute to.

Arguably, for these students, the aspect of the NOS that needs to be emphasised in teaching is the set of common values (such as seeking to explain a broad range of phenomena in terms of the minimum number of basic concepts) which underpin the scientific enterprise as an intellectual pursuit. Again arguably, the stress on scientific literacy for all could distract from the need to also support those aspects of learning *about* science most relevant to potential future scientists.

What do we mean by 'the nature of science'?

As soon as we accept that it is educationally desirable that students should learn their science within a broader context of appreciating some of the NOS, we are faced with the question of defining, or at least offering some kind of characterisation of, what we mean by the 'nature' of science. Something as complex and varied as science is hardly likely to have a simple 'nature', and indeed science has been studied from a number of perspectives. The following are among the most significant.

- Philosophy of science – for example, considering such questions as:

  What counts as science?

  What is the status of scientific knowledge?

  How does science produce knowledge?

- History of science – considering how the scientific ideas that are widely accepted today were developed, and why they came to be generally accepted by scientists.

- Sociology of science – considering such issues as whether extra-scientific factors (such as personal or cultural bias or the institutional 'culture' of the laboratory) influence the processes or products of science, as well as the relationships between science and the wider society:

  how science is supported (or not) by public funding and institutions

  how science is communicated beyond the scientific community

  how the knowledge produced by science is used in public decision making, and so on.

Clearly these areas overlap, and are informed by other disciplines. For example, psychologists and other cognitive scientists have been interested in how individual scientists come to develop (or discard) ideas – a theme that can link to philosophy (which tells us about the formal logic of scientific decision making); history (which provides cases to be studied); and sociology (which will consider how an individual is inevitably influenced by the wider cultural context – for example, geneticists working in the Stalinist Soviet Union where Darwin's ideas were not acceptable on ideological grounds).

The natures of the sciences?

In this brief treatment, I refer to 'the' NOS, but there are important differences between different science disciplines that could be interpreted as suggesting that they do not share a single 'nature'. It is certainly true that each scientific field develops its own set of key commitments (to core concepts, methodology, preferred forms of representation and so on), and therefore scientific work can vary quite considerably (Kuhn, 1996). So for example, the traditional controlled experiment is central to some sciences, but impractical in others. However, it is arguably also the case that there is a core set of values informing practices in all science disciplines that act as a demarcation criterion for what counts as a science – so, for example, all sciences develop explanations based upon the interpretation of evidence that builds upon, and is used to critique, existing theories (Taber, 2009). All secondary students should be introduced to this common core NOS, as a background for further learning about the particular natures of different science disciplines.

The notion of How Science Works

In the UK curriculum context, revisions of the statutory requirements for what must be taught in schools brought to prominence the phrase 'How Science Works' (HSW) as a central focus of science teaching, and for the formal assessment of science learning.

Recent revisions of the National Curriculum (NC) in England were presented to teachers in a format that was very different to earlier versions. In place of a substantive prescription of topics to be taught, dominated by the science content, the new secondary curriculum documents are minimal and provide only outlines of the topic areas to be covered. More significantly, arguably, the specification of science topics is presented as only one strand of what needs to be taught, given no more prominence than other aspects.

The NC document for Key Stage 3 (ages 11 to 14) organises the curriculum (in a format parallel to other subjects areas) under *Key concepts*, *Key processes*, *Range and content* and *Curriculum opportunities* (QCA, 2007a). The document for Key Stage 4 (ages 14 to 16) is divided into *Knowledge, skills and understanding* and *Breadth of study* (QCA, 2007b). The Key Stage 3 document introduces the notion of key concepts by explaining that:

> 'There are a number of key concepts that underpin the study of science and How Science Works.'
>
> QCA (2007a)

The Key Stage 4 document prefaces both sections with statements to the effect that:

> '… the knowledge, skills and understanding of How Science Works are integrated into the teaching of the Breadth of Study.'
>
> QCA (2007b, p. 221)

Despite the different format, both documents suggest that learning aims should concern both understanding some science, and understanding *about* science itself (that is, the nature of science). It is also suggested that teaching and learning about HSW should not be seen as something discrete from teaching the concepts of particular science topics, but rather that students should learn about the nature of science (NOS) through science topics such as electricity, elements and compounds, variation among living things or the apparent motion of celestial bodies. That is, teachers are asked to make sure that students *learn about science through learning some science*.

Research into teaching and learning NOS

There is actually a considerable body of literature discussing aspects of teaching and learning of the NOS (Arnold and Millar, 1993). Much of this work is spread across a wide range of books, journal articles and conference papers. However, there are some very useful introductions to this area of work (Hodson, 2009; Matthews, 1994), and the journal of the International History and Philosophy of Science Teaching Group, called *Science and Education*, publishes many relevant articles.

One important area of research explores how students and teachers understand aspects of NOS. This can be considered as part of the extensive 'constructivist' research into learning in science, which not only explores the extent to which students learn the ideas presented in science classes, but also reveals how often learners come to lessons holding 'alternative' conceptions of scientific concepts (Taber, 2009). Professor Reinders Duit (at the Institute for Science and Mathematics Education at the University of Kiel) has produced a bibliography entitled *Students' and teachers' conceptions and science education,* which is freely available to download from the web (Duit, 2009).

Student understanding of the NOS

It is not possible to summarise such a large body of work here, but it is possible to offer some flavour of what research has suggested. The research suggests that, in general, secondary age students can be considered to have relatively unsophisticated understanding of key concepts about science. For example, models of many different kinds are widely used in science, and often they have limited ranges of application, and may include features which are known to oversimplify or even contradict some aspects of the system being modelled. To appreciate how such flawed representations can be useful, it is important to appreciate their status and role (often as exploratory thinking tools) within the scientific process. Yet learners commonly see models as intended as little more than scale replicas of real systems (Grosslight *et al.* 1991). Of course, some teaching models *are* meant to have this role, but most scientific models are something quite different.

A key issue in the philosophy of science is the status of scientific knowledge, and the processes by which such knowledge is developed. These are issues where different philosophers have presented different accounts, but there is what might be called a 'post-positivist' consensus (Taber, 2009, Chapter 2) that:

1   scientific knowledge should always be considered to some extent *provisional,* in that we are always open to consider new evidence
2   however, scientific knowledge is also *reliable,* so that it is reasonable to use well-established scientific ideas as the basis for action.

At first glance these points may seem to be somewhat contradictory: how can we rely on knowledge that we acknowledge is tentative? An example would be Newtonian mechanics, which was long known to lead to anomalies (for example, its predictions did not match the precise details of the observed orbit of Mercury), yet despite these anomalies remained the best available account until it was succeeded by Einstein's theory of time and space. Indeed, a century later, the imperfect Newtonian model remains an immensely powerful instrument for planning such human actions as the space missions to other planets.

The philosophy of science suggests that technically we can never be sure that our scientific knowledge offers a true account of the nature of things, and indeed the history of science shows how ideas that are at one time widely accepted by scientists may turn out to need modification. This need not be limited to esoteric areas of science that are well outside the scope of the school curriculum. One example might be the so-called 'central dogma' of molecular biology, which considered a one-way flow of information from DNA to RNA to proteins. While this was originally a fruitful new idea in the field, it is contradicted by the action of retroviruses, which – given the extent of HIV infection in many parts of the world – are a focus of scientific study of major economic and social importance.

Research suggests that secondary students tend to have rather simplistic notions of the nature of scientific ideas (Driver *et al.* 1996) – for example, thinking that scientific theories are just imaginative guesses at how the world is, which can then be unproblematically 'proved' to be true, or refuted. This needs to be a key focus of teaching about NOS, as appreciating why scientific knowledge should be considered both provisional and yet reliable is central to scientific literacy, allowing people to make sense of the nature of scientific debates about climate change, nuclear power, vaccination programmes and so forth.

Reassuringly, research also suggests that secondary students are capable of learning about NOS under supportive conditions (Solomon, 1995).

Teacher understanding of the NOS

It is possible to suggest three interlinked factors that are likely to contribute to school students' limited appreciation of the NOS. One of these is hinted at above: the material itself is quite complicated. For example, appreciating exactly what people like Popper, Kuhn, Lakatos and Feyerabend said about the limits or methods of science is quite complex. But then, of course, much of the science in the curriculum is equally complex when studied at the highest levels. When a topic becomes established in the curriculum it becomes clear at what level it needs to be understood, and over time curriculum and teaching models are developed to match different age groups. Just as there are 'suitable' levels of treatment for teaching about photosynthesis or volcanoes, so must curriculum models of the NOS be developed and refined (Taber, 2008).

This relates to a second point. As teaching about the NOS has previously had limited emphasis in school science, we should not be surprised if students have not learned much about it. Indeed, part of the rationale behind the HSW emphasis in the recent English curriculum developments, was the recognition that the intention that teachers would teach about the NOS through teaching the science topics specified in the previous National Curriculum was never realised because the intended implicit NOS context was not widely recognised by teachers as a central aspect of the curriculum.

This in turn was not only due to the lack of explicit specification in the curriculum documents, but also because teachers themselves were largely uninformed about (at least the formal aspects of) the NOS. Indeed, some research seems to suggest that teacher knowledge about the NOS may be as weak as that found among school children (Abd-El-Khalick, 2002), and that remediation may involve something more than simply providing NOS-based inputs into higher education courses (Abd-El-Khalick and Lederman, 2000). Teachers not suitably prepared to teach about something that was not clearly specified provide an understandable context for limited student learning.

Teaching about aspects of the NOS

Given the general message from research, the challenge of effective teaching about HSW should not be underestimated. Yet teaching and learning about the NOS is now a core part of school science:

> 'Pupils should be taught ... about the use of contemporary scientific and technological developments and their benefits, drawbacks and risks ... to consider how and why decisions about science and technology are made, including those that raise ethical issues, and about the social, economic and environmental effects of such decisions ... how uncertainties in scientific knowledge and scientific ideas change over time and about the role of the scientific community in validating these changes.'
>
> QCA (2007b, p. 223)

Thematic review of research in science education

There has in recent years been increasing interest in teaching about aspects of the NOS, and there is certainly material to support teachers looking for ideas (some examples are suggested in the table). One important area is that of supporting students to learn about the relationship between ideas and evidence in science, including developing students' argumentation skills (see Chapter 13 in this Guide). Another strand concerns teaching about controversial issues that are informed by science (Levinson, 2007). Another area concerns teaching that is inclusive of ideas from students' own diverse cultural backgrounds (Aikenhead, 2006). However, there remains considerable scope for further research and resource development to inform effective teaching.

Table 1 Some examples of resources to support the teaching of the NOS.

Resource	Comment	Availability
SATIS (Science and Technology in Society)	These ASE materials were produced in paper format during the 1980s. Many are useful for teaching about NOS, and there is now a dedicated website presenting materials, and providing support for teachers.	The site may be found at http://www.satisrevisited.co.uk/
IDEAS (Ideas, Evidence and Argument in Science)	A pack of materials was produced to support teachers in teaching about ideas and evidence in lower secondary science.	This project was funded by the Nuffield Foundation and materials published by King's College London.
Ideas and evidence in science research project	A project initiated as part of the (UK Government funded) National Strategies, and with additional support from the Gatsby Science Enhancement Programme	Summary materials are posted at the teachfind website http://www.teachfind.com/
Enriching school science for the gifted learner	Deriving from a project to provide science enhancement through focus on the NOS. A set of classroom resources and an accompanying book. Includes activities that focus on what is science?; scientific method; laws in science; integrating science; critiquing models; use of analogy in science. Published by the Science Enhancement Programme	pdf of book may be downloaded from https://camtools.cam.ac.uk/wiki/site/%7Ekst24/gifted.html Full set of materials available from http://www.mindsetsonline.co.uk/index.php
FaradaySchools website	This website offers resources exploring the 'big questions' in science. In particular it includes materials looking at different perspectives on the relationship between science and religion.	http://www.faradayschools.com

The need for further research

To summarise, teachers are now being told that the NOS is not only a prescribed part of the school curriculum, but is essential to meeting key aims of science education. Yet research suggests that students, and even many teachers, currently fall well short of the expected levels of knowledge and understanding. Other research is more promising, offering materials and approaches that are reported to be effective at engaging and teaching students.

That may seen incongruent, but only if we lose sight of the diversity of contexts in which science is taught and learned. One initiative produced a series of NOS-based activities that were generally well received by 14 to 15-year-old students, and suggested that these learners were quite able to engage with learning activities relating to the philosophy of science, the nature of scientific laws and models, the interaction of scientific and social concerns, the nature of scientific explanations and so forth (Taber, 2007). However, the particular context was an after-school enrichment programme for able students. The materials produced in that project are likely to be effective when used with other comparable teaching groups – but cannot be *assumed* to be suitable without at least some modification for, say, 11-year-olds or students in lower ability sets.

This seems to be a general issue: there are plenty of claims for things that have been shown to work in particular situations, but these claims must be seen against the generally negative picture offered by much research into what is more typical. Perhaps in time this picture will shift. As more teachers develop their knowledge and skills in teaching about the NOS, the general situation will improve. Perhaps, also, research in a wide range of teaching contexts will offer a better picture of what 'works' under different conditions (allowing us to refine curriculum and teaching models of the NOS).

In the meantime, individual teachers would be best advised to seek examples of teaching approaches and materials that have been shown to be effective, and to test out whether they can be adapted for use in their own teaching contexts – that is, to undertake their own small-scale classroom inquiry. Just as when teaching content areas such as forces, acids or plant nutrition, such innovation is most likely to be effective when it is informed by first eliciting the students' current levels of understanding and existing conceptions. This need not depend upon sophisticated methodology (see Box 1). Here, the existing research into student understanding of the NOS can provide guidance on what to expect, and how to best go about eliciting student ideas.

Box I Key Stage 3 students' understanding of the term 'theory' as elicited by trainee teachers interviewing students in top science sets (as reported in *School Science Review*).

Student perceptions of the term 'theory'

'Pupils [in top science sets in Y7, Y8 in one school, and Y9 in another school] were asked "Have you come across the word 'theory' in science?" (and, if yes) "Can you explain what a theory is?"

In common with previous research, pupils' responses tended to be quite vague. About half of the pupils in Y7–8 (9/19 in Y7, 8/17 in Y8) and most of those in Y9 (21/28) gave responses at the level of a theory being an idea, or something people think. A much smaller number (2/19 in Y7, 4/17 in Y8, 7/28 in Y9) gave responses suggesting that a theory had an uncertain aspect and should be considered "unproven".

... Most of the pupils could suggest at least one theory, although the range of suggestions was narrow. The common responses were Newton's theory of gravity, Darwin's theory of evolution and Einstein's theory of relativity – each being mentioned at least five times in each of the classes. However, the only other acceptable suggestion was the big bang theory. Pythagoras' theorem and Hooke's law were both offered despite their names, and four of the Y7 students and four of the Y9 pupils were unable to make a single suggestion of a scientific theory.'

Taber (2006)

Recommended reading

Brown, S., Fauvel, J. and Finnegan, R. (eds) (1981) *Conceptions of Inquiry*. London: Routledge.

Chalmers, A.F. (1982) *What is This Thing Called Science?* (second edition). Milton Keynes: Open University Press.

Gjertson, D. (1989) *Science and Philosophy: past and present*. Harmondsworth: Penguin.

Losee, J. (1993) *A Historical Introduction to the Philosophy of Science* (third edition). Oxford: Oxford University Press.

Riggs, P.J. (1992) *Whys and Ways of Science: introducing philosophical and sociological theories of science*. Melbourne: Melbourne University Press.

School Science Review, **87**(321) – 2006 theme issue on teaching about ideas and evidence in science.

References

Abd-El-Khalick, F. (2002) *The influence of a philosophy of science course on preservice secondary teachers' views of nature of science*. Paper presented at the Annual International Conference of the Association for the Education of Teachers in Science, Charlotte, North Carolina 10–13 January 2002.

Abd-El-Khalick, F. and Lederman, N. G. (2000) The influence of history of science courses on students' views of nature of science. *Journal of Research in Science Teaching*, **37**(10), 1057–1095.

Aikenhead, G. S. (2006) *Science Education for Everyday Life: Evidence-based practice*. New York: Teachers College Press.

Arnold, M. and Millar, R. (1993) *Students' Understanding of the Nature of Science: Annotated Bibliography* (Vol. Working paper 11). Leeds/York: Children's Learning in Science Research Group, University of Leeds/University of York Science Education Group.

Cerini, B., Murray, I. and Reiss, M. (2003) *Student Review of the Science Curriculum: Major findings*. London: Planet Science/Institute of Education/Science Museum.

Driver, R., Leach, J., Millar, R. and Scott, P. (1996) *Young People's Images of Science*. Buckingham: Open University Press.

Duit, R. (2009) *Students' and teachers' conceptions and science education*. Available at: www.ipn.uni-kiel.de/aktuell/stcse/stcse.html

Duschl, R.A. (2000) Making the nature of science explicit. In Millar, R., Leach, J. and Osborne, J. (eds) *Improving Science Education: the contribution of research* (pp. 187–206). Buckingham: Open University Press.

Grosslight, L., Unger, C., Jay, E. and Smith, C. L. (1991) Understanding models and their use in science: conceptions of middle and high school students and experts. *Journal of Research in Science Teaching*, **28**(9), 799–822.

Hodson, D. (2009) *Teaching and Learning About Science: Language, theories, methods, history, tradiitons and values*. Rotterdam, The Netherlands: Sense Publishers.

Kuhn, T.S. (1996) *The Structure of Scientific Revolutions* (3rd ed.). Chicago: University of Chicago.

Levinson, R. (2007) Teaching controversial socio-scientific issues to gifted and talented students. In Taber, K.S. (ed) *Science Education for Gifted Learners* (pp. 128–141). London: Routledge.

Matthews, M.R. (1994) *Science Teaching: The role of history and philosophy of science*. London: Routledge.

Millar R. and Osborne J. (1998) *Beyond 2000: Science education for the future*. London: King's College.

Osborne, J. (2002) Learning and teaching about the nature of science. In Amos, S. and Boohan, R. (eds) *Teaching Science in Secondary Schools: Perspectives on practice* (pp. 227–237). London: Routledge Falmer.

QCA (2007a) *Science: Programme of study for Key Stage 3 and attainment targets*. London: Qualifications and Curriculum Authority.

QCA (2007b) *Science: Programme of study for Key Stage 4*. London: Qualifications and Curriculum Authority.

Solomon, J. (1995) Higher level understanding of the nature of science. *School Science Review,* **76**(276), 15–22.

Taber, K.S. (2006) Exploring pupils' understanding of key 'nature of science' terms though research as part of initial teacher education. *School Science Review,* **87**(321) 51–61.

Taber, K.S. (2007) *Enriching School Science for the Gifted Learner.* London: Gatsby Science Enhancement Programme.

Taber, K.S. (2008) Towards a curricular model of the nature of science. *Science and Education,* **17**(2–3), 179–218.

Taber, K.S. (2009) *Progressing Science Education: Constructing the scientific research programme into the contingent nature of learning science.* Dordrecht: Springer.

Taber, K.S. (2011) The natures of scientific thinking: creativity as the handmaiden to logic in the development of public and personal knowledge. In Khine, M.S. (ed.) *Advances in the Nature of Science Research Concepts and Methodologies* (pp. 51-74). Dordrecht: Springer.

Chapter 4

Pedagogical content knowledge (PCK): a summary review of PCK in the context of science education research

Amanda Berry

The term 'pedagogical content knowledge' (PCK) was introduced by Lee Shulman, an American educationalist, in his 1986 presidential address to the American Educational Research Association (Shulman, 1986). Shulman was seeking to draw attention to a missing dimension in educational research, which had overlooked the central role of subject matter content in teaching. Shulman presented a strong case for PCK as a specific and unique form of knowledge for teaching:

> '... that special amalgam of content and pedagogy that is uniquely the province of teachers.'
>
> Shulman (1986, p. 9)

In this way, PCK refers to the kind of knowledge possessed by a subject specialist in a particular field (such as a specialist in chemistry, physics or biology) as distinct from a teacher's skill of combining content and pedagogy in meaningful ways in order to promote student learning. Shulman conceptualised PCK as including:

> '... the most powerful analogies, illustrations, examples, explanations, and demonstrations – in a word, the ways of representing and formulating the subject that makes it comprehensible for others.'
>
> Shulman (1986, p. 9).

He asserted that teachers need this type of knowledge to structure the content of their lessons, to choose or develop specific representations or analogies, to understand and anticipate particular preconceptions or learning difficulties of their students, and so on. He suggested that the more representations and strategies teachers have at their disposal within a certain subject domain, and the better they understand their students' learning processes in the same domain, the more effectively they can teach in that domain.

In a later publication, Shulman (1987, p. 8) included PCK in what he called 'the knowledge base for teaching'. This knowledge base consisted of seven categories that include:

1   content knowledge
2   general pedagogical knowledge, with special reference to those broad principles and strategies of classroom management and organisation that appear to transcend subject matter
3   curriculum knowledge, with particular grasp of the materials and programs that serve as 'tools of the trade' for teachers
4   pedagogical content knowledge
5   knowledge of learners and their characteristics
6   knowledge of educational contexts, ranging from workings of the group or classroom, the governance and financing of school districts, to the character of communities and cultures
7   knowledge of educational ends, purposes and values, and their philosophical and historical grounds.

These categories were derived from scholarship in the content discipline of science, educational materials and structures, science education research and the wisdom of practice (Shulman, 1987) and were intended to highlight the special role of content knowledge and to situate it within a larger landscape of professional knowledge for teaching.

Conceptualising PCK

Since its introduction, there has been a great deal of research on PCK, much of which has developed within the field of science education. One of the major issues researchers have focused on is what comprises PCK and whether it is a separate category of knowledge, or a transformation of other kinds of knowledge (such as subject matter knowledge, pedagogical knowledge and knowledge of context) into a teachable form. Since Shulman himself did not offer a precise definition of PCK (rather he put it forward as an important idea for discussion), this situation has led to researchers conceptualising PCK in a range of ways. Most have drawn on Shulman's knowledge base for teaching as a starting point, and in particular two key elements of PCK – knowledge of comprehensible representations of subject matter, and understanding of content-related learning difficulties.

In an often-cited paper, Magnusson, Krajcik and Borko (1999) presented PCK as a separate domain of teacher knowledge that exists alongside other domains, such as pedagogical knowledge and beliefs. In their discussion of the nature of PCK, they presented a model in which PCK for science teaching consists of five aspects or components:

1 orientations toward teaching science

2 knowledge of science curricula

3 knowledge of students' understanding of science

4 knowledge of assessment in science

5 knowledge of subject-specific and topic-specific strategies.

Acknowledging that these components may interact in very complex ways, these authors claim that effective teachers need to develop expertise in all aspects of pedagogical content knowledge, and with respect to all topics they teach. Orientations toward teaching science, in particular, have been identified as a critical component within this PCK model (Friedrichsen and Dana, 2005). Sources that shape teachers' orientations towards teaching science include: prior work experiences, professional development choices, beliefs about students and about learning, as well as time constraints.

Some researchers have pointed out that investigating PCK in terms of specific components or categories may lead to an overly simplistic or fragmented representation of teachers' knowledge. To acknowledge its constantly evolving nature, Cochran, DeRuiter and King (1993) preferred to speak of pedagogical content *knowing* (PCKg). Similarly, Mason (1999) emphasised the dynamic nature of PCK in research and in teaching, respectively. Rather than representing PCK as a fixed or static body of knowledge, Mason perceived PCK as an *ability* to combine content knowledge of a discipline with the teaching of that discipline. Adding to this, Hashweh (2005) proposed that PCK should be considered a collection or repertoire of pedagogical constructions, which teachers acquire when repeatedly teaching a certain topic.

Loughran and colleagues argued that researchers often fail to acknowledge the complex relationships and interactions existing within a teacher's personal professional knowledge base (Loughran *et al.* 2001, 2004). Attempting to portray PCK in a way that is valid and useful from a science teacher's point of view, these authors constructed a series of Resource Folios for various science topics consisting of a CoRe in combination with so-called PaP-eRs (Pedagogical and Professional-experience Repertoire). For example, a Resource Folio for the topic of 'Particle Theory' includes a CoRe and PaP-eRs about teaching and learning this topic. A CoRe is structured around questions related to some of the elements of Shulman's knowledge base, in particular knowledge of the main content ideas associated with a specific topic, teaching procedures and purposes, and knowledge about students' thinking. Table 1 shows an example of a CoRe.

Each CoRe is connected to a collection of PaP-eRs, which illustrate aspects of PCK 'in action' of the topic under consideration. PaP-eRs are short narratives based on teachers' accounts of teaching a specific topic and are intended to make explicit teachers' pedagogical reasoning, that is, the thinking and actions of a capable teacher in teaching a specific aspect of the content. PaP-eRs include a variety of narrative representations, for example: a dialogue between two teachers exploring their approach to the teaching of particular content and student responses to it; a teacher's annotated curriculum document; or a student's perspective of a teaching/learning situation. The function of PaP-eRs is to elaborate and give insight into the various interacting elements that comprise a teacher's PCK. (See Box 1 for an example of a PaP-eR.)

To summarise, while the idea of PCK has been an attractive one to researchers and much research has been generated about it, particularly in science education research, there is no universally agreed upon definition of PCK. The boundaries around the concept have remained fuzzy which has meant that what researchers have looked for and how they have interpreted their findings has varied considerably. Several dilemmas also arise in looking across the research that has been produced. These include:

1   a lack of clarity about whether PCK should be thought of as knowledge which is very specific for each topic that teachers teach, or whether there are ideas or approaches that are useful across topics or even across a whole discipline area (e.g. element – concept, chemical reactions – topic, science – discipline)

2   the difficulties of trying to research PCK in a way that avoids breaking it into separate and static parts that may result in a simplistic and hence a misleading picture of teachers' knowledge

3   how PCK can become a useful and relevant construct for science teachers, as well as researchers.

Investigating PCK

Investigating PCK in science education has developed through a variety of approaches. Often this research has involved exploring what teachers do and do not know about some aspect of teaching a particular topic, and typically includes comparisons of knowledge between different teachers (e.g. Magnusson and Krajcik, 1993: heat energy and temperature), between novice and expert teachers (e.g. Clermont, Borko and Krajcik, 1994: density and air pressure), or as a result of some kind of intervention, such as a workshop or pre-service course (e.g. van Driel, Verloop and de Vos, 1998: chemical equilibrium; Veal, Tippins and Bell, 1998: linear motion, thermodynamics). The relationship between teachers' subject matter knowledge and PCK has also been explored (e.g. Geddis et al. 1993: isotopes; Parker and Heywood, 2000: forces in floating and sinking). Thus much of the research has been trying to understand aspects of teachers' PCK rather than exploring the whole of a teacher's PCK about a particular topic.

The development of PCK

The development of PCK is thought to be a complex and nonlinear process that is rooted in teachers' classroom practice (Magnusson et al. 1999) and revolves around teachers' interpretation of subject matter knowledge and general pedagogical knowledge (Marks, 1990). It is apparent that the PCK development of primary school teachers may differ from that of secondary school teachers because usually the former do not specialise in a specific subject area. Therefore, they may not develop specific PCK for all of the different topic and subjects that they teach, but instead develop PCK on a more general level (Appleton, 2008).

Three main themes characterise research on how PCK develops, as described below. Much of this work draws on research with pre-service teachers and is located predominantly in the context of science education.

1   **The role of subject matter knowledge:** Most researchers agree that subject matter knowledge is prerequisite to the development of PCK and that limited content knowledge restricts the development of teachers' PCK.

2 **Teaching experience with a focus on student learning:** Lack of content knowledge combined with lack of experience (and confidence) is thought to delay the development of PCK. Since PCK is considered to develop with experience, the implication is that pre-service or beginning teachers usually have little or no PCK (van Driel et al. 1998). On the other hand, an expert teacher will have well-formed PCK for the topics that are commonly taught. Some teacher education programs have been directed towards improving these aspects of knowledge and experience – for example, through providing primary pre-service teachers with science 'activities that work' (Appleton, 2003), or opportunities to observe school students' learning in practice, and, in connection to this, to study the research literature (e.g. on misconceptions regarding specific science topics).

3 **The design of teacher education:** The design of pre-service programs can restrict the development of PCK where courses on content and pedagogy are separate and pre-service teachers are not encouraged to link their learning in these areas.

From studies on experienced teachers, however, it appears that strong and well-integrated subject matter knowledge does not guarantee the smooth development of a teacher's PCK. In particular, when teaching unfamiliar topics, it appears that PCK cannot simply be 'imported' from one topic area into another. This is because the development of teaching approaches that respond to a deep knowledge of the content is something that is built up and developed over time. This also suggests that the development of PCK should be an important element of the continuing education of all teachers.

The role of teaching experience was highlighted in a ten-year study of one primary science teacher (Mulholland and Wallace, 2005). This study found that the various knowledge bases that comprise PCK all grew over time, although in different ways. In particular, general teaching knowledge bases and interactive knowledge bases, such as knowledge about learners, developed substantially, whereas subject knowledge bases remained relatively stable. This study also illustrated the development of PCK as a complex pattern of interactions between these various components, which is situated in the teacher's classroom. In this particular study, new curriculum materials appeared to be an important source for this development.

To date, research on the development of PCK presents an ambiguous picture. Teaching experience and subject matter knowledge are obviously important but contextual and personal factors apparently may lead to quite different processes of knowledge development. The development of PCK is perhaps then best viewed as a complex interplay between knowledge of subject matter, teaching and learning, and context, and the way in which teachers combine and use this knowledge to express their expertise. In the context of pre-service teacher education, PCK can be promoted by addressing both pre-service teachers' subject matter knowledge and their educational beliefs, in combination with providing them with opportunities to gain teaching experience, and, in particular, to reflect on these experiences. Specific workshops may serve as an intermediate measure, helping to set a frame for subsequent teaching experiences.

Conclusion

In terms of science learning at the level of specific topics there is little research to inform us about the ways in which teachers transform subject matter knowledge and how they relate their transformations to student understanding. Neither has there been specific input for teacher education in this respect. Instead, most recommendations regarding PCK development for pre-service and in-service teacher education are of a rather general nature.

In the view of this author, PCK implies a transformation of subject matter knowledge so that it can be used effectively and flexibly in the communication process between teachers and learners during classroom practice. From this perspective, the main aim in studying science teachers' PCK is to understand how and why teachers teach a certain science topic the way they do, and, in particular, how their teaching approach is related to, or focused on, student learning in science. Achieving such understanding is vital to the development of effective pre-service and in-service programs.

However, much of the research on PCK so far has not served this purpose very well. This can be explained partly by the tacit nature of teachers' personal professional knowledge, which has urged scholars to develop instruments and procedures that help to make this knowledge explicit and measure PCK in a valid manner, rather than exploring what the construct might offer for the practice of teaching and teacher education. Also, it must be noted that PCK is quite sensitive to personal characteristics of teachers, and their working contexts. Several studies (e.g. Henze, 2006) have reported substantial differences between the PCK of experienced science teachers around the same topic area, even when their subject matter knowledge is similar and when they teach the same curriculum. These differences appear to stem from a range of factors including different orientations towards teaching, different purposes and practices.

Nevertheless, it seems possible to capture and portray PCK in such a way that key notions of teaching and learning a specific topic are made explicit (van Driel et al. 1998). Also, discussing and sharing such key notions among teachers may contribute to the establishment of a 'collective' PCK – that is, a shared or common form of teachers' professional practical knowledge about teaching certain subject matter. At the same time, there should, of course, be room for individual teachers to adapt or complement this shared knowledge to their own situations (cf. the above-mentioned Resource Folios of Loughran and colleagues).

In reflecting on PCK research in science education, Abell (2008) questioned whether PCK is still a useful construct 20 years after its introduction by Shulman. She convincingly gave an affirmative answer to this question stating:

> 'We still do not know enough about what PCK science teachers have, how they come to have it, or what they do with it.'
>
> Abell (2008, p. 1413)

Abell highlighted a range of research areas and questions for further study using PCK as a theoretical framework. These areas include:

- examining PCK across different grade levels, career stages, disciplines and topics
- investigating the *quality* of teachers' PCK in addition to measuring the *amount* of PCK they have

- understanding more about PCK development, particularly at critical points in a teacher's career, and generating models of PCK development
- putting in place systematic, long-term programmes of study.

Introducing the construct of PCK – and examining, analysing and modelling it in pre-service teacher education practice (both at university and in school-based practice) – makes it more likely that teaching will be seen as a specialised and sophisticated practice. In this way, PCK may emerge as a way of thinking about teaching subject matter that encourages learning about teaching as going beyond the acquisition of instructional strategies and techniques, to include an understanding of how learners develop insight in specific school subjects.

Table 1 (pages 36–38) CoRe for Particle Theory. This table offers some of the range of ideas that might be covered in teaching Year 7–9 science students on the topic of Particle Theory. The list of important science ideas/concepts is not designed to imply that these are the 'only' or the 'correct' ideas/concepts for this topic. They are, however, those important science ideas/concepts that teachers in this project suggested and discussed as pertaining to Particle Theory.

Important science ideas/concepts

	A	B	C	D	E	F	G
1 What you intend the students to learn about this idea	A. That matter is made up of small bits that are called particles.	B. That there is empty space between particles.	C. That particles are different (their speed is changed by temperature) and that they appear in a certain arrangement.	D. That particles of different substances are different from one another.	E. That there are different kinds of particles that, when joined, are different again. There are different 'smallest bits'.	F. That there is conservation of matter. Particles don't disappear or get created – rather their arrangements change.	G. That the concept of a model is used to explain the things we observe.
2 Why it is important for students to know this	Because it helps to explain the behaviour of everyday things; e.g. diffusion.	Because it explains the ability to compress things and helps to explain events such as expansion and dissolving.	Because it explains what happens in phase changes, e.g. the need to contain gases is evidence that the particles are moving.	Because it explains the observable behaviours of different substances.	Because it explains why there are a limited number of elements, but many different kinds of compounds. It also accounts for the concept of atoms and molecules.	Because in any reaction involving matter, all of that matter must be accounted for.	Because the use of models links to important ideas about the way we explore and express views about the nature of science, e.g. the particle theory was constructed rather than discovered.
3 What else you know about this idea (that you do not intend students to know yet)	Subatomic structure. Chemical reactions. Ions (links to electricity). Generalisations about properties of materials. More complicated models of matter. Links to diffusion and thermal properties of matter.					That the bits themselves are different when combined (e.g. ionic and molecular formation).	
4 Difficulties/ limitations connected with teaching this idea	Particles are too small to see. The use of models is not necessary to comprehend science in every day life. Substances 'appear to' disappear when dissolved. What holds particles together? Why don't substances automatically become a gas?	There is a big difference between macro (seen) and micro (unseen) levels, e.g. wood seems solid so it is hard to picture empty space between the 'wood particles.	The term 'state' implies that things are separate and fixed. It is difficult to imagine particles in a solid moving. There are problems with some representations of liquid, e.g. particles are often shown as being much further apart than they are in solids. 'Melt' and 'dissolve' are often used interchangeably in everyday life.	That macro properties are a result of micro arrangements is hard to understand.	Students can come to think that molecules 'disassociate' in boiling water (the confusion between atoms and molecules).	Bits are rearranged to create a different substance from existing bits (integrity of particles).	

Important science ideas/concepts

5 Knowledge about students' thinking which influences your teaching of this idea	Many students will use a continuous model (despite former teaching).	The notion of 'space' is very difficult to think about – most students propose that there is other 'stuff' between the particles. Students think that particles get bigger during expansion.	Students have commonly encountered states of matter but do not understand it in terms of particle movement. Students can be confused by the notion of melting and think a particular particle melts.	Students tend to internalise a model from textbooks that shows circles all of the same size.	Students use the terms 'molecule' and 'atom' without understanding concepts. They simply adopt the language.	Students believe that new stuff can appear.
6 Other factors that influence your teaching of this idea	Maturity – stage of psychological development, readiness to grapple with abstract ideas. Dealing with many different student conceptions at once. Knowledge of context (students' and teacher's). Using the term 'phase' suggests the idea of a continuum and helps to address the difficulties associated with the term 'state'.					
7 Teaching procedures (and particular reasons for using these to engage with this idea)	**Probes** of student understanding, e.g. students draw a flask containing air, then re-draw the same flask with some of the air removed. Probes promote student thinking and uncover individual's views of situations. **Analogies:** Use of analogies to draw parallel between new ideas and specific/similar situations. For example, although something may appear to be made up of one thing – like a pipe is made up of one piece of metal – it is really the combination of lots of small things. This can be analogous to a jar of sand. From a distance it looks like one thing, but up close you can see the individual grains of sand.	**POE** (Predict, Observe, Explain): e.g. squashing syringe of air (ask students to predict the outcome based on different models of matter). **Mixing activities:** e.g. methylated spirits and water or salt and water (the outcome can be explained by empty space between the bits). **Comparing models.**	**Translation activities:** e.g. role play, modelling, drawing. **Creative writing:** Compare pieces with and without misconceptions, i.e. share students' work around the class and encourage students' comments on aspects of understanding in them. **Using models and demonstrations:** e.g. a jar of marbles as model: packed tight to illustrate a solid; remove one and shake to demonstrate movement in a liquid. **Observation:** Dry ice sublimating – what's happening?	**Mixing activities:** it can be helpful to model the mixing of different substances by, for example, using different sized balls for the mixing of water and methylated spirits.	**POE** (Predict, Observe, Explain): e.g. water boiling (this can create a need for different kinds of smallest bits). **Modelling with specific materials:** e.g. explore the possible combinations in new things.	

Important science ideas/concepts

7 Cont. **Teaching** **procedures** **(and particular** **reasons for** **using these to** **engage with** **this idea)**	**Linking activities:** Behaviour of everyday things, e.g. putting a marshmallow in a gas jar and changing the pressure so the behaviour of the marshmallow is affected. It helps to illustrate the point that small bits move or act differently in response to changes in conditions. The marshmallow is good because it is an example of something they are familiar with – it links to their everyday experience.					
8 Specific **ways of** **ascertaining** **students'** **understanding** **or confusion** **around this** **idea (include** **likely range of** **responses)**	Explaining thinking and defending views. Making predictions about new situations. Tracking one's own learning e.g. 'I used to think . . .' Ask questions such as 'What is something that has been bothering you from yesterday's lesson?'	Concept Map using the terms solid, liquid, gas, particles, air, nothing.		Draw a picture to show what happens to water particles when water boils.		
	Questions such as: 'Explain why popcorn pops' 'Why when popcorn is pierced does it not pop?' 'Why can we smell onions being cooked when we are at a distance from them?' 'Why does a syringe containing NO_2 appear darker when it is compressed?'					

Put on your 'Magic Glasses' (which are glasses that enable you to see the particles in substances) – What do you see? (i.e. discuss what might be seen through the magic glasses) OR Draw what you see (then compare and discuss these drawings).

Box 1 A PaP-eR on the Particle Model: Seeing things differently

Introduction

This PaP-eR illustrates how important the teacher's understanding of the content is in influencing how she approaches her teaching about the Particle Model of matter. In this PaP-eR, the teaching unfolds over a number of lessons and is based on the view that understanding how a model can help to explain everyday phenomena requires continual revisiting and reinforcement with students. The PaP-eR closes with an illustration of how inherent contradictions in teaching resources need to be recognised and addressed in order to minimise their level of 'interference' in learning specific concepts and how important that is in teaching about models.

Rhonda is a chemistry specialist with a commitment to making science meaningful for her students. She enjoys teaching about states of matter and has developed a number of important 'frames' for approaching the content so that her students will better grasp the ideas rather than simply learn how to 'parrot' the appropriate science responses in a test.

Rhonda's framing in the interview – the content

At year 7 level it really is only a very limited particle theory that I teach – I don't go into atomic structure in any serious way. I try to introduce the students to the idea that everything around them is not continuous but is made up of small particles that fit together. I don't try to give any detail about how they fit together but I do talk with them about the particles being roughly spherical objects that are very, very, very, very tiny.

I know that getting students to use a particle model is not going to fully happen: they will revert to a continuous model when they are pushed. But it is important to start moving them some way along the path – to get them to consider that there may be another way of looking at the things around us. The ideas of the particle model also need to be linked to what is happening during phase changes (melting, freezing etc.) and that link needs to be at the very tiny level rather than at the macroscopic level. So these two ideas influence how I approach the teaching.

It's important to continually remind yourself that particle theory at years 7 and 8 needs to be presented in helpful ways. I believe that maturity plays an important part in what students can actually grasp at a certain age. It's easy, as the teacher, to forget how conceptually difficult and conceptually abstract this topic is. It is an important topic to teach about though, because it's one of those building blocks of chemistry that you can build on in layers over the years in science classes rather than trying to do it all at once. It's conceptually meaty so I enjoy teaching it!

So what do I do? Well I suppose the first issue is helping the students to start thinking differently about what they're looking at. It's important to help them realise that although the things they are looking at appear to be made up of one thing – like a piece of pipe is made up of one piece of metal – you can break it down until it is made up of lots of small things combining together. A simple analogy is a jar of sand. From a distance it looks like one thing, but up close you can see the individual grains of sand.

From this, you can begin to explain the behaviour of everyday things in terms of movements of particles. This is a big shift in thinking for students. Again, you can play with this idea by getting something like a marshmallow and putting it in a gas jar and changing the pressure so the behaviour of the marshmallow is affected. (The behaviour is described below.) It helps to illustrate the point about small bits moving or acting differently in response to the conditions. The marshmallow is also good because it is an example of something they are familiar with – it links to their everyday experiences and that really matters. I've built up quite a few of these examples in my teaching over the years; it's good fun too.

The other idea to try and aim for is the idea of space, nothing, between the particles; it's really hard. One way of helping to address this is by using the demonstration of mixing water and methylated spirits. You add equal volumes of them together, if each liquid is one big block of water or of methylated spirits, then the combined volume should be double, but it isn't, so – how come? That helps to make the point about the spaces, so that in this case things can fit between the spaces.

So overall I suppose really I'm only concentrating on three things:

1   *Things are made up of tiny little bits.*
2   *There is space between the tiny little bits.*
3   *You can use the model to explain phase changes, etc.*

But I don't mean to make it sound as simple as that because really what I do is respond to what's happening in the class. Last year I went 'down the density path' even though I wasn't intending to. But, because it was students' questions that took us there, I let it go on and followed it for longer. The point really is that the use of the particle model is a way of thinking and it's something that the students have to be reminded of so that they think about things from that perspective, rather than reverting to their continuous model perspective.

Rhonda's framing in the classroom – 'Imagine'

The unit starts with Rhonda asking the students to imagine that they have been shrunk down so that they are very tiny and then they fall into a droplet of water on the lab bench. They have to imagine what the droplet looks like from the inside, and then they write a short adventure story and draw a picture of what they can see. The students' pictures show a range of responses; a handful contain dots but most of these are explained as being 'the dirt and stuff in the water'. Through a number of activities and discussions over several lessons Rhonda introduces the class to the content ideas that she outlined in the interview.

Then Rhonda gets all of the students to make a pair of cardboard glasses. They decorate these in whatever way they wish. She encourages them to use their imagination in designing their 'magic glasses'. Putting the glasses on is a cue for them to think in terms of particles.

One of the problems I find is that they easily revert back to a continuous model, so putting them in a situation where they wear the glasses and look at something helps them to better understand how the model works to explain what they are seeing. You can get them to put them on at different times throughout the unit and it helps them make the transition to particle model thinking.

In one lesson Rhonda fries onions on the front bench in the laboratory. The students call out from their seats when they start to smell the onions. They track the progress of the smell towards the back of the lab. Rhonda asks them to put on their glasses and look around the room. Can they explain the smell through particle theory? She asks them to think about when they mixed the methylated spirits and water together. With their glasses on they need to describe what is happening as the two liquids combine.

Rhonda shows the class a marshmallow inside a gas jar. By reducing the air pressure in the jar she causes the marshmallow to swell up and then eventually collapse. She asks the students to think about the air inside the marshmallow. If they could 'see' it through their glasses how could they explain what was happening to the marshmallow?

The class revisits the shrinking adventure in the drop of water. Rhonda asks them to think carefully and draw what the inside of a drop of water would be like with the 'magic glasses' on. Later in the unit, Rhonda will introduce a new activity based around the way that textbooks represent water as a liquid.

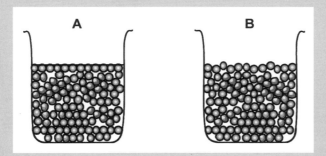

If you look at the pictures in books they often show liquid as particles but the liquid is capped by a continuous line (diagram A), which inadvertently undermines what we're trying to get students to understand by these representations of a particulate model. The students end up thinking that the water is the clear stuff and the particles are just dots in the water.

Rhonda decides that this year she will ask the class to look at a beaker of water through their glasses and to decide which of the two diagrams best represents water and why they think so.

If the students are wearing their glasses when they look at a beaker of water they should see diagram B rather than diagram A. And be able to explain why they do!

Acknowledgement

The author wishes to acknowledge her on-going collaborative PCK research with Professor Jan van Driel of Leiden University, which this paper draws upon.

References

Abell, S.K. (2008) Twenty Years Later: does pedagogical content knowledge remain a useful idea? *International Journal of Science Education* **30**(10), 1405–1416.

Appleton, K. (2003) How do beginning primary school teachers cope with science? Toward an understanding of science teaching practice. *Research in Science Education* 33, 1–25.

Appleton, K. (2008) Developing science pedagogical knowledge through mentoring elementary teachers. *Journal of Science Teacher Education,* **19**(6), 523–545.

Clermont, C.P., Borko, H. and Krajcik, J.S. (1994) Comparative study of the pedagogical content knowledge of experienced and novice chemical demonstrators. *Journal of Research in Science Teaching,* **31**, 419–441

Cochran, K.F., DeRuiter, J.A. and King, R.A. (1993) Pedagogical content knowing: an integrative model for teacher preparation. *Journal of Teacher Education* **44**, 263–272.

Friedrichsen, P.F. and Dana, T.M. (2005) Substantive-level theory of highly regarded secondary biology teachers' science teaching orientations. *Journal of Research in Science Teaching* **42**, 218–244.

Geddis, A.N., Onslow, B., Beynon, C. and Oesch, J. (1993) Transforming Content Knowledge: Learning to teach about isotopes. *Science Education* **77**(6), 575–591.

Hashweh, M.Z. (2005) Teacher pedagogical constructions: a reconfiguration of pedagogical content knowledge. *Teachers and Teaching: theory and practice* 11, 273–292.

Henze, I. (2006) *Science Teachers' Knowledge Development in the Context of Educational Innovation.* PhD Dissertation. Leiden: ICLON, Universiteit Leiden.

Loughran, J., Milroy, P., Berry, A., Gunstone, R. and Mulhall, P. (2001) Documenting science teachers' pedagogical content knowledge through PaP-eRs. *Research in Science Education* **31**, 289–307.

Loughran, J., Mulhall, P. and Berry, A. (2004) In search of pedagogical content knowledge for science: Developing ways of articulating and documenting professional practice. *Journal of Research in Science Teaching* **41**, 370–391.

Magnusson, S. and Krajcik, J.S. (1993) *Teacher Knowledge and Representation of Content in Instruction about Heat Energy and Temperature.* Paper presented at the annual meeting of the National Association for Research in Science Teaching (Atlanta, GA, April 1993) ED387313

Magnusson, S., Krajcik, J. and Borko, H. (1999) Nature, sources, and development of pedagogical content knowledge for science teaching. In Gess-Newsome, J. and Lederman, N.G. (eds) *Examining Pedagogical Content Knowledge* (pp. 95–132). Dordrecht: Kluwer Academic Publishers.

Marks, R. (1990) Pedagogical content knowledge: From a mathematical case to a modified conception. *Journal of Teacher Education* **41**, 3–11.

Mason, C.L. (1999) The TRIAD approach: A consensus for science teaching and learning. In Gess-Newsome, J. and Lederman, N.G. (eds) *Examining Pedagogical Content Knowledge* (pp. 277–292). Dordrecht: Kluwer Academic Publishers.

Mulholland, J. and Wallace, J. (2005) Growing the tree of teacher knowledge: ten years of learning to teach elementary science. *Journal of Research in Science Teaching* **42**, 767–790.

Parker, J. and Heywood, D. (2000) Exploring the relationship between subject knowledge and pedagogic content knowledge in primary teachers' learning about forces. *International Journal of Science Education* **22**(1), 89–111.

Shulman, L.S. (1986) Those who understand: Knowledge growth in teaching. *Educational Researcher* **15**(2), 4–14.

Shulman, L.S. (1987) Knowledge and teaching: foundations of the new reform. *Harvard Educational Review* **57**, 1–22.

van Driel, J.H., Verloop, N. and de Vos, W. (1998) Developing science teachers' pedagogical content knowledge. *Journal of Research in Science Teaching* **35**, 673–695.

Veal, W.R., Tippins, D.J. and Bell, J. (1998) *The Evolution of Pedagogical Content Knowledge in Prospective Secondary Physics Teachers*. Paper presented at the annual meeting of the National Association for Research in Science Teaching, San Diego, CA.

Chapter 5

What do we know about learners' ideas at the Primary level?

Wynne Harlen

What we know about the ideas that learners bring to their science education has changed approaches to teaching science. No longer is this seen as just providing new ideas and facts but rather as changing the ideas and ways of thinking that learners already have and linking them into broader networks of ideas. This chapter begins with research evidence that infants are learning about the world around them right from birth. Thus they already have ideas that they take with them into the Primary school. We then look at some examples of ideas about physical and biological objects and events that have been found to be widely held, and which teachers can expect to find their students to hold. The final section brings together some ways of helping children to form more scientific ideas, basing these on the characteristics of the ideas that they have developed for themselves.

Learning from birth

The reactions of infants have been studied by Gopnik, Meltzoff and Kuhl (1999), using observations of how babies move their heads and their eyes as indications of what interests and what surprises them. One of the findings from studying babies soon after birth is that they look particularly at straight lines and contrasts – they like stripes and corners – and their eyes will trace round the outline of objects shown to them. In this way, they are distinguishing objects from their surroundings. They are also fascinated by movement and, by following the movement of objects they see around them, soon become able to predict where a particular moving object will be even though part of its path is obscured. For instance, if a rolling ball passes behind a screen they look at the point where it ought to appear again. Thus Gopnik *et al.* (1999, p. 70) conclude that:

'In the first few months of life, babies ... know how to use edges and patterns of movement to segregate the world into separate objects. They know something about how these object characteristically move. They also know that objects are part of three-dimensional space.'

Using these methods, which enable infants' understanding to be inferred before they have developed speech, researchers have shown that in the first year of life infants understand that inanimate objects cannot move themselves. At the same time they realise that animate objects do have the potential to move by themselves (Spelke, 1990), confirming Piaget's earlier observation of his own children (Piaget, 1952).

Two ideas are particularly important in understanding the world around us: the permanence of objects, and causality. If the ball does not appear from behind the screen, the very young baby shows puzzlement but seems not to consider that it is still there. So even if they see an object being hidden under a cloth they may not look for it there. The idea that objects which seem to disappear must still exist somewhere takes time to develop. Causality is inferred from observation that some effect invariably follows some action or change. Infants very soon find that they can cause something to happen but it takes time for them to distinguish between psychological causality (getting a response from a parent by smiling or crying) and physical causality. This has happened by about their first birthday, when they can work out how to make something happen and seem to have some idea of how objects can influence each other. This means that they begin to give explanations of events in terms of something that might be a cause.

Duschl, Schweingruber and Shouse (2007, p. 54) conclude from an extensive review of research that there is a pattern in young children's understanding of events and phenomena that reflects differences between domains: *'These include mechanics, folk biology, some aspects of chemistry (e.g. an initial understanding of different substances) and folk psychology.'* Such patterns are found in children's understanding in the many countries where studies of this kind have been carried out. Duschl *et al.* also note that:

> 'Not only does the growth of scientific understanding involve a sense of the patterns special to such domains as physics and biology, but it also requires much broader cognitive skills that cut across domains. These include an ability to stand back and look at one's knowledge and learning, heuristics that enable one to efficiently process large amounts of information, and strategies for acquiring, maintaining and transmitting information.'

Duschl et al. (2007, p. 55)

Ideas of Primary school children

Given this intense mental activity in pre-school years, it is not surprising that children enter school with some ideas already formed about how things in the physical and biological world are explained. Although these ideas are frequently referred to as 'misconceptions', it is clear that they are the result of reasoning, albeit limited, based on their particular experience. Rather than thinking of these ideas as mistaken and needing correction, it is more productive to think of them as indicating that children are eager to make sense of things around them, as the following examples show.

Forces

Although most of the research into children's ideas has been with Secondary-aged children, the ideas of Primary and Middle school students have been studied, particularly by Osborne and Freyberg (1985) in New Zealand, Vosniadou (1997) in Greece, Smith, di Sessa and Roschelle (1993) in the USA and in England by the Science Processes and Concepts Exploration (SPACE) project (1990–1998).

Osborne and Freyberg (1985), in the New Zealand Learning Science Project, interviewed children about instances drawn on cards. For example, one card showed a man trying to move a car by pushing, but not succeeding in moving in. When the children were asked if there was a force on the car, the common response was that there was no movement and so no force. When asked about the forces on a ball thrown upwards, they claimed an upward force while the ball is rising after it has left the hand and then a downward force once it has reached its highest point and is falling.

Russell, McGuigan and Hughes (1998), in the SPACE report on Forces, identify a sequence in understanding the concept of force. Younger Primary children refer to pushes and pulls, but not often to these as forces. Russell *et al.* (p. 137) suggest that children should be guided to use the terms 'push' and 'pull': *'… as precursors to the more generalized term 'force', rather than as instances of the term force'* (author's emphasis). Young Primary children initially refer to pushes and pulls as actions of themselves as agents, then extend this to other living things and then to inanimate agents such as the wind and machines.

Gravity is a universally experienced force and it is perhaps because it is always present that children do not take it into account. Things that are dropped fall downwards 'naturally'. The SPACE research showed that various kinds of activities designed to help children to see gravity as a force acting towards the Earth from all directions resulted in a large shift in Primary children's recognition of gravity as a force pulling things down, although few described the force as being towards the centre of the Earth.

Floating is a phenomenon depending on the balance of forces acting on an object in a fluid, such as water, but children often consider that other factors are involved, such as the speed of movement of the object and the depth of water. Biddulph and Osborne (1984) asked children about a range of possible variables that might affect floating, such as the size of the object or the depth of water. The results show a definite trend with age. Only 10% of the 8-year-olds thought that a whole candle would float at the same level as a short piece of the candle. This proportion was 30% for 10-year-olds and 65% for 12-year-olds. Even at the age of 12 years, however, a quarter of the children thought the full-length candle would float lower than the short piece. To investigate the effect of changing the depth of water the children were shown a cross-sectional drawing of a boat being launched in shallow water and then moving to deep water. Half of the 8-year-olds said it would float lower in the deeper water; about a fifth of 10 and 12-year-olds also gave this answer.

Research across a variety of static and dynamic events indicates that Primary-aged children:

- consider that moving objects need a constant force to keep them moving in the same way
- believe that an object that is not moving has no forces acting on it
- believe that a moving body has a force acting on it in the direction of motion.

These are all ideas that have certain logic in relation to limited everyday experience and are held by many Secondary school students and not a few adults. Their apparent 'common sense' makes them difficult to change.

Sound and light

Children's ideas about how they hear and see things were investigated in the SPACE project by interview, and by asking children to represent their explanation of events in drawings, which they annotate themselves or tell an adult how to annotate. For instance, after some experience with making sounds with different objects, children were asked about how a drum makes a sound and how they hear it. It was typical of younger Primary children to 'explain' in terms of the actions rather than a mechanism. For instance, they might state: *'I think I hear the sound by listening hard and I think it could be because the drum sound is very loud'*.

Older children used the term 'vibration' as the source of the sound but often in an ambiguous way – as being the same as the sound, as in this description of how a string telephone (string connecting two yoghurt pots) works:

'The voices went to the string and were then transferred into vibrations which went down the string and when it got to the other yoghurt pot and were then transferred back into a voice.'

In relation to sight, children past the stage of believing that objects no longer exist if they are hidden from view or if they close their eyes nevertheless commonly describe the process of seeing as if it is their eyes that produce the light that makes the objects appear. When asked to show how they see an object, they draw and describe something like a ray of light directed out of the eye to the object along the line of sight. This is an understandable interpretation of the subjective experience of 'looking'. When we choose to look at something we do feel our eyes turn as if we are the active agent in the process. This is a persistent and widespread conception, which can interfere with later learning.

Living things and life processes

The concept of 'living things' as including plants and animals does not seem to appear until the upper Primary years (Carey, 1988). Even then, the meaning of 'animal' may not be the biological one. Research carried out by Bell and Barker (1982), involving interviews and a survey of children from age 5 to 17 years, showed that children's initial idea of what is an animal is restricted to large land mammals. For instance, a high proportion of their sample of 5-year-olds recognised a cow as an animal and the proportion rose to 100% by the age of 7 years. However, creatures such as worms and spiders were not considered to be animals by three-quarters of the 9-year-olds and only a slightly lower proportion of 12-year-olds. Only a fifth of the sample of 5-year-olds considered a human being to be an animal and this proportion rose to just over a half for children aged 9–12.

They recognise that plants need soil, water and light but younger children do not attempt to explain why. When asked to explain, a 10-year-old wrote:

'I think the plant needs water to keep it alive. I also think that it needs some soil to help the plant to grow. The plant sucks the soil up the stem. The soil has got something in it to help the plant grow. The plant needs sun because if it did not have light it would never open its petals'.

unpublished SPACE research, quoted in Harlen and Qualter (2009)

The 'explanation' here is not in terms of processes but only of need. Similarly, in relation to their own bodies, Primary children have little idea about processes of digestion, reproduction, or how muscles work. This is hardly surprising since many adults have misconceptions about biological processes (Driver *et al.* 1994).

SPACE research into children's ideas about the processes of life shows that young children become aware of separate organs each with a single function inside their bodies, starting with the heart. Later they come to perceive connecting channels between the organs that enable them to work together. When children were asked to draw, on an outline of the human body, what they thought was in their own bodies, it was found that children drew those parts that they could feel. For example, they identified the heart and bones. They also were aware of the brain. But in general they did not know about organs such as kidneys, lungs and intestines, which are not sensed (Osborn, Wadsworth and Black, 1992).

Matter and materials

Children's ideas about matter change quite dramatically in the Primary years (Duschl et al. 2007). Their early ideas are grounded in how things appear to their senses. Weight is judged from how heavy things feel in their hands, size is judged overall rather than from particular dimensions and there is no conception of density. Their understanding of matter changes when they come to measure weight/mass and volume. However, they still have difficulty when going beyond what they can see and feel (Smith, Solomon and Carey, 2005). So the idea that gases are material is difficult. For instance, a child explained: *'You can't see the air, but sometimes you think there is nothing in there 'cos you can't see anything but it isn't a matter of seeing, it's a matter of knowing.'* Similarly the idea of matter being composed of particles far too small to be seen is not entertained by many in the Primary years.

However, at the macroscopic level, even pre-school children relate properties of different materials to their uses and know that breaking something up may change its appearance but not the material from which it is made (Smith, Carey and Wider, 1985). Later the use of materials is recognised as being directly related to the children's experience of the properties required by various objects. For example, chalk is used for writing on the blackboard because it is soft and white, glass is used for windows because you can see through it, wood is used for doors and furniture because it is strong, firm, keeps out the rain and doesn't tear or bend (Russell, Longden and McGuigan, 1991).

The Earth in space

Children's early ideas about the movement of the Sun and Moon derive from their perceptions of the apparent rapid movements of the positions of these bodies caused by the children's own movement from one place to another. The fact that they can see the Sun wherever they are gives them the idea that it follows them around. Older children can distinguish this apparent rapid and irregular movement from the regular patterns of movement day by day, although these will inevitably be interpreted as the Sun moving round the Earth.

In their drawings, children represent the Moon and stars in conventional manner – a crescent moon and pointed stars, since they frequently see representations like this. They also see globes, drawings and even photographs from space, showing that the Earth is spherical and this experience is reflected in their drawings. However, this information is difficult to reconcile with their direct observations and leaves them having to *'deal with incompatible pieces of information, some stemming from everyday experience and some coming from the surrounding culture'* (Vosniadou, 1997, p. 48). Here Vosniadou was drawing on findings about children's ideas about the Earth. She found that most children above the age of about three had been exposed to information in one form or another that the Earth is spherical, while their everyday experience told them that it was flat. Their struggle to reconcile these two concepts led to some seemingly odd ideas – of a hollow sphere in which there is a flat surface on which people live, or of two Earths, a round one in the sky with all the characteristics of the adult model, and a flat one on which people live. This is an example of constructs that may result from providing new information without regard to ideas that the children may already have.

Some general characteristics of Primary children's ideas

A key feature emerging even from these few examples of children's ideas has been that they are clearly the result of reasoning. Children have worked out these ideas for themselves and believe in them. The fact that similar ideas are found from working with children of quite different backgrounds suggests that the ideas are the product of children's reasoning about things that are experienced everywhere – the weather, the sky, different kinds of living things including human beings, materials, rocks and soil, and so on. This makes it particularly important to take these ideas seriously, not brush them aside and expect children to accept more 'accurate' but different explanations of events. From a child's point of view, their ideas make more sense than the 'scientific' view, which is often counter-intuitive. The scientific view frequently makes use of ideas based on things that are not observable by children, such as water vapour, unseen forces, vibrations in air, and so on. For example, the notion that moving things come to a stop if you stop pushing them suggests that it is 'natural' for movement to stop, whereas the scientific view is that there must be a force to stop the movement. The teacher's role is indeed to help children to develop scientific understanding, and close study of how children reach the ideas they already have will give clues about how best to do this.

Inevitably children's ideas are based on limited experience and the relatively few examples that they will have encountered. Anyone might conclude that 'all wood floats' if they have not come across ebony or lignum vitae. So extending experience is a central aim of Primary school science. However, experience alone is not enough. In addition, it is necessary to ensure that the cognitive skills mentioned on page 45 in this chapter, in quoting Duschl *et al.* (2007), are being developed so that children have the ability to gather and interpret evidence in a scientific way.

It may also be necessary to offer and scaffold alternative ways of explaining events and to provide the appropriate vocabulary. Quite often the everyday use of words – such as 'animal' (as excluding humans) and 'energy' (as a property of a person), for example – has a considerable effect on children's concepts. This is particularly strong in the case of the concept of 'animal'. For example, notices in shops saying 'No animals allowed' would reinforce a narrow view of the notion of 'animal'. These everyday ways of using the word conflict with the scientific use, based on the common features shared by all animals. The conflict can have serious consequences in children's misunderstanding if there is any uncertainty as to which meaning of the word is being used in a particular instance. A teacher can do nothing to prevent the word being used loosely in everyday situations, but can help children to recognise that the words have different meanings in different contexts.

Finally, children often use different ideas to explain what, from an adult point of view, is the same phenomenon encountered in different contexts. For instance, children may realise that moving air helps wet clothes to dry yet may consider that puddles dry up only because water leaks through the ground. A key aim of science education is to enable learners to develop 'big' ideas that allow them to make sense of a range of experiences. Their 'small' ideas, relating to specific situations, need to be linked together to give more powerful networks of ideas, a process that can be helped by teachers asking for ideas to be tried and tested in new situations.

References

Bell, B. and Barker, M. (1982) Towards a scientific concept of 'animal'. *Journal of Biological Education* **16**(3), 197–200.

Biddulph, F. and Osborne, R. (1984) Pupils' ideas about floating and sinking. *Research in Science Education* **14**, 114–124.

Carey, S. (1988) Conceptual difference between children and adults. *Mind and Language* **3**, 167–181.

Driver, R., Squires, A., Rushworth, P. and Wood-Robinson, V. (1994) *Making Sense of Secondary Science: Research into children's ideas.* London: Routledge.

Duschl, R.A., Schweingruber, H. A. and Shouse, A.W. (2007) *Taking Science to School: learning and teaching science in grades K–8.* Washington: National Academies Press.

Gopnik, A., Meltzoff, A. and Kuhl, P. (1999) *The Scientist in the Crib.* New York: William Morrow.

Harlen, W. and Qualter, A. (2009) *The Teaching of Science in Primary Schools* (fifth edition). London: Routledge.

Osborn, J., Wadsworth, P. and Black, P. (1992) *SPACE Research Report: Processes of Life.* Liverpool: Liverpool University Press.

Osborne, R. and Freyberg, P. (1985) Learning science. *The Implications of Children's Science.* Auckland: Heineman.

Piaget, J. (1952) *The Origins of Intelligence in Children.* New York: International Universities Press.

Russell, T., Longden, K. and McGuigan, L. (1991) *SPACE Research Report: Materials.* Liverpool: Liverpool University Press.

Russell, T., McGuigan, L. and Hughes, A. (1998) *SPACE Research Report: Forces.* Liverpool: Liverpool University Press.

Smith, C., Carey, S. and Wider, M. (1985) On differentiation: a case study of the development of size, weight, and density. *Cognition* **21**(3), 177–237.

Smith, C., diSessa, A. and Roschelle, J. (1993) Misconceptions reconceived: a constructivist analysis of knowledge in transition. *Journal of the Learning Sciences* **3**, 115–163.

Smith, C., Solomon, G. and Carey, S. (2005) Never getting to zero: elementary school students' understanding of the infinite divisibility of number and matter. *Cognitive Psycholgy* **51**(2), 101–140.

SPACE (Science Processes and Concepts Exploration) Research Reports. *Evaporation and Condensation* (1990), *Growth* (1990), *Light* (1990), *Sound* (1990), *Electricity* (1991), *Materials* (1991), *Processes of Life* (1992), *Rocks, Soil and Weather* (1992), *Forces* (1998). Liverpool: Liverpool University Press.

Spelke, E.S. (1990) Principles of object perception. *Cognitive Science* **14**, 29–56.

Vosniadou, S. (1997) On the development of the understanding of abstract ideas. In Harnqvist, K. and Burgen, A. (eds) *Growing Up with Science.* London: Jessica Kingsley.

Chapter 6

What do we know about what students are thinking at Secondary level?

Virginia Kearton and Penny Robotham
with John Oversby

Learning science at Secondary level takes place throughout the period of adolescence, from Primary school where enthusiasm for learning in general is strong and the sense of curiosity about the world is often dominant, to a point where some learners can be very focused on a future career in sciences or not, or may be quite disillusioned about the learning process in school altogether. The Secondary stage is a time of great change in their lives. In the UK, at Primary level, the inquiry process is a major feature in Primary science education. Inquiry often focuses on scientific procedures such as designing an inquiry, planning observations through experimentation that may include controlling variables in a fair test model, collecting and interpreting data in a search for patterns of behaviour, and forming explanations embodying concepts and theories. At Secondary level, increasing factual knowledge is a mainstay of science lessons with practical work often devoted to illustrating underpinning concepts. Explanations are increasingly quantitative, with an emphasis on abstract algebraic reasoning and a greater focus on applying generalisations to novel situations. Scientific investigations are dominant in formal, teacher-assessed activities that contribute to the learner's final grade.

Researching students' subject knowledge

Research about subject matter knowledge among learners – factual and conceptual – has been investigated using a variety of methodologies. For example:

- Gilbert and Watts (1983) created their 'interviews about concepts' and 'interviews about instances' to inquire, through a semi-structured process, about domain-specific knowledge, such as in forces, and electricity

- the Assessment of Performance Unit in the 1980s used a variety of methods such as pencil-and-paper tests, practical work and interviews (see www.nationalstemcentre. org.uk/elibrary/collection/727/assessment-of-performance-unit-science-reports-for-teachers)
- Oversby (1996) used multiple choice tests in the domain of earth science.

While these examples do not constitute a systematic review of the available literature on methods, they serve to exemplify the range that has been used. Interviews, since they are time-intensive in analysis, sample only a few learners but provide deep and rich information about individual learning. Multiple choice and structured tests provide data on a large population, although often at a rather superficial level.

One issue about much of the methodology undertaken by large-scale projects on what learners learn is that they rarely refer to the socio-cultural background of the learners; they are 'socio-culturally blind'. Anderson (2007) suggests that this simply reinforces the 'culture of power' (p. 21) that focuses on the concepts and theories and omits the *people, tools and social contexts involved in the construction of science*' (Brickhouse, 1994, cited in Barton and Yang, 2000). Learners are required to ignore humanistic aspects and learn the socially disembedded facts, concepts and theories prescribed for them.

Concept learning

Scott, Asoko and Leach (2007) have identified two contrasting positions about concept learning: acquisition and participation.

Acquisition

Scott *et al.* (2007) focus on conceptual change, where often one concept is exchanged for another. This can be seen in the concept of 'work', where everyday meaning is exchanged in the science laboratory for a more scientific meaning. It seems, though, that *addition* of the scientific idea is often the case, rather than exchange, so that both meanings are retained, sometimes muddled and confused, and the learner tries to remember which learning to recall in different contexts. The learner too often simply returns the idea that the teacher clearly wants in the classroom, while reverting to the more common understanding at other times. Sometimes, though, an inappropriate meaning is recalled in science examinations and tests. The Scott *et al.* report attributes this conflict to relatively stable concept formation, which is quite resistant to change. The acquisition model can be seen as a transmissive model where the scientific explanation or concept is given to the learner from outside, and is *more or less* received and incorporated into the mental framework of the learner. The phrase 'more or less' points to the problems of this approach, especially when the acquisition is 'less'.

Acquisition is further complicated by the action of the learner in constructing a new and idiosyncratic understanding that depends on what they already know and exactly how the new ideas have been given and received. What seems so obvious to the teacher might not be so to the learner! This process is known as constructivism. Learning in the classroom is, though, rarely a completely individual process, especially when discussion between learners takes place during practical work. We thus have individual constructivism, and social constructivism, as two polarised facets of learners trying to make sense of what goes on in the classroom.

Participation

Scott *et al.* also discuss participative approaches to learning science. They summarise the following insights (further explanation has been added here, in brackets):

'Learning is seen as a process of developing participation in the practices of a particular community (the science community, in this case).

The learner takes on the role of apprentice, whereas the teacher is seen as the expert participant (the teacher acts as some kind of representative of the scientific community – that is, as a scientist).

That which is to be learned involves some aspect of practice or discourse (the learning involves an inquiry through experimentation or discussion).'

Scott *et al.* (2007, p. 47)

Participation frequently uses the notion of 'authentic inquiry', often working with ill-defined problems, experiencing ambiguities and uncertainty, experiencing the shared social nature of scientific work by working with others, and drawing on expertise of others in the classroom or in the wider community. There are critics of 'authentic inquiry' who point out that it is often based in the culture of the scientists and not the culture of the learner.

Modes of learning

Learning science takes place in a multimodal setting: language (written and spoken), diagrams, pictures, graphs, models, gestures, mathematical functions, practical work inside and outside classrooms. An ever-present danger is when the teacher smoothly glides between these modes, leaving the learner unaware of the value and significance of each mode.

Learning in different science disciplines

Physics

Duit, Niedderer and Scheker (2007) have reviewed research in physics education, so this section will simply provide an overview. They note that about 64% of constructivist research is in the domain of physics. They attribute this to the abstract, highly idealised and mathematical nature of the discipline at school level. They also mention that these reasons may well be why girls, in particular, have the least interest in physics, although generally boys are also unmotivated by physics compared with the other sciences.

The most popular topic for research is mechanics (forces) where the issue of invisibility appears to cause severe problems. In addition, physical explanations apply frequently to ideal and simplified situations – for example, where there is no air resistance in objects falling through air, or where friction is treated as being negligible. In some contexts, the acting force is treated as though it is composed of two forces acting at right angles (resolved forces) so that calculations can be carried out using ideal mathematical equations. These abstractions, coupled with insufficient algebraic and geometric understanding, form strong challenges to understanding for many learners. Diagrammatic representations include conventions such as arrows to indicate both direction and magnitude, consistent with force being a vector quantity. Better learning seems to take place when these conventions are made explicit and used consistently. Learners appear to find it difficult to conceive of force as a detached idea, and think of force as being associated with a body, and transferable to another body. Most of the successful methods described in Duit *et al.* (2007) link the motion and forces directly, by using a picture of the motion with a superimposed diagram of the acting forces.

Electrical circuits comprise the next most common area to be researched, according to Duit *et al.* The effects of electricity, such as bulbs lighting up, are often obvious but this topic suffers from similar problems to the ones on forces, previously discussed. Electricity itself is invisible, with three features (current, potential difference and resistance) being abstract and quantitative. The diagrammatic representations often contain many conventions, such as symbols for cells, bulbs, ammeters, voltmeters, and even the wires themselves, so that the working memory of many learners is severely stretched. Algebraic manipulations of these abstract features constitute a major part of studying electricity, providing a strong clue to the difficulties faced in teaching this topic.

Particle modelling is another common area for study of learners' concepts. Linking macroscopic properties, such as pressure, volume and shape, to sub-microscopic particles requires the use of modelling and conventional diagrams. What has been rarely investigated is how learners link two-dimensional representations of sub-microscopic particles to three-dimensional macroscopic properties such as shape and pressure. Conflict between diagrams, with some showing spaces between adjoining particles in solids, and others showing them touching, hardly dispel confusion.

Duit *et al.* suggest that much of the physics curriculum may only be accessible to the more able or gifted learners, while noting that sales of popular science books on quantum physics and relativity are booming. This dichotomy has not yet been resolved.

Chemistry

This discipline has been reviewed by De Jong and Taber (2007). They also discuss the gap between observable macroscopic features of chemical changes and the imaginary sub-microscopic and symbolic representations frequently used in explanations. This gap is at the heart of many difficulties in chemistry learning for adolescents. Even at the macroscopic level, not all the change is visible, with invisible gases entering and leaving the systems unnoticed, causing some misunderstandings. Historical events showed that careful and accurate weighing gave precious insights into the total nature of the changes being investigated, but such accurate instruments are not readily available to adolescents, and their skills in manipulation are such that the errors of measurement often outweigh the small differences they are looking for. Two other confounding features also conspire to cause problems. Many reactions in the curriculum take place in solution, where many solutes are colourless so that it is difficult to distinguish between them. Another tool adopted by historical chemists was measurement of temperature changes, firstly to indicate that a change was taking place, but secondly as part of measuring energy changes to account for the driving imperative for the chemical change. Unfortunately, many of the cheap thermometers presently in use with adolescents are too imprecise to be used for the second purpose.

The sub-microscopic domain of chemistry is essential for explanatory success. However, introductory particle science usually represents the particles as identical spheres (circles) whereas it is the differences between particles (molecules) of different substances that are significant and support learners making sense of the notion of substance itself. One of the areas of this section that seems to have been ignored by researchers so far is the distinction between molecules, atoms and ions, not least as evidenced by statements such as 'water molecules contain hydrogen atoms' that usually go unchallenged.

The third aspect of chemistry that poses many problems is the symbolic representational form. De Jong and Taber note the following.

- The meaning of a chemical formula as representing a single unit, rather than a collection of particles, causes difficulties – the algorithmic methods adopted to balance chemical equations do little to dislodge this misunderstanding.
- Major differences between algebraic equations and chemical equations are not discussed. The distinctive use of coefficients and subscripts are well documented in researches on balancing equations but the plus sign does not have the same meaning, while chemical equations usually use an arrow rather than the equals sign, consistent with the different meaning. There are other features of chemical equations, such as state symbols, and inclusion of energy changes and conditions, that further confuse what should be included. It seems that what expert chemists find useful, and of no consequence to their interpretation of the meaning, may well be a source of difficulty for novice learners.
- Chemistry for adolescents usually only focuses, in symbolic representations at least, on the start and end points of the change, and not at all on the intermediate stages of how the particles rearrange.
- Diagrams of chemical reactions provide a source of confusion in two ways. Firstly, they often mix the macroscopic (for example, a beaker of solution) with a symbolic representation of the solute. Secondly, they frequently omit a major item, such as the solvent, without making this explicit.

De Jong and Taber also mention serious confusion about chemical bonding explanations. This is partly related to being unable to distinguish between different sub-microscopic entities (molecules, atoms and ions), partly because they lack understanding of how these entities change in apparently simple processes, such as dissolution, and partly because they use oversimplified ideas, such as the octet rule with insufficient understanding.

De Jong and Taber make radical suggestions about alternative strategies, such as that based on research into the use of story lines in a context-based approach. They suggest explaining bonding in terms of forces rather than octets, and avoiding animistic language. They also suggest a progression from metallic bonding, to ionic (as the force between oppositely charged ions), to giant structures, and then to simple covalent bonding. Whether this will be easily adopted in opposition to the strong traditional approach of textbooks remains to be seen.

Biology

Driver et al. (1994) report research concerning children's ideas in biology in the following sections:

1 living things
2 nutrition
3 growth
4 responding to the environment

5   reproduction and inheritance

6   microbes

7   ecosystems.

This sequence establishes the discipline by differentiating the living world from the physical world through various specific characteristics that are obvious features. Microbes are not visible to the naked eye, except in colonies, but readily observable through microscopes. This 'direct access' to characteristics of living things provides a ready appreciation of the living world, making it possible to learn biology at a young age.

Driver and her colleagues did not mention research evidence about biochemistry. Abell and Lederman (2007) similarly pay little attention to this area in their *Handbook of Research on Science Education*. As noted in the chemistry section above, this may be because that area of scientific knowledge concerns invisibles that are only accessible through models such as diagrams, symbols, and ICT-based animations. Ecosystems, in contrast, have been quite well researched. Driver *et al.* report challenges in two respects:

- understanding of representations such as food and energy changes involving confusion of arrows, which parallel similar confusions in force diagrams
- abstract concepts such as populations, environments, competition, and matter cycles.

Since ecosystems are super-macroscopic, and rarely directly observable, it seems that difficulties in learning about them resolve into problems about learning through analogies and models.

Earth sciences and astronomy

We have included these two topics together since they demonstrate similarities. They have been significantly documented in Driver *et al.* (1994).

Earth sciences have aspects that learners find challenging, such as the large scale of plate tectonics. Again, animations and diagrams have been widely used to access these unobservable events. In addition, the enormously long timescale of many geological events has proved a barrier to learning even for postgraduates (Oversby, 1996).

Astronomical systems, such as galaxies and the solar system, have the disadvantage of also being large scale. In astronomy education, many explanations require the learner to be able to see the system from two viewpoints simultaneously. Eclipse diagrams, for example, have to be understood by imagining the observer positioned on the Earth in a shadow, while imagining, at the same time, being somewhere in space looking down on the Sun, Moon and Earth system, and being able to interpret lines as the edge of envelopes of light. It is no wonder that many never really appreciate how these events can happen.

Summary

There have been many investigations into content learning, as Abell and Lederman (2007) have carefully documented. This chapter can only point the way to some of the compendia of evidence that have been collected. Since there are many topics that have not been explored, or only lightly studied, it is possible that we may never know the full extent of the field. We have tried, in this chapter, to give some indication of the underlying causes, such as invisibles, abstractions and large scales. It is likely that we shall continue to have recourse to analogies and models for accessible explanations, and innovative ones using ICT and drama. These are not without their own disadvantages since the learners have to see the benefits and limitations of these forms of explanation, to avoid the traps of over-interpretation and oversimplification. Perhaps we need more of a framework for understanding types of difficulties, rather than simply collecting more examples. This may be a significant challenge for science education researchers.

References

Abell, S.K. and Lederman, N.G. (2007) *Handbook of Research on Science Education*. New York: Routledge.

Anderson, C.W. (2007) Perspectives on science learning. In Abell, S.K. and Lederman, N.G. (eds) *Handbook of Research on Science Education* (pp. 3–30). New York: Routledge.

Barton, A.C. and Yang, K. (2000) The culture of power and science education: learning from Miguel. *Journal of Research in Science Teaching* **37**, 379–394.

De Jong, O. and Taber, K.S. (2007) Teaching and learning the many faces of chemistry. In Abell, S.K. and Lederman, N.G. (eds) *Handbook of Research on Science Education* (pp. 631–652). New York: Routledge.

Driver, R., Squires, A., Rushworth, P. and Wood-Robinson V. (1994) *Making Sense of Secondary Science: Research into children's ideas*. London: Routledge.

Duit, R., Niedderer H. and Scheker, H. (2007) Teaching physics. In Abell, S.K. and Lederman, N.G. (eds) *Handbook of Research on Science Education* (pp. 599–630). New York: Routledge.

Gilbert, J.K. and Watts, D.M. (1983) Enigmas in school science: students' conceptions for scientifically associated words. *Research in Science and Technological Education* **1**(2), 161–171.

Oversby, J. (1996) Knowledge of earth science and the potential for its development. *School Science Review* **78**, 91–97.

Scott, P., Asoko, H. and Leach, J. (2007) Student conceptions and conceptual learning in science. In Abell, S.K. and Lederman, N.G. (eds) *Handbook of Research on Science Education* (pp. 31–56). New York: Routledge.

Chapter 7

Science teachers' knowledge of science

Vanessa Kind

Can a chemist change her spots?

I once taught students taking physics at GCSE (16+ examination). Despite my specialist subject being chemistry, initially I felt capable: I was (am) enthusiastic about physics and, as an experienced teacher, had confidence in my teaching skills. But after a few lessons in my new realm I knew something was missing – simply, I lacked familiarity with, and extensive, detailed knowledge of, physics. As a result, my lessons were limited to fairly boring tasks that were not stimulating for students. On-going support from a physics specialist helped me deliver reasonably successful lessons, in the sense that students probably 'learned something', but it was surprising to me that, despite my long-standing interest in physics, I felt uncomfortable teaching it – I was aware that my being a 'non-specialist physicist' meant the students did not receive consistently high quality learning experiences. I couldn't 'change my spots': my chemistry teaching skills did not transfer easily into physics teaching expertise. My experience is not unique – many science teachers teach outside their specialism, with varying degrees of success. This chapter illustrates how science educators have investigated these experiences.

Two issues are apparent. First, the role played by subject knowledge. In teaching physics, I was presenting subject knowledge I had acquired 15 years earlier, at the age of 16. Recall of facts, familiarity and depth of knowledge about concepts were all challenges for me. Second, poor subject knowledge impacts on teaching quality. Again, my own experience shows I was forced to seek advice, as I could only prepare simple activities myself. My experience as a chemistry teacher made me conscious that my physics lessons lacked quality and impact.

This chapter is divided to discuss these issues in turn. However, to begin, let us establish what is meant by 'subject knowledge' in research terms.

Knowledge of science is 'subject matter knowledge' (SMK)

American educationalist Joseph Schwab (1978) coined the term 'subject matter knowledge' (SMK) to embrace a teacher's knowledge about his/her subject. The importance of this to teachers' classroom roles was captured by another American, Lee Shulman (1986, 1987).

He identified SMK as the knowledge transformed by a teacher using his/her pedagogical content knowledge (PCK), the ways a teacher has of making a topic comprehensible to others. Since then, both SMK and PCK have been investigated extensively (Abell, 2007; Kind, 2009a). SMK is regarded as an 'umbrella conception' (Cochran and Jones, 1998) comprising four components, here applied to science:

- **content knowledge** – the facts and concepts of science
- **substantive knowledge** – the explanatory structures and/or paradigms of science
- **syntactic knowledge** – the methods and processes of generating scientific knowledge
- **beliefs about science as a subject** – the feelings learners and teachers have about various aspects of science.

Science content knowledge has received the most extensive attention from researchers, but evidence is available in all four areas. Content knowledge and its impact on teaching provide the foci for this chapter.

Science teachers' content knowledge

Science teachers' content knowledge (CK) has been investigated by researchers since the 1930s: Ralya and Ralya (1938) reported Primary teachers' misconceptions about causes of the seasons, heat and temperature and force and motion. The Second World War and the post-Sputnik era of intense curriculum development in science education intervened, but researchers began revisiting these issues eventually.

Studies of teachers' content knowledge (CK) proliferated from the 1980s as constructivist-inspired misconceptions research became established. Some researchers probed a range of ideas across the sciences simultaneously. For example, New Zealand researchers Hope and Townsend (1983) reported that teachers understood biology concepts such as 'plant', 'animal' and 'living' relatively well, but their understandings of physics concepts ('force', 'friction', 'gravity') were similar to those of 14 and 15-year-olds. Ameh and Gunstone (1985, 1986) found that teachers in Australia and Nigeria (regardless of cultural differences) had misconceptions about life *and* physical science concepts: only 26% had a scientific understanding of 'animal', 30% of 'force', 40% of 'electric current' and 66% of gravity. About 71% understood 'living' in a scientific sense. A consistent picture of teachers holding identical misconceptions to students they taught built up from research worldwide (for example, Carré, 1993; Wandersee, Mintzes and Novak, 1994; Lloyd et al. 1998; Schoon and Boone, 1998). However, there is evidence that fewer misconceptions are observed among teachers than students due to their additional maturity and education. Nevertheless, evidence that misconceptions are a consistent and persistent feature of teachers' CK is apparent,

Rice (2005) found significant weaknesses in pre-service Primary teachers' science understanding of ten different science topics, including the perception that oxygen could not boil.

Teachers' CK of physics

Teachers' physics CK has been more extensively studied than that in chemistry and biology. A contributory factor is that as a majority of Secondary science teaching entrants are biology graduates, researchers assume their understanding of physics is relatively poor. Teachers' CK about ten physics topics has been investigated consistently:

- light and shadows (Jones, Carter and Rua, 1999)
- electricity (Daehler and Shinohara, 2001)
- sound (Jones, Carter and Rua, 1999)
- force and motion (Kruger, Summers and Palacio, 1990b)
- energy (Summers and Kruger, 1992)
- heat and temperature (Jasien and Oberem, 2002)
- thermal properties of materials (Sciarretta, Stilli and Vicentini Missoni, 1990)
- sinking and floating (Parker and Heywood, 2000)
- air pressure (Rollnick and Rutherford, 1990)
- gravity (Kruger, Summers and Palacio, 1990a).

In general, findings mirror those reported for students' misconceptions, suggesting that many faulty ideas remain unchanged and unchallenged from childhood. Other research includes that of US-based Lawrenz (1986), who gave Primary teachers a multiple-choice test about physics topics. She found that questions on atomic structure, density and stars were answered correctly by more than 50% of respondents. In contrast, less than 50% gave correct answers to questions on electric current, temperature, motion and light. In the UK, Primary science gained importance in the 1980s, leading to probing of Primary teachers' understanding of basic physics. Kruger and colleagues' major project (for example, Kruger and Summers, 1988) investigated teachers' ideas about energy, materials, gravity and forces, followed by development of support materials to shore up any deficiencies.

Teachers' CK of space and earth sciences

The enhanced role for Primary science in the UK led to investigations of primary teachers' understandings of astronomical phenomena. Parker and Heywood (1998) found that only about 10% of trainees and 34% of experienced Primary teachers held scientific ideas about seasonal changes. In contrast, Kikas (2004) found that around 60% of Estonian science teachers could explain seasonal changes correctly. Among the misconceptions she revealed was the notion that in summer the angle of the Earth moved Estonia closer to the Equator. Parker and Heywood found a similar common idea was that 'the Earth is closer to the Sun' in summer.

Phases of the Moon pose considerable difficulties. Few teachers in Mant and Summers's study (1993) or Parker and Heywood's work (1998) could give scientific explanations for these. A commonly held idea was that our view of the Moon is obscured by the Sun/Earth's shadow/'something'. Teachers also confused eclipses and phases.

Geological ideas have received relatively little attention from researchers. Trend (2001) studied Primary teachers' understanding of deep time, finding that relative time was much more significant to teachers' perceptions than absolute time. Thus, they found it difficult to place key events accurately on a geological timescale, often conflating major occurrences as having occurred roughly simultaneously, rather than being separated by long time periods. For example, teachers found it hard to distinguish between the formation of the Sun and the Big Bang in time; similarly, the appearance of the first humans was placed in time with the disappearance of the woolly mammoth. Some teachers grossly misjudged events, reasoning, for example, that the first fish appeared less than 1000 years ago or that space-time began 1 million million years ago.

Teachers' CK of chemistry

Primary (elementary) teachers' understanding about science ideas – notably particles, conservation of mass and changes of state – have been investigated widely, yielding the consistent finding that observable, macroscopic phenomena rather than particle ideas are used to explain behaviour of matter. Gabel, Samuel and Hunn (1987) found that over 50% of pre-service Primary teachers ignored conservation and orderly organisation of particles when drawing pictures of atomic or molecular arrangements. Roth (1992) and Kruger and Summers (1989) also found teachers ignored particles when explaining changes in materials such as water and ice. Ball and McDiarmid (1990) suggest these teachers' science CK is grounded in everyday and pre-higher education experiences rather than being based on information gained during a teacher education course.

Secondary chemistry teachers also hold misconceptions. Kind and Kind (2009) report that all pre-service science teachers find chemical bonding problematic – a mean score of 46% was achieved by about 170 graduates on a test of basic chemical bonding ideas, compared to 71% on conservation of mass questions. A tendency to think of hydrochloric acid as comprising hydrogen chloride molecules in water was one finding. A tendency to use macroscopic language rather than particle terminology to describe the behaviour of particles is reported by Kruse and Roehrig (2005), echoing data relating to Primary teachers. Lin, Cheng and Lawrenz's (2000) research on states of matter shows teachers and students share misunderstandings about gases and misuses of the gas laws.

Inevitably, teachers' understanding of more advanced chemical concepts reveals difficulties. Banerjee (1991), for example, explored teachers' knowledge of chemical equilibrium. He found that 49% of teachers and 35% of students confuse rate and the extent of a reaction, reasoning that if the temperature of an exothermic reaction is decreased, the rate of the forward reaction will increase. In Sweden, Gorin (1994) found that some teachers and students did not realise that a mole of any substance contains the same number of particles. Haidar's (1997) study on the mole concept in Yemen showed that teachers relied on recall of facts, concepts and algorithms, but lacked problem-solving skills. In the UK, Kind and Kind (2009) report that about 11% (of around 170) graduates could not use reacting mass reasoning to answer a very simple question about carbon combusting in oxygen.

Teachers' CK of biology

In contrast to work in physical sciences, relatively few studies in biology education have focused on teachers' understanding of specific topics. One reason for this may be that many science teachers have biology backgrounds, so fewer misconceptions are judged likely, making research potentially less fruitful in terms of revealing teacher CK weaknesses. Extant research includes that of Liarakou, Gavrilakis and Flouri (2009), who found that only 11.6% of teacher respondents on the Greek island of Rhodes could give a scientifically correct definition of 'sustainable development', even though over 60% had heard of the term. Gayford (1998) investigated UK teachers' understanding of sustainability. He revealed that science teachers express interest and expertise on this topic, developing their knowledge on specific aspects such as climate change, recycling and conservation work over time.

Teachers' ideas about respiration were probed by Sanders (1993) in South Africa. She found that about 77% of respondents thought respiration provides oxygen and removes carbon dioxide, an error leading to misunderstandings such as plants only respiring at night and photosynthesis and digestion (rather than respiration) being the processes that provide energy for life processes. Greene (1990) investigated education students' understanding of natural selection. He reports that about 46% had '*at least a functional understanding*' (p. 884) of the topic, while Lamarckism (inheritance of acquired characteristics) and the existence of a pool of variations in a population were alternatives. Greene notes the logic with which participants sustained their arguments in each case.

Teachers' CK of science: a summary

The wealth of evidence on teachers' CK generates a consistent pattern: teachers possess identical misconceptions to their students, although teachers' misconceptions are fewer in number. Possible reasons for the persistence and consistency of faulty understanding of even basic scientific concepts are worth exploring. Teachers are academically successful – many are high quality end-products of educational systems worldwide. As such, they are competent rote-learners, memorisers, experimenters and problem solvers. However, data described above suggest that university-level education in science does not challenge misconceptions or faulty thinking gained at school. University science is 'science', while school science is an amalgam of scientific facts and information presented in a format deemed suitable for young students. The two are not the same. Deng (2007) reflects on this, noting logical, social, psychological and epistemological (that is, to do with the structure of the subject) differences. Thus, misconceptions are unsurprising, as these relate to faults in learning school science, not academic science. In learning to teach, teachers must master the ways in which school science interprets their specialism, as well as other aspects. Perhaps inevitably teachers fall back on recalling their own pre-university experiences, innocently perpetuating misunderstandings among the next generation. Teacher education has a clear role to play in breaking this cycle. In engaging with school science, teachers set aside their 'expert science' knowledge. Consequences arising from this are discussed in the next section.

The impact of CK on science teaching

Significant research evidence indicates that the quality of a teacher's CK (or SMK, to use the umbrella term) impacts on his/her classroom practice. Khourey-Bowers and Fenk (2009) note that:

> '*Teachers with broad and deep … subject specific knowledge, awareness of common alternative conceptions and … scientific models can provide rich learning opportunities for their students.*'

Khourey-Bowers and Fenk (2009, pp. 437–438)

To return to the opening scenario, my physics teaching missed these – I 'knew' basic physics, but any 'advanced' understanding was from reading about specific topics of interest, not rigorous study. My depth of knowledge was inadequate to answer 16+ students' challenging questions. I knew about students' misconceptions, but more so in chemistry than in physics. Reliance on mathematical models for teaching key concepts exposed my poor understanding, prohibiting effective use. Borko (2004) summarises other characteristics I lacked:

> '*Teachers must have rich and flexible knowledge of the subjects they teach … understand the central facts and concepts of the discipline, how these ideas are connected and the processes used to establish new knowledge and determine the validity of claims.*'

Borko (2004, p. 5)

Clearly, experience of teaching any (even relevant) field is insufficient – 'knowing your subject' is vital to ensure students experience positive learning outcomes. In this section, we explore two aspects of the impact that weak or strong SMK/CK has on science teaching: in within-specialism and outside-specialism teaching, and in novice and expert (experienced) teachers. (Note that these studies report CK and SMK. Hence both these terms are used in this section.)

The impact of CK on within-specialism and outside-specialism teaching

Evidence for perpetuation of misconceptions by teachers working outside specialism was revealed by Hashweh (1987), who showed that teachers with insecure understanding of a science concept, such as when teaching outside specialism, tended to embed their misconceptions into lesson plans. Intervention by colleagues prevented these being taught. Examples of the impact of weak CK on lesson activities are reported by Sanders, Borko and Lockard (1993). Their work with experienced teachers teaching outside specialism revealed that when working in areas of science in which they had weak CK, teachers tended to act 'like novices' (p. 723), resorting to 'less risky' activities and more teacher talk. Conversely, within specialism, teaching areas in which they had expertise, teachers planned lessons that included more student involvement, such as setting up opportunities for students to ask questions. Arzi and White (2007) followed teachers in a longitudinal study (discussed below), which included probing outside-specialism teaching. They note that teachers used within specialism are more likely to develop and retain good CK than those used as a 'Jack of all trades', and suggest that imposing outside-specialism teaching could prove counterproductive in achieving good outcomes for students.

Poor-quality subject-specific SMK also impacts on teachers' abilities to teach broader aspects of science. For example, Taylor and Dana (2003) note that physics specialists and non-specialists differ in their approaches to producing reliable data in physics experiments. They found that the high quality of SMK possessed by specialists contributed to their being able to know and understand how instruments – that is, physics equipment – could be used to produce reliable data. Non-specialists, they suggest, would not have the SMK necessary to design their own activity, or note faults in a student-designed experiment. Ratcliffe and Millar (2009) probed teachers' abilities in implementing scientific literacy approaches in their lessons. They found that teachers with weak CK in handling scientific evidence and processes of inquiry led to over-reliance on copying and worksheet tasks in lessons. The authors note that 'unrealised potential' existed in many classroom activities, as teachers lacked confidence to initiate discussions through use of open questions.

The novice–expert shift

Geddis et al. (1993) showed that pre-service teachers experience difficulties teaching their specialist subjects because they lack the ability to transform their knowledge in ways that enable students to learn. They describe how two pre-service chemistry teachers approached teaching isotopes: both taught students 'what they knew', using inappropriate strategies that did not take learners' prior knowledge into account. An experienced teacher used a strategy that helped students learn key principles about the concept. Thus, in the initial stages of learning to teach, good SMK alone is insufficient to ensure high quality lessons.

Kind (2009b) showed that some trainee science teachers who found their within-specialism lessons were less successful than those taught on outside-specialism topics did not seek help from school-based mentors (experienced teachers) in preparing lessons. This was because trainees felt they were expected to 'know' their specialist subject, and to teach it without support. Consequently, they over-pitched knowledge or prepared inappropriate activities. One novice likened within-specialism teaching as 'a conflict' in his head, as he agonised over what to teach and what to leave out. Outside-specialism teaching prompted attention on learning the necessary science, seeking help to teach appropriately, with consequent feelings of greater success.

The impact of teaching experience on CK was assessed in a 17-year longitudinal study by Arzi and White (2007). They followed Secondary science teachers from their first year in post. They report that teachers' CK changed in subtle ways as experience built up. Unused CK was forgotten, while little accretion of new knowledge occurred. However, teachers showed improved understanding and integration of concepts over time. The authors noted crucially that school curricula became a major factor influencing teachers' CK, acting as an organiser and source. In consequence, teachers only occasionally refreshed or updated their CK beyond studying the student texts, and where this occurred, magazine and general science books were common sources of new material. Thus, teachers become more expert at teaching school science, but with the consequence that their knowledge of academic science diminishes. The dangers of this position are noted thus:

> '… rich knowledge which is not confined to curriculum and evaluation requirements provides teachers with degrees of freedom that enable them to experiment pedagogically and to instil curiosity and zest in their students.'

> Arzi and White (2007, p. 246)

Heywood (2007) reflects on science SMK in Primary teacher education, making the point that *'few primary trainees are likely to have studied science beyond the age of 16'* (p. 520), resulting in a lack of confidence for teaching science. He notes that in the early years *'naïve views'* (p. 536) of teaching and learning science, perhaps as 'telling', are likely to be apparent as trainees gain confidence in using a wider range of classroom practices.

Implications and conclusions

Subject knowledge plays a vital role in science teaching. Research evidence shows that teachers need accurate, deep and rich science knowledge to teach their specialism and other aspects effectively. Deep knowledge linked with rigorous, advanced academic study, provides a sound background for teaching a subject. However, evidence is clear that this alone is insufficient – teachers must acquire appropriate pedagogical skills in order to make knowledge available to their students. A complicating (or perhaps simplifying) factor is that the actual knowledge they need to deliver in the classroom is 'school science', the nature of which is determined by social and political influence. Thus, possessing good science subject knowledge from an academic degree acts as a starting point – but, as Arzi and White (2007) showed, the key driver for SMK/CK over time becomes school science. This means that exposing and 'treating' science teachers' misconceptions of any science topic they need to teach is essential, as these arise from school science. A fair assumption is that a majority of science teachers hold misconceptions about at least one science concept. Teacher education has a defined role to play in correcting misconceptions relating to school science topics.

The switch to 'school science' becoming the mainstay of a teacher's SMK has the effect of reducing knowledge of academic science. Evidence suggests that maintaining a high level of science knowledge in a specialist area helps to enrich lessons, providing a source of background information and stimulation for students. Ratcliffe and Millar (2009) showed that lack of confidence stemming from poor CK in general areas of science led to poor quality lessons. There is a need, therefore, to provide teachers with opportunities to 'keep in touch' with their specialist subjects. In England, the Science Learning Centre network (www.sciencelearningcentres.org.uk) was planned with this remit in mind.

Changing spots? Or adaptation?

There is a need for realism, however. A majority of science teachers have biology as their specialist subject – yet school science demands knowledge of physical and earth sciences in addition. Teaching outside specialism will remain realistic and necessary for many science teachers in many schools. Evidence shows the potential hazards of this position. My own experience showed I could not easily 'change my spots' to become a physicist – after years of teaching chemistry, I was attuned to its foibles, experiments and patterns knowing appropriate strategies to address these with a range of students. I could at best adapt – alter my spots' colour, maybe – to account for new experiences, but changing entirely or even gaining parity across the two sciences was highly unlikely. The extent to which any science education system can ensure equality and high quality of CK/SMK and PCK in all science teachers for all science subjects will be a determining measure of success.

References

Abell, S.K. (2007) Research on science teacher knowledge. In Abell, S.K. and Lederman, N.G. (eds) *Handbook of Research on Science Education* (Chapter 36). New Jersey, USA: Lawrence Erlbaum Associates Inc.

Ameh, C. and Gunstone, R. (1985) Teachers' concepts in science. *Research in Science Education* **15**, 151–157.

Ameh, C. and Gunstone, R. (1986) Science teachers' concepts in Nigeria and Australia. *Research in Science Education* **16**, 73–81.

Arzi, H.J. and White, R.T. (2007) Change in teachers' knowledge of subject matter: a 17-year longitudinal study. *Science Education* **92**(2) 221–251.

Ball, D. and McDiarmid, G. (1990) The subject matter preparation of teachers. In Houston, W., Haberman, M. and Sikula, J. (eds) *Handbook of Research in Teacher Education* (pp. 437–449). New York: Macmillan

Banerjee, A.C. (1991) Misconceptions of students and teachers in chemical equilibrium. *International Journal of Science Education* **13**(4) 487–494.

Borko, H. (2004) Professional development and teacher learning: mapping the terrain. *Educational Researcher* **33**(8) 3–15.

Carré, C. (1993) Performance in subject matter knowledge in science. In Bennett, N. and Carré, C. (eds) *Learning to Teach.* London: Routledge.

Cochran, K.F. and Jones, L.L. (1998) The subject matter knowledge of pre-service science teachers. In Fraser, B.J. and Tobin, K.G. (eds) *International Handbook of Science Education* (Chapter 6.5). Dordrecht: Kluwer Academic Publishers.

Daehler, K.R. and Shinohara, M. (2001) A complete circuit is a complete circle: exploring the potential of case materials and methods to develop teachers' content knowledge and pedagogical content knowledge of science. *Research in Science Education* **31**, 267–288.

Deng, Z. (2007) Knowing the subject matter of a secondary school science subject. *Journal of Curriculum Studies* **39**(5) 503–535.

Gabel, D.L., Samuel, K.V. and Hunn, D. (1987) Understanding the particulate nature of matter. *Journal of Chemical Education* **64**, 695–697.

Gayford, C. (1998) The perspectives of science teachers in relation to current thinking about environmental education. *Research in Science and Technological Education* **16**, 101–113.

Geddis, A.N., Onslow, B., Beynon, C. and Oesch, J. (1993) Transforming content knowledge: learning to teach about isotopes. *Science Education* **77**(6) 575–591.

Gorin, G. (1994) Mole and chemical amount: A discussion of the fundamental measurements of chemistry. *Journal of Chemical Education* **71**, 114–116.

Greene, E.D. (1990) The logic of university students' misunderstandings of natural selection. *Journal of Research in Science Teaching* **27**(9) 875–885.

Haidar, A.H. (1997) Prospective chemistry teachers' conceptions of the conservation of matter and related concepts. *Journal of Research in Science Teaching* **34**, 181–197.

Hashweh, M.Z. (1987) Effects of subject matter knowledge in the teaching of biology and physics. *Teaching and Teacher Education* **3**, 109–120.

Heywood, D.S. (2007) Problematising science subject matter knowledge as a legitimate enterprise in primary teacher education. *Cambridge Journal of Education* **37**(4) 519–542.

Hope, J. and Townsend, M. (1983) Student teachers' understanding of science concepts. *Research in Science Education* **13**, 177–183.

Jasien, P.G. and Oberem, G.E. (2002) Understanding of elementary concepts in heat and temperature among college students and K–12 teachers. *Journal of Chemical Education* **79**, 889–895.

Jones, M.G., Carter, G. and Rua, M.J. (1999) Children's concepts: tools for transforming science teachers' knowledge. *Science Education* **83**, 545–557.

Khourey-Bowers, C. and Fenk, C. (2009) Influence of constructivist professional development on chemistry content knowledge and scientific model development. *Journal of Science Teacher Education* **20**(5) 437–457.

Kikas, E. (2004) Teachers' conceptions and misconceptions concerning three natural phenomena. *Journal of Research in Science Teaching* **41**(5) 432–448.

Kind, V. (2009a) Pedagogical content knowledge in science education: perspectives and potential for progress. *Studies in Science Education* **45**(2) 169–204.

Kind, V. (2009b) A conflict in your head: an exploration of trainees' subject matter knowledge development and its impact on teacher self-confidence. *International Journal of Science Education* **31**(11) 1529–1562.

Kind, V. and Kind, P.M. (2009) Qualified to teach? How personal and academic characteristics of pre-service science teachers compare with their understandings of basic chemical ideas. *International Journal of Science Education*. (under review)

Kruger, C. and Summers, M. (1988) Primary school teachers' understanding of science concepts. *Journal of Education for Teaching* **14**, 259–265.

Kruger, C. and Summers, M. (1989) An investigation of some primary school teachers' understanding of changes in materials. *School Science Review* **71**, 17–27.

Kruger, C., Summers, M. and Palacio, D. (1990a) An investigation of some English Primary school teachers' understanding of the concepts force and gravity. *British Educational Research Journal* **16**, 383–397.

Kruger, C., Summers, M. and Palacio, D. (1990b) A survey of Primary school teachers' conceptions of force and motion. *Education Research* **32**, 83–95.

Kruse, R.A. and Roehrig, G.H. (2005) A comparison study: assessing teachers' conceptions with the chemistry concepts inventory. *Journal of Chemical Education* **82**, 1246–1250.

Lawrenz, F. (1986) Misconceptions of physical science concepts among elementary school teachers. *School Science and Mathematics* **86**, 654–660.

Liarakou, G., Gavrilakis, C. and Flouri, E. (2009) Secondary school teachers' knowledge and attitudes towards renewable energy sources. *Journal of Science Education and Technology* **18**, 120–129.

Lin, H., Cheng, H. and Lawrenz, F. (2000) The assessment of students' and teachers' understanding of gas laws. *Journal of Chemical Education* **77**, 235–238.

Lloyd, J.K., Smith, R.G., Fay, C.L., Khang, G.N., Kam Wah, L.L. and Sai, C.L. (1998) Subject knowledge for teaching at primary level: A comparison of pre-service teacher in England and Singapore. *International Journal of Science Education* **20**, 521–532.

Mant, J. and Summers, M. (1993) Some Primary teachers' understanding of the Earth's place in the Universe. *Research Papers in Education* **8**(1) 101–129.

Parker, J. and Heywood, D. (1998) The Earth and beyond: developing primary science teachers' understanding of basic astronomical events. *International Journal of Science Education* **20**(5) 503–520.

Parker, J. and Heywood, D. (2000) Exploring the relationship between subject knowledge and pedagogic knowledge in Primary teachers' learning about forces. *International Journal of Science Education* **22**, 89–111.

Ralya, L.L. and Ralya, L.L. (1938) Some misconceptions in science held by prospective elementary teachers. *Science Education* **22**, 241–251.

Ratcliffe, M. and Millar, R. (2009) Teaching for understanding of science in context: Evidence from the pilot trials of the Twenty-First Century Science courses. *Journal of Research in Science Teaching* **46**(8) 946–959.

Rice, D. (2005) I didn't know oxygen could boil! What pre-service and inservice elementary teachers' answers to 'simple' science questions reveals about their subject matter knowledge. *International Journal of Science Education* **27**(9) 1059–1082.

Rollnick, M. and Rutherford, M. (1990) African Primary school teachers – what ideas do they hold on air and air pressure? *International Journal of Science Education* **12**, 101–113.

Roth, W.-M. (1992) The particulate theory of matter for pre-service elementary teachers. *Journal of Science Teacher Education* **3**, 115–122.

Sanders, M. (1993) Erroneous ideas about respiration: The teacher factor. *Journal of Research in Science Teaching* **30**(8) 919–934.

Sanders, L.R., Borko, H. and Lockard, J.D. (1993) Secondary science teachers' knowledge base when teaching science courses in and out of their area of certification. *Journal of Research in Science Teaching* **30**(7) 723–736.

Schwab, J.J. (1978) *Science, Curriculum and Liberal Education.* Chicago: University of Chicago Press.

Schoon K.J. and Boone, W.J. (1998) Self-efficacy and alternative conceptions of science of pre-service elementary teachers. *Science Education* **82**, 553–568.

Sciarretta, M.R., Stilli, R. and Vicentini Missoni, M. (1990) On the thermal properties of materials: common-sense knowledge of Italian students and teachers. *International Journal of Science Education* **12**, 369–379.

Shulman, L.S. (1986) Those who understand: a conception of teacher knowledge. *American Educator* Spring 1986, 9–44.

Shulman, L.S. (1987) Knowledge and teaching: foundations of the new reform. *Harvard Educational Review* **57**(1) 1–22.

Summers, M. and Kruger, C. (1992) Research into English Primary school teachers' understanding of the concept of energy. *Evaluation and Research in Education* **6**, 95–111.

Taylor, J.A. and Dana, T.M. (2003) Secondary school physics teachers' conceptions of scientific evidence: an exploratory case study. *Journal of Research in Science Teaching* **40**(8) 721–736.

Trend, R.D. (2001) Deep time framework: a preliminary study of UK Primary teachers' conceptions of geological time and perceptions of geoscience. *Journal of Research in Science Teaching* **38**(2) 191–221.

Wandersee, J.H., Mintzes, J.J. and Novak, J.D. (1994) Research on alternative conceptions in science. In Gabel, D. (ed) *Handbook of Research on Science Teaching and Learning* (Chapter 5). New York: Macmillan.

Chapter 8

The role and value of practical work

Rob Toplis

'Are we doing a practical today?' is a question that greets many science teachers as they open the laboratory door to a group of students. Practical work is seen by many science teachers to be an integral part of their teaching, a belief that 'doing' helps learning; 'I do and I understand.' This belief has arisen from the practical exercises of the mid 1900s, through the Nuffield projects of the 1960s and 1970s to process science in the 1980s and the inclusion of scientific inquiry, Sc1, in the National Curriculum for England from 1989 (Wellington, 1998). Similar adherence to the value of practical work is also present in the curricula of other countries ranging from scientific inquiry in the US (National Science Education Standards, 1996) to developing investigative skills and attitudes in the New Zealand science curriculum (New Zealand Ministry of Education, 1993). A lot of time, money and effort have been devoted to practical work in school science (Toplis, 2007), so what does research tell us about its role and its worth?

Wellington (1998, p. 7) provides three main arguments for carrying out practical work in school science:

- cognitive arguments for improving understanding and conceptual development
- affective arguments for generating interest, motivation and enthusiasm
- the skills argument for transferable skills such as observation, prediction and inference, as well as manipulative skills.

These divisions may not be quite so simple: research by Toh (1991) into the factors affecting success in science investigation found that affective and cognitive factors correlated with successful performance; Alsop (2005, p. 3) notes that *'affect and cognition cannot be meaningfully understood as disparate entities'*.

An early questionnaire survey of teachers' reasons for doing practical work (Kerr, 1963, cited in Wellington, 2000, pp. 145–147) indicates that observation and scientific thinking were ranked highly, as was encouraging accurate observation and careful recording for the 16–18 years age group. However, Ormerod and Duckworth (1975, p. 45) report somewhat conflicting results between teachers and students: teachers placed promotion of interest low on their list whereas the 624 students polled placed 'interest and reality' at the top of their list for the value of practical work.

While there is anecdote and opinion about the value of practical work, there is relatively little recent direct research evidence of the most effective ways of doing practical work or of what students gain from it. Hodson makes the scathing comment:

'A major cause of the unsatisfactory nature of much school practical work is that teachers use it unthinkingly. Not because they are unthinking people, but because they have been subject to the powerful, myth-making rhetoric of the profession that sees hands-on practical work as the universal panacea, the educational solution to all learning problems.'

Hodson (1990, pp. 33–34)

The cognitive argument

Few researchers have addressed questions about whether or not learning is better, worse or just different with practical work. A web-based survey (Murray and Reiss, 2005, p. 86) showed that of 1451 responses to the question 'How does practical work help learning?', 47% thought practical work made understanding theory easier and 12% believed it provided a deeper understanding. Recent research (Abrahams and Millar, 2008) has addressed the effectiveness of practical work as a teaching and learning method in school science. It reports the use of a framework model developed from a model of the process of design and evaluation (Millar, Le Maréchal and Tiberghien, 1999) to analyse specific practical tasks from 25 case study lessons using observation and interview data. The findings from analysis of the data indicate that the teachers' focus on the practical lessons was predominantly one of developing scientific knowledge rather than developing scientific inquiry and that practical work was generally effective at getting students to do what was intended with physical objects rather than use scientific ideas and reflect on the data. Abrahams and Millar (2008) note that there was little evidence of a cognitive challenge in linking observables to ideas, and that practical tasks rarely incorporated explicit strategies to help students make these links. This concurs with a view from a study with grade 7 students in the US that, 'The standard curriculum is reinforcing students' own common-sense views about the nature of scientific knowledge' (Carey et al. 1989, p. 515).

Is the cognitive argument for improving understanding and conceptual development of science limited solely to understanding substantive ideas – the facts, laws and theories of science? It has been argued (Gott and Duggan, 1995, 1996) that procedural understanding – the thinking behind the doing – involves a set of ideas that are complementary to conceptual understanding and include a cognitive demand. This procedural understanding requires 'concepts of evidence' which refer to, for example, the design, measurement, data handling and evaluation of practical work (Gott and Duggan, 1995, p. 30), the thinking needed to solve problems as part of scientific inquiry. The Procedural and Conceptual Knowledge in Science (PACKS) project in the 1990s (Millar et al. 1994) carried out extensive research into the role of this procedural knowledge and its relationship to the knowledge of the laws and theories of science. Some of the conclusions related to how students used knowledge and thought about investigation tasks, with many being prepared to draw conclusions on the basis of evidence that would be regarded as unreliable or invalid, or both. There are complex links between understanding and performance that show the importance of both procedural and substantive knowledge in each stage of an investigation. Students use different 'frames' for understanding tasks, ranging from an engagement frame for wanting to do a task, through a modelling frame, an engineering frame that adopts a 'which works best?' approach, to a scientific frame that involves comparisons and generalisations. Furthermore, the project found that some children can apply their understanding when responding to the demands of an investigation but cannot express this understanding explicitly. Work by Pekmez, Johnson and Gott (2005) in schools in England groups teachers' understanding of the nature and purpose of practical work into three distinct categories:

- those who represent thinking consistent with the National Curriculum in distinguishing investigations as a type of practical work concerned with problem solving, and drawing on both substantive and procedural knowledge
- those who believe the only aim of practical work is to support substantive explanations of science, with practical activities as a means to this end
- a group that is less easy to categorise in that their interpretation of investigations involves skills rather than ideas, which is more in line with the process movement.

The limited research evidence here indicates that the cognitive argument for practical work in school science is not as clear as it appears, that learning science with practical work is successful when it is incorporated as an explicit strategy to help students make links or as part of the kinds of procedural understanding needed to carry out more open-ended investigative work.

The skills argument

The skills argument appears to be a straightforward one at first – that of allowing students to develop the skills of handling apparatus, and making measurements. However, there must be cognitive dimensions to this as decisions need to be made about which apparatus to use, which measuring device to choose and the degree of accuracy of the measurement. Skills are more than just the 'mechanical' aspects of practical work that students acquire, store and draw upon at a later date (Gott and Duggan, 1995, p. 26). They may extend to those processes of predicting, observing and interpreting and may be transferable to new contexts (Wellington, 1998). There are two problems with these assumptions: first, that some of these skills may not be as straightforward as they appear; and second, that transfer is more easily said than done.

Taking the skill of observation, Millar (1991) makes the point that the relevance of an observation in science depends on prior expectation or theory in order to decide what is relevant, that we bring our own set of 'spectacles' to an observation (Millar, 1998, p. 18). Allen's research (2010) shows that the spectacles may be clouded to the extent that observations may be a result of expectations, that students' actually see what they think they are supposed to see. Ideas that skills can be transferred may be wishful thinking: Chapman counters the argument that education in the sciences develops skills which have applications in many other areas of human activities with:

> 'Claims made for transferable skills are always suspect. Those made on behalf of the sciences are no more – or less – suspect than those made on behalf of many other areas of the curriculum. Furthermore if a skill has general applicability it is clearly illogical to specify an area of experience through which it must be delivered.'

Chapman (1993, p. 262)

If skills are theory laden and not necessarily transferable, they must be limited only to the domain of school science practical work rather than general education. Additionally, it could be argued that acquiring some of the practical skills of measurement and handling apparatus are, or will be, redundant in a digital age and with remote handling technologies.

It appears that practical work features highly in students' attitudes towards, and enjoyment of, school science. When this author asked small groups of students about their experiences of science practicals at Secondary school, their reported sentiments compared their experiences of practical work with those of other aspects of science lessons: for example, they said it was 'fun to do something, not just writing', 'all working together' and 'more interesting than reading or listening to teachers' (reported in Wellington, 2005, p. 103). Jarman's survey (1993) reports that when students transfer from Primary to Secondary school they note that there is more practical work and with different equipment, including that icon of school science, the Bunsen burner.

Research carried out by a team from Sheffield for the Qualifications and Curriculum Authority in 1998 surveyed the views of students, teachers, advisers and inspectors at Key Stages 3 and 4 to investigate a number of issues, including practical work and investigations (Nott and Wellington, 1999). They found that most teachers interviewed believed that practical work motivates and enthuses students, and this view was echoed with student interviews and questionnaire responses, which showed that they were very positive about practical work and expressed enjoyment of it. However, four in ten teachers believed that students frequently lose sight of the purpose of practical work whereas just over half believe they are able to keep the purpose of practical work in mind. In interviews, teachers claimed that practical work is not always effective and efficient, a view shared by advisers and inspectors, and also commented that students were reluctant to write up work, and thought investigations took too long to mark and too long to give feedback. Most teachers used set investigations that had been developed over the years and saw them primarily as assessment exercises. This summative rather than formative role of investigations, of being able to 'jump through hoops' (Nott and Wellington, 1999, p. 14), was reflected in the year 12 students' questionnaires where most felt they knew how to get good marks in investigations at GCSE; a situation paralleled in Keiler's work (Keiler and Woolnough, 2002) where gaining marks – even to the extent of falsifying practical results – was seen to be important by students in the GCSE years.

The affective argument

Students' attitudes have been the subject of large-scale surveys with most measurements based on quantitative questionnaires and with a few case studies involving interviews that have provided rich qualitative data. A number of these attitude studies make specific mention of practical work in school science. A wide-ranging survey by Bennett and Hogarth (2005) covered attitudes to science, to the individual sciences, to school science and to future science careers of cohorts of school students from ages 11 to 15. When agreeing to the response item 'Science lessons are among my favourite lessons', 26 students produced 'other' comments. Of these, 11 made reference to the fun, exciting, interesting or enjoyable aspects of science lessons and 7 students mentioned that they particularly liked the experimental and practical activities.

Another survey, this time using a web-based format, produced 1450 responses to questions about effective and enjoyable ways of learning. Although the item on discussions and debates in class scored the highest (48%) for being useful and effective, 'doing a science experiment in class' came third out of 11 items for being enjoyable, below 'going on a science trip or excursion' and 'looking at videos' (Murray and Reiss, 2005, p. 86). Reporting research based on questionnaire and interview methods conducted in South Wales with students aged 11 to 14, Parkinson *et al.* (1998) show that practical work was high on the list of 'likes' from both boys and girls and comment that:

> *'Many of the responses indicated that students enjoyed the opportunity of working with others during experimental work.'*

> Parkinson *et al.* (1998, p. 172)

Although questionnaire surveys provide detailed numerical data in response to specific items and are useful for identifying the nature of the problem (Osborne, Simon and Collins, 2003), they provide little information on their own about why students have preferences for practical work. An exception is where free response items are included, as with the survey reported by Bennett and Hogarth (2005). Two qualitative studies can provide further information: the first by Osborne and Collins (2000, 2001) about views of the school science curriculum, and the second on the affective value of practical work from Abraham's study (2008). Osborne and Collins (2000) interviewed 144 students in focus groups of between six and eight. Their findings cover a wide range of views on the importance of science, the curriculum, interest in science topics, and content. On the area of practical work, they found that students expressed a great interest, they enjoyed the personal autonomy, the fun (for example, dissection) and found practical work made science more accessible and more easily retained. However, students said they had too few opportunities to carry out practical work or for discussion (Osborne and Collins, 2001). Abrahams (2008) indicates that practical work provides situational interest, an interest that is stimulated in an individual as a result of being in a particular environment or situation and which, unlike a personal interest, can be stimulated by teachers. The students in Abraham's study found that students have a *relative* preference for practical work, where they claim to like practical work in preference to alternative methods of teaching:

> *'It is important to point out that some of the reasons for claiming to like practical work within this [affective] category ... are less of a positive endorsement of practical work than a desire to avoid having to write and/or do too much work.'*

> Abrahams (2008, p. 11)

Only a small minority claimed that it helped them to learn, understand or recollect ideas and concepts.

Where is practical work going?

The research on practical work discussed in this chapter indicates that it is enjoyed by the majority of students as an alternative to other teaching approaches and as an approach to autonomous working. Furthermore, practical work may provide some cognitive advantage in helping them to learn science, especially when an explicit strategy is used to link ideas and activities. The jury is still out when it comes to considering the role of practical work for acquiring skills, particularly if they cannot be transferred to other areas. Relatively few students will go into science-based careers and the skills they have used in school science are likely to be overtaken by new technologies.

So where will practical work go from here? Jenkins (1998) has written a very thought-provoking review of the history of practical work in laboratories and it seems that the school science laboratory may well be here to stay. It is how the space is used that will change: there will be new designs, new and flexible spaces, new ways of engaging learning such as group activities, more open-ended styles of investigations and the use of data-logging equipment. There may be criticisms of some of these. Is data-logging 'authentic' practical work? Can open-ended work be compatible with the pressures to obtain results and rankings on examination league tables? The Science Community Representing Education (SCORE) report (2008) notes that we need an evidence base to better define issues relating to the effectiveness of practical work.

In a sense, practical work is an integral part of the culture of school science and the laboratory is the home of science lessons and science teachers. It may be very difficult to imagine the class waiting at the door *not* asking if they are going to do a practical today.

References

Abrahams, I. (2008) Does practical work really motivate? A study of the affective value of practical work in secondary school science. *International Journal of Science Education*. First Article, 1–19.

Abrahams, I. and Millar, R. (2008) Does practical work really work? A study of the effectiveness of practical work as a teaching and learning method in school science. *International Journal of Science Education* **30**(14) 1945–1969.

Allen, M. (2010) Learner error, affectual stimulation, and conceptual change. *Journal of Research in Science Teaching* **47**(2) 151–173.

Alsop, S. (2005) Bridging the Cartesian divide: science education and affect. In Alsop, S. (ed) *Beyond Cartesian Dualism* (pp. 3–16). Dordrect: Springer.

Bennett, J. and Hogarth, S. (2005) *Would You Want to Talk to a Scientist at a Party? Students' attitudes to school science and science.* York: Department of Educational Studies, the University of York.

Carey, S., Evans, R., Honda, M., Jay, E. and Unger, C. (1989) 'An experiment is when you try it and see if it works': a study of grade 7 students' understanding of the construction of scientific knowledge. *International Journal of Science Education* **11**(5) 514–529.

Chapman, B. (1993) The overselling of science education in the eighties. In Whitelegg, E., Thomas, J. and Tresman, S. (eds) *Challenges and Opportunities for Science Education* (pp. 256–277). London: Paul Chapman Publishing.

Gott, R. and Duggan, S. (1995) *Investigative Work in the Science Curriculum.* Buckingham: Open University Press.

Gott, R. and Duggan, S. (1996) Practical work: its role in the understanding of evidence in science. *International Journal of Science Education* **18**(7) 791–806.

Hodson, D. (1990) A critical look at practical work in school science. *School Science Review*, **70**(256) 33–40.

Jarman, R. (1993) Real experiments with Bunsen burners: pupils' perceptions of the similarities and differences between primary science and secondary science. *School Science Review* **74**(268) 19–29.

Jenkins, E. (1998) The schooling of laboratory science. In Wellington, J. (ed) *Practical Work in School Science: Which way now?* London: Routledge.

Keiler, L.S. and Woolnough, B.E. (2002) Practical work in school science: the dominance of assessment. *School Science Review* **83**(304) 83–88.

Kerr, J.F. (1963) *Practical Work in School Science*. Leicester: Leicester University Press.

Millar, R. (1991) A means to an end: the role of process in science education. In Woolnough, B. (ed) *Practical Science* (pp. 43–52). Buckingham: Open University Press.

Millar, R. (1998) Rhetoric and reality. In Wellington, J. (ed.) *Practical Work In School Science: Which way now?* (pp. 16–31). London: Routledge.

Millar, R., Lubben, F., Gott, R. and Duggan, S. (1994) Investigating in the school science laboratory: conceptual and procedural knowledge and their influence on performance. *Research Papers in Education* **9**(2) 207–248.

Millar, R., Le Maréchal, J.-F. and Tiberghien, A. (1999) 'Mapping' the domain. Varieties of practical work. In Leach, J. and Paulsen, A. (eds) *Practical Work in Science Education – Recent Research Studies* (pp. 33–42). Roskilde/Dordrecht, The Netherlands: Roskilde University Press/Kluwer.

Murray, I. and Reiss, M. (2005) The student review of the science curriculum. *School Science Review* **87**(318) 83–93.

National Committee on Science Education Standards and Assessment; National Research Council (1996) *National Science Education Standards*. Washington: The National Academies Press.

New Zealand Ministry of Education (1993) *Science in the New Zealand Curriculum*. Wellington: Learning Media.

Nott, M. and Wellington, J. (1999) The state we're in: issues in Key Stage 3 and 4 science. *School Science Review.* **81**(294) 13–18.

Ormerod, M.B. and Duckworth, D. (1975) *Pupils' Attitudes to Science. A review of research*. Windsor, Berks: NFER Publishing Company.

Osborne, J. and Collins, S. (2000) *Pupils' and Parents' Views of the School Science Curriculum*. London: King's College London.

Osborne, J. and Collins, S. (2001) Pupils' views of the role and value of the science curriculum: a focus group study. *International Journal of Science Education* **23**(5) 441–467.

Osborne, J., Simon, S. and Collins, S. (2003) Attitudes towards science: a review of the literature and its implications. *International Journal of Science Education* **25**(9) 1049–1079.

Parkinson, J., Hendley, D., Tanner, H. and Stables, A. (1998) Pupils' attitudes to science in Key Stage 3 of the National Curriculum: a study of pupils in South Wales. *Research in Science and Technological Education* **16**(1) 165–176.

Pekmez, O.P., Johnson, P. and Gott, R. (2005) Teachers' understanding of the nature and purpose of practical work. *Research in Science and Technological Education* **23**(1) 3–23.

SCORE (2008) *Practical Work in Science: A report and proposal for a strategic framework*. London: SCORE.

Toh, K.-A. (1991) Factors affecting success in science investigation. In Woolnough, B. (ed) *Practical Science* (pp. 89–100). Buckingham: Open University Press.

Toplis, R. (2007) Practical work in science. *Education in Science* **221**, 28–29.

Wellington, J. (1998) (ed) *Practical Work in School Science: Which way now?* London: Routledge.

Wellington, J. (2000) *Teaching and Learning Secondary Science.* London: Routledge.

Wellington, J. (2005) Practical work and the affective domain: what do we know, what should we ask, and what is worth exploring further? In Alsop, S. (ed) *Beyond Cartesian Dualism* (pp. 99–109). Dordrecht: Springer.

Chapter 9

Group work: what does research say about its effect on learning?

Deb McGregor

Defining group work

Group work is used in many different ways to support learning in science. However, the ways in which group work is often described do not clearly convey *how* children or students are learning together. Labels used to define group work are often used loosely, including 'collaborative', which Bennett *et al.* (2005, p. 7) propose indicates most activities that do not involve teacher exposition. There are many different ways in which group work *could* be categorised, including:

- by the learning process being supported (as indicated below)
- by the technique being used (jigsaw or snowballing, for example)
- by the composition of the group (mixed ability or mixed learning styles, for example)
- by the size of the group (pair, trio, quad and so on).

This chapter, however, focuses on the nature of group work, the ways in which small groups, ranging from two to five or six students, might work together in either a Primary or Secondary science classroom.

The nature of group work

Group work activity can vary widely and could include, for example, a pair of students carrying out an illustrative experiment to show how an increase in temperature results in a faster rate of reaction, or a trio or quad deliberating over the ethical considerations of gene counselling for a presentation, or five or six children rehearsing how they are going to enact sound waves being transferred through a solid, liquid and gas. The ways in which learners are 'set up' or prepared to work together and the task they are given on which to work together can shape different forms of social interaction arising through group work. It may be that they:

- work **cooperatively** – each student working on an individual but related task, and then sharing outcomes with other group members
- work **collaboratively** – participating in joint activity that is mutually supportive, working towards a common goal and developing shared understanding
- engage in **peer tutoring** – where more expert students structure and support the work of less expert others
- engage in formative **peer assessment** – where a peer critiques another's work and offers constructive modifications.

This chapter outlines factors influencing the occurrence, type and effectiveness of group work and suggests 'what next' regarding extending, enhancing or enriching effective group work in science classrooms.

Potentially influencing factors

There are many factors that influence the nature of group work in school science. Policies prescribing school practices (such as streaming, banding or setting) and routines (such as mixed ability in-class groupings or mixing learning styles) will influence teaching (see Box 1).

Box 1 Some definitions of groupings.

Streaming usually refers to the 'ability' group a child may be placed in. This remains the same for all subjects.

Banding involves placing students in broadly similar ability groupings. There may be two or three bands across a year, and students may be setted within bands.

Setting usually refers to students being placed in groups of similar ability (as perceived by the school). Setting may vary for individuals in different subjects.

Learning preferences (visual, auditory and kinaesthetic) are more commonly referred to as learning styles.

The ways in which classrooms are physically laid out – whether in regimented rows, with movable benches or tables, fixed teaching podia or with interactive whiteboards on only one wall – shapes the way teachers manage and organise students to work together.

The nature of tasks will also influence the types of contributions individuals will offer within a group and the subsequent learning achieved. When task scaffolding, for example, is semi-structured, it can offer learners opportunities to deliberate, but provides sufficient support to focus attention on key aspects of experimentation (McGregor, 2008). Tasks providing decision-making opportunities can support higher levels of engagement, discussion, inferential reasoning and less disruptive behaviour (Baines, Davies and Blatchford, 2009, p. 95).

Composition of groups – whether single sex, mixed ability, friendship groups, trios or quads, for example – can also influence learning processes and outcomes. Alexopoulou and Driver's (1996) study indicated how discussion was constrained when students worked in pairs, but was richer in nature when in fours. McGregor's (2003) study highlighted how trios appear to support, given appropriate guidance, extended constructive deliberations of plausible possibilities in investigational situations. Some students will feel more or less confident suggesting ideas or proposing alternative viewpoints, and this can be modified by the way that teachers organise for and encourage social exchange of ideas, critique of suggestions and engagement in peer–peer reflection.

Finally, the perceptions that students hold about *why* and *how* they should interact, question each other, or comment constructively on ideas also influences the nature and development of group work.

Research findings about effective group work in science

Although Galton, Hargreaves and Pell (2009, p. 1) highlight how group work is still a neglected art in many classrooms, they emphasise how it is the quality of talk that appears to contribute to improving group work. In Primary science education, there are many studies exploring good practice that indicate how preparatory training, the application of conflict, development of trust and argumentation are also key influences supporting learning. The lack of evidence, however, to indicate what constitutes effective practice in Secondary science classrooms can be supplemented by studies in other disciplines that offer insight into the ways students *could* learn more effectively through social interaction.

Group work in Primary science

Research on group work in Primary science provides substantial evidence that collaborative learning can have positive effects on the quality of discourse, decision-making processes and conceptual grasp. The studies that illustrate this highlight the importance of discussion, emotional ease and trust when working with others and understanding about what is expected of them (Simon and Maloney, 2007) when working without direct and continual teacher guidance. Talk that involves peers explaining their individual ideas to each other (for example, 'My idea is …', 'I think that … because …' or 'Well, I thought …') or responding to peers' queries about their ideas (for example, 'What is your reason for thinking that?') has been found to indicate more effective discursive exchange. Tasks that encourage this kind of open discussion support more collaborative responses to problems, providing the opportunity to explore reasoning – for example, collectively reflecting after reading about the life cycle of a penguin, and then asking 'Why does the father do that?', or 'How is a penguin father different to a human father or a human mother?' To support inclusivity and shared engagement involving every member of a group, the teacher needs thoughtfully to organise for symmetrical (equal) contributions, or the students need to be routinely practiced in equitably offering ideas and freely elaborating on discussions in small clusters.

Other kinds of tasks that involve teachers asking children to 'explain to their partner', 'describe your reasons to the group', 'highlight what is good', 'describe how it can be improved', for example, have also been shown to extend discussion, argumentation and consideration of alternative perspectives to encourage exploratory talk. Howe *et al.* (1992) showed how children grouped on the basis of their different ideas, about forces acting on inclined planes, socially engaged in co-constructing understandings and performed better in post-task tests. This kind of talk between peers in a group encourages critical but constructive engagement with each other's ideas. Statements and suggestions are offered for joint reflection and consideration. These may be challenged and counter-challenged, but challenges are justified and alternative possibilities are offered. Compared with other types of talk, understanding is made more 'publicly accountable' and reasoning more 'visible' (Mercer, 2000). This approach underpins the *Thinking Together* programme (Dawes, Mercer and Wegerif 2000) and links with Chapter 13 on dialogue and argumentation. There are also indications that the collective focus helps sensitise and alert students to make connections to more familiar contexts, ensuring ideas become better embedded. Approaches embracing dialogic teaching, argumentation, concept cartoons, thinking together, empathising with puppets and techniques such as snowballing and jigsaw can all be used to good effect to support small-group learning through promotion of questioning, consideration of conflicting perspectives, exploratory discussion, reasoned justifications and constructive reflection.

There is also some evidence that friendship groupings may positively influence productivity (although there is contradictory evidence about this at the Secondary level). More recently, attention has turned to the ways in which children might be better prepared for engaging in group work in Primary science. A study by Howe et al. (2007) indicates that where children received systematic preliminary training in various skills, including how to listen, question, provide explanations and reach agreement, they gained markedly in their conceptual understanding. These skills appear to be critical for preventing social friction being caused by the disagreements that spark the discussion of ideas. Group members need to trust each other to disagree (Tolmie et al. 2009) in order to sustain and facilitate discussion to support effective group work. Kutnick and Berdondini's (2009) work emphasised how emotional factors such as trust and respect were key in training children to work together. Their findings re-enforced the importance of both communication and social skills.

Group work in Secondary science

A fairly recent national study (Kutnick et al. 2005) reviewing teachers' practice within Secondary science lessons indicates that group work is a well-integrated teaching strategy. However, pedagogic decisions about why group work should be used were often informed by resourcing implications (limited equipment, fixed furniture, size of tables and so on). Rather alarmingly, it appears that little consideration is given to the learning purpose, objectives and the processes in which different sized groups might interactively engage. Student groupings were rarely determined by the type and demands of the learning task (Galton et al. 2009) and teachers even made decisions about using small group working to relieve boredom or, conversely, halted collaborative learning to control behaviour of some individuals (Kutnick et al. 2005). The ways that students might equally contribute in a collaborative way towards an agreed group goal is often assumed but not clearly described or supported and teachers even organise pairs of working students as a strategy for more control and less disruption (ibid).

Several other studies have also shown that science teachers (under significant content delivery pressures) have not regularly planned for different ways in which social interaction may arise within small groups to purposely enrich and enhance learning. However, complementing the Primary studies, Baggott and Erduran (2007) have described how argumentation can be promoted in GCSE courses courses and Bennett et al. (2005) have emphasised how metacognition is important for effective discussion. McGregor (2008) has illustrated how the nature of task can shape the kinds of interactions, talk and learning of group members. Differentiated tasks (open, scaffolded, prescriptive) can support more or less exploratory talk about different aspects of the experimental process, influencing the quality of learning and understanding of science.

Learning from the research

Science teachers are concerned about how to use group work effectively (Galton *et al.* 2009) to ensure equality of involvement and quality engagement of *all* participants in a group. Teaching approaches that encourage peer tutoring or cooperative learning, or – even more effectively – that support effective collaboration, should be the aim in group work. In the brief review above, group work has been shown to be an effective strategy to support social constructivist teaching, but it does require careful organisation and management to work effectively.

Current research findings signal what approaches appear to work in Primary schools. Indeed, Thurston *et al.* (2010) indicate that children look forward to continuing to work co-operatively at Secondary school, but these hopes are not commonly fulfilled. Developing and sustaining social interactions and discussions to support effective collaboration in Secondary science classrooms requires somewhat different pedagogical strategies. More detailed research, it seems, is needed to explore further how teenagers could continue to learn together more effectively. Certainly, researching further how different kinds of groupings, and participant roles therein, could influence thinking processes and learning outcomes should be high on the group work agenda.

References

Alexopoulou, E. and Driver, R. (1996) Small-group discussion in physics: peer interaction modes in pairs and fours. *Journal of Research in Science Teaching* **33**(10) 1099–1114.

Baggott, S. and Erduran, S. (2007) Argument and developments in the science curriculum. *School Science Review* **88**(324) 31–40.

Baines, E., Davies, C. and Blatchford, P. (2009) Improving pupil group work interaction and dialogue in primary classrooms: results from a year-long intervention study. *Cambridge Journal of Education* **39**(1) 95–117

Bennett, J., Lubben, F., Hogarth, S. and Campbell, B. (2005) *A Systematic Review of the Use of Small-Group Discussions in Science Teaching with Students Aged 11–18, and their Effects on Students' Understanding in Science or Attitude to Science: review summary*. York: Department of Educational Studies, University of York.

Dawes, L., Mercer, N. and Wegerif, R. (2000) *Thinking Together: a programme of activities for developing speaking, listening and thinking skills for children aged 8–11*. Birmingham: Imaginative Minds Ltd.

Galton, M. and Hargreaves, L. (2009) Group work: still a neglected art? *Cambridge Journal of Education* **39**(1) 1-6.

Howe, C., Tolmie, A. and Rodgers, C. (1992) The acquisition of conceptual knowledge in science by primary school children: group interaction and the understanding of motion down an incline. *British Journal of Developmental Psychology* **10**, 113-130.

Howe, C.J., Tolmie, A., Greer, K. and Mackenzie, M. (1995) Peer collaboration and conceptual growth in Physics: Task influences on children's understanding of heating and cooling. *Cognition and Instruction* **13**, 483–503.

Howe, C., Tolmie, A., Thurston, A., Topping, K., Christie, D., Livingston, K., Jessimen, E. and Donaldson, C. (2007) Group work in elementary science: towards organisational principles for supporting pupil learning. *Learning and Instruction* **17**, 549–563.

Kutnick, P. and Berdondini, L. (2009) Can the enhancement of group working in classrooms provide a basis for effective communication in support of school-based cognitive achievement in classrooms of young learners? *Cambridge Journal of Education* **39**(1) 71–94.

Kutnick, P., Blatchford, P., Clark, H., MacIntyre, H. and Baines, E. (2005) Teachers' understandings of the relationship between within-class (pupil) grouping and learning in secondary schools. *Educational Research* **47**(1) 1–24.

Mercer, N. (2000) *Words and Minds: How we use language to think together*. London: Routledge.

McGregor, D. (2003) Applying learning theories reflexively to understand and support the use of group work in the learning of science. Unpublished PhD Thesis: Keele University.

McGregor, D. (2008) The influence of task structure on students' learning processes: observations from case studies in secondary school science. *Journal of Curriculum Studies* **40**(4) 509–540.

Simon, S. and Maloney, J. (2007) Activities for promoting small-group discussion and argumentation. *School Science Review* **88**(324) 49–58.

Thurston, A., Topping, K.J., Tolmie, A.K., Christie, D., Karagiannidou, E. and Murray, P. (2010) Cooperative learning in science: Follow-up from primary to high school. *International Journal of Science Education* **32**(4) 501-522.

Tolmie, A., Topping, K., Christie, D., Donaldson, C., Howe, C., Jessiman, E., Livingston, K. and Thurston, A. (2009) Social effects of collaborative learning in primary schools. *Learning and Instruction* **20**(2010) 177–191. DOI:10.1016/j.learninstruc.2009.01.005.

Chapter 10

Creativity in teaching science

Stuart Naylor and Brenda Keogh

Some time ago, the authors were collecting data for research in the Puppets Promoting Engagement and Talk in Science (PUPPETS) project (Simon *et al.* 2008). Two of the teachers involved in the research talked about being more creative in their science teaching. However, the two teachers – let's call them Ged and Chris – seemed to have rather different views about what being creative in teaching science, using the puppets, meant to them.

Ged's view of using a puppet was that it allowed him to use a more creative approach in his science lessons. He described how he was able to be more adventurous and relaxed with his students, more open to new ideas that emerged during a lesson, and more willing to take risks in what he did and what he allowed the students to do. He listened to the students' ideas more, was more flexible in how he responded to their ideas, and was more willing to allow them to develop their ideas in ways that he hadn't anticipated. We could say that his teaching became more dialogic (Alexander, 2008).

By contrast, Chris talked about how using a puppet helped him to be more creative in teaching science by making stronger links between science and the arts. He made more effort to identify different modes of artistic expression that students could use to communicate their ideas about science. This included using role play to act out scientific concepts, using art to capture scientific ideas, and using scientific ideas as inspiration for music, dance and drama, so that science lessons also met learning objectives from other subject areas. We could say that his teaching became more cross-curricular.

Clearly Chris and Ged's comments indicate that they held different views about what being creative in their teaching meant. Their comments are indicative of a more general issue – of how teachers make sense of creativity and what kind of support can be offered to teachers who wish to be more creative. They also illustrate some of the tensions in writing about creativity in teaching science, since we see different views about creativity reflected in the literature. In this chapter, we attempt to explore these issues, considering what we understand by creativity in teaching science, identifying its benefits, and suggesting how creativity can be encouraged and achieved realistically in the classroom.

What is creativity in teaching science?

Is creativity something that is embedded in typical science lessons (Ged's view), or does the creativity come more from linking science creatively with other subjects such as art, poetry, music or drama (as Chris would advocate)?

Taking the cross-curricular perspective, Nickerson (2009) describes using drama to represent what happens to particles of solid as they dissolve in a liquid, or to illustrate pushes, pulls and balanced forces. Similarly, Rosen (2000) uses poems as a starting point for science activity, while Feasey (2001) uses poetry as a means of learners recording their ideas. If external funding is an indicator, then links between science and other subjects seem to be a reasonably high priority. The Wellcome Trust has funded a range of projects, such as the Pulse Project and Science Centrestage, which support performing arts projects enabling young people to engage with biomedical science issues. Similarly, the National Endowment for Science, Technology and the Arts (NESTA), uses lottery funding to support a variety of initiatives, including using performing arts to represent scientific ideas.

However, many teachers would claim that creativity is inherent in science – in hypothesising, solving problems of experimental design, finding patterns in data, linking disparate concepts, and so on – rather than needing to be artificially injected through cross-curricular channels. They may feel that they don't know enough about the creative arts to make sensible curriculum links, and may question whether such links are either necessary or sufficient for science to be creative. Some may suggest that a cross-curricular perspective is a blind alley if the majority of science lessons are dull and descriptive, with only brief forays into more creative arts-based territory. Very creative scientists who make dramatic conceptual leaps – the Einsteins, Darwins or Feynmans – don't seem to feel any necessity to link science overtly with other subjects, but of course that doesn't mean that we shouldn't do it in science education.

Issue No 332 of the journal *School Science Review* (March 2009) was a special issue on creativity in science, in which nine articles gave a reasonably comprehensive view of creativity in science teaching and learning. Of the nine articles published, five of them were written largely from the standpoint of creativity being embedded in typical science lessons, while the other four described some kind of cross-curricular work in which science is linked with other subjects. This balance seems to reflect the overall dichotomy of approaches to creativity in science teaching – it can be embedded within science lessons, and it can be evident in cross-curricular connections.

Defining creativity

While we acknowledge that creativity in science teaching can take different forms, it is helpful to try to pin down at least some aspects of what we mean by creativity. There are plenty of definitions of creativity in the literature.

- Fisher (1990, p. 40) suggests that creativity *'consists largely of rearranging what we know in order to find out what we do not know'*, and that the task of teaching is to spark off the creative impulse within the child.

- Best and Thomas (2007, p. 27) define creativity as *'the intentional and purposeful search for innovation in problem solving'*, with a more user-friendly definition as *'the process of finding and implementing new and appropriate ways of doing things.'*

- Davies, Rosso and Bell-Scott (2002) describe creative thinking skills as generating and extending ideas, suggesting hypotheses, applying imagination and looking for imaginative outcomes.

Probably the most authoritative source is the National Advisory Committee on Creative and Cultural Education (NACCCE). This committee recognised that creativity is a term used in different ways by different people in different contexts. With a range of possible definitions to choose from, they settled on one that they felt was the most useful, stating that creativity is:

'imaginative activity fashioned so as to produce outcomes that are both original and of value.'

NACCCE (1999, p. 29)

They helpfully refer to four characteristics that underpin this definition, these being imaginative thinking, purposeful activity, a degree of originality for the individual and some type of critical evaluation.

Presumably, the NACCCE definition must be viewed as authoritative, since it has been incorporated into various National Curriculum and QCDA documents since then (QCDA, 2010, for example). The QCDA website has a whole section about creativity, explaining why it is important and how teachers can promote it (QCDA, 2010). Ofsted has written about it too (Ofsted, 2003), though how Einstein's comment that 'Imagination is more important than knowledge. Knowledge is limited. Imagination encircles the world' (Einstein, 1929) would be judged using the current Ofsted framework remains to be seen. In any case, the NACCCE definition is, arguably, one that meets our needs, since it could apply to both science-specific and cross-curricular activities.

Creative learners or creative teachers?

Is it the learner who needs to be creative, or the teacher, or both? Definitions of creativity tend to focus more on what learners do, and clearly learners can be creative in their responses in the classroom. For example, Roberts (2009) describes how open-ended investigations can give learners the opportunity to work creatively to solve a problem, and how teaching concepts of evidence and uncertainty help them to do this. However, the title of Best and Thomas's (2007) book is the *Creative Teaching and Learning Toolkit*, with a clear implication that teachers and learners are both involved. Similarly NACCCE (1999) recognises that teachers can be creative in their teaching, and that they have a responsibility to recognise and develop young people's creative capacities. Millar and Osborne's (1998) seminal report on the future of science education doesn't appear to address creativity directly, but they do describe the aims of science education as being to:

'… sustain and develop the curiosity of young people about the natural world … and to foster a sense of wonder, enthusiasm and interest in science …'

Millar and Osborne (1998, p. 5)

It's difficult to read that without a strong sense of teachers being creative as well as learners responding creatively to their teaching. Wardle (2009) sees a strong connection between teaching that is creative and learners who are engaged, inspired and stimulated by their study of science, and he views creative teaching as 'good' teaching in terms of its approach, strategy, interventions and activities.

Who is creativity for?

It has been suggested that creativity enhances learning for gifted and talented students in particular. This is highlighted by Ponchaud's description of a PGCE Enhancement Programme designed to help newly qualified teachers work creatively with gifted and talented learners (Ponchaud, 2009), with suggestions for how activities might be incorporated into typical science lessons without detracting from the learning experiences of other students. Similarly O'Brien notes that creative and critical thinking is particularly well-suited to gifted learners (O'Brien, 2003).

Are the benefits of creative teaching therefore restricted to particular groups, or is creativity something from which all learners will benefit? Our experience suggests the latter, and that any relationship between levels of achievement in school and levels of creativity is tenuous at best. We can't be alone in seeing examples of high achieving conscientious plodders, working alongside learners with high potential but low achievement – creative, bored and disengaged. Even if there were such a relationship, we may not want to reinforce it. Maybe creativity is a bit like 'intelligence', something that most people have the potential to develop, but how much it develops is profoundly influenced by relationships, environment and experiences.

What is the purpose of being creative?

Creative science teaching can be a vehicle to develop appropriate knowledge, understanding and skills. A wide range of programmes such as CASE (Adey, Shayer and Yates, 2001), Let's Think (Adey, 2008) and the IDEAS project (Osborne, Erduran and Simon, 2004) use a variety of creative approaches to get learners to engage with science and develop specific skills. In these programmes, the purpose of creative teaching is to make teaching more effective. Alternatively, scientific concepts and ideas can be used creatively to solve real-life problems, as described in the materials produced by the Science Enhancement Programme (2010). From this perspective, creativity is something embedded in science as a subject, and this has value in relation to external situations. A third perspective suggests that science can be used as a context in which learners develop their own creative skills and attitudes. For example, Claxton describes how teachers can help learners to become more resilient, resourceful, reflective and reciprocal, how this helps them to become better learners and how it leads to more creative engagement by both learners and teachers (Claxton, 2002). Similarly, Bianchi and Barnett (2006) use science learning activities to develop personal capabilities such as self-management, problem solving and creativity.

How to be creative

From this brief review, it is apparent is that there is no overall consensus about the meaning or purpose of creativity as it applies to science lessons, and that different authors have different perspectives. In some ways, it is a bit like the situation that has developed with constructivist learning and teaching over the past couple of decades (Skamp, 2004, gives a helpful overview of this). It may sound great in principle, but there are so many different perspectives on what it looks like (Taber, 2009) that it is really hard for teachers to be confident about how to implement it in typical classrooms. Implementation requires teachers to understand how to make creativity meaningful and manageable, but the range of writing makes it sound rather complex.

Teachers also need to consider the breadth of their ambitions – what do they see as the outcome of more creative teaching and/or more creative learners? The National College for School Leadership (2004) suggests a number of spectrum lines by which we can judge the degree of creativity in a situation, ranging from virtually none to very high levels, with various stages in between. These apply to planning and teaching, the nature of the curriculum, the nature of the learning environment, and so on. What is apparent is that with high levels of creativity we would expect learners to have lots of opportunities to influence their own learning environment and how the school operates, and that there will be high levels of unpredictability in how lessons develop. Teachers would not only have to plan for flexibility but would also have to adapt lessons in ways not envisaged in their planning. Not all teachers will see that as a desirable outcome!

Cost and sustainability raise other questions for teachers of science, in both Primary and Secondary schools. High-profile creative demonstrations, outings, projects, special events and programmes can make a lasting impression on learners and, in some cases, stimulate a lifelong commitment to science as a career. However, the cost of these can be quite high, not only in financial terms but also in energy, staff development, curriculum time, and disruption to the curriculum. How sustainable are they? Some might suggest that programmes such as CASE and Let's Think, for example, are great for the enthusiasts, but for more typical teachers the cost in terms of curriculum time is too high. Many teachers will also find that small-scale, 'generalisable' strategies are more manageable than occasional big events, and that most of the costs involved in putting on creative science lessons can be avoided with a focus on small-scale changes to practice.

Linked with this is the question of what happens the rest of the time. What does a typical lesson look like? Is creativity reserved for special occasions? If so, what impression does that give to learners? There is a clear parallel here with the practice of separating out special 'thinking lessons' – the obvious implication is that most lessons aren't. The most widely cited alternative to the 'special occasion' lesson is the infusion lesson, in which ideas such as creativity are included in typical lessons on a drip-feed basis. Teachers making use of an infusion lesson strategy will use a variety of suitable strategies to embed creativity into their teaching as often as possible (Schwarz, Fischer and Parks, 1998). For example, research into using concept cartoons (Naylor and Keogh, 2010) as part of a lesson shows that they can provide a space in which learners' ideas become significant, and their ideas can then become a creative stimulus around which the rest of the lesson is constructed (Keogh and Naylor, 1999).

Conclusion

So where does all this leave us? Is it a case of 'anything goes' for creativity, or is there any kind of consensus about its purpose and characteristics? Hattie (2009) leaves us in no doubt about its value in raising student achievement. Manning, Glackin and Dillon (2009) provide a helpful outline of some interrelated principles:

- creativity is actively advocated in the various curriculum documents that provide guidance for teachers

- creativity can be taught and learned
- teachers have to be creative themselves (at least to some extent) in order to teach science creatively
- creativity is an important outcome of education, and science lessons should provide opportunities for learners to become more creative.

We can also recognise that creativity is largely an attitude of mind, for teachers and for learners. Since creativity is a way of thinking, and ways of thinking mould attitudes, creativity is also a process of developing attitudes (Fisher, 1990, p. 39). It is absolutely the opposite of what Joan Solomon captured in her incisive phrase, 'frog-marched discovery' (Solomon, 1980), where everything about the lesson is organised in advance, and there is no space for learners' ideas or for following up the unexpected.

Creativity is encouraged when:

- teachers provide a suitable learning environment
- scientific ideas are contextualised so that learners have some sense of purpose to the lesson
- teachers use a variety of creative approaches
- teaching is truly dialogic.

This is achievable gradually, in small steps. Many teachers are much more willing to accept small-scale, evolutionary changes rather than more radical and fundamental changes to their practice (Keogh and Naylor, 2007). Maybe teachers will feel more empowered to change their professional practice in relation to creativity if they don't feel that they have to make major changes in what they do in the classroom.

Dedication

We dedicate this chapter to the memory of Joan Solomon, who was a role model for creative science educators everywhere. In Glen Aikenhead's words, 'science education today is more advanced, more student-oriented and more human as a result of Joan' (Aikenhead, 2009).

References

Adey, P. (ed) (2008) *Let's Think Handbook*. London: GL Assessment.

Adey, P., Shayer, M. and Yates, C. (2001) *Thinking Science: The curriculum materials of the CASE Project* (third edition). London: Nelson Thornes.

Aikenhead, G. (2009) Joan Solomon: a life remembered. *Education in Science*, September 2009, 8–9.

Alexander, R. (2008) *Towards Dialogic Teaching: Rethinking classroom talk* (fourth edition). York: Dialogos.

Best, B. and Thomas, W. (2007) *Creative Teaching and Learning Toolkit*. London: Continuum.

Bianchi, L. and Barnett, R. (2006) *Smart Science*. Sheffield: Sheffield Hallam University.

Claxton, G. (2002) *Building Learning Power*. Bristol: TLO.

Davies, S., Rosso, R. and Bell-Scott, L. (2002) Using TASC to foster the development of problem-solving and thinking skills in science. In Wallace, B. and Bentley, R. (eds) *Teaching Thinking Skills Across the Middle Years* (pp. 95–114). London: David Fulton.

Einstein, A. (1929) quoted in 'What life means to Einstein: an interview by George Sylvester Viereck'. *Saturday Evening Post*, 202, p. 113.

Feasey, R. (2001) *Science is Like a Tub of Ice Cream – Cool and Fun.* Hatfield: ASE.

Fisher, R. (1990) *Teaching Children to Think.* Hemel Hempstead: Simon and Schuster.

Hattie, J. (2009) *Visible Learning: A synthesis of over 800 meta-analyses relating to achievement.* Abingdon: Routledge.

Keogh, B. and Naylor, S. (1999) Concept cartoons, teaching and learning in science: an evaluation. *International Journal of Science Education* **21**(4) 431–446.

Keogh, B. and Naylor, S. (2007) Talking and thinking in science. *School Science Review*, **88**(324) 85–90.

Manning, A., Glackin, M. and Dillon, J. (2009) Creative science lessons? Prospective science teachers reflect on good practice. *School Science Review* **90**(332) 53–58.

Millar, R. and Osborne, J. (1998) *Beyond 2000: Science education for the future.* London: King's College.

NACCCE (National Advisory Committee on Creativity, Culture and Education) (1999) *All Our Futures: Creativity, culture and education.* London: DfEE.

National College for School Leadership (2004) *Developing Creativity in the Primary School: a practical guide for school leaders.* Nottingham: NCSL.

Naylor, S. and Keogh, B. (2010) *Concept Cartoons in Science Education* (second edition). Sandbach: Millgate House Publishers.

Nickerson, L. (2009) Science drama. *School Science Review*, **90**(332) 83–89.

O'Brien, P. (2003) *Using Science to Develop Thinking Skills at Key Stage 3: Materials for gifted children.* London: David Fulton.

Ofsted (2003) *Expecting the Unexpected: Developing creativity in primary and secondary schools.* London: Ofsted.

Osborne, J., Erduran, S. and Simon, S. (2004) *Ideas, Evidence and Argument in Science.* London: Nuffield Foundation.

Ponchaud, B. (2009) Expanding horizons – giftedness and thinking activities in science. *School Science Review* **90**(332) 59–63.

QCDA (2010) *Creativity.* The primary materials are now available at: www.cciproject.org/creativity/index.htm

Roberts, R. (2009) Can teaching about evidence encourage a creative approach in open-ended investigations? *School Science Review* **90**(332) 31–38.

Rosen, M. (2000) *Star Science, Technology and Reading.* Van Dyck, E. (ed) Hatfield: ASE.

Schwarz, R., Fischer, S. and Parks, S. (1998) *Infusing the Teaching of Creative and Critical Thinking into Secondary Science: A lesson design handbook.* Pacific Grove: Critical thinking books and software.

Science Enhancement Programme (2010) available at: www.sep.org.uk. Primary Science Enhancement Programme, available at: www.cciproject.org/creativity (accessed 14 July 2011).

Simon, S., Naylor S., Keogh B., Maloney, J. and Downing, B. (2008) Puppets promoting engagement and talk in science. *International Journal of Science Education* **30**(9) 1229–1248.

Skamp, K. (2004) *Teaching Primary Science Constructively* (second edition). Victoria, Australia: Thomson.

Solomon, J. (1980) *Teaching Children in the Laboratory.* London: Croom Helm.

Taber, K. (2009) *Progressing Science Education.* Dordrecht: Springer.

Wardle, J. (2009) Creativity in science. *School Science Review* **90**(332) 29–30.

Chapter 11

Learning out of the classroom

Michael Reiss

The UK has, for about a century, had a strong tradition of practical work in school science education. As a result, a well-equipped laboratory has long been considered highly desirable for Secondary science teaching, and the advent of the National Curriculum in England, Northern Ireland and Wales in 1989 led to Primary science being influenced more by the assumptions of Secondary science than vice versa. When this emphasis on laboratory work is put alongside the various pressures operating to make it ever more difficult to take students outside the classroom, it is little wonder that learning out of the classroom has often been the *Cinderella* of science teaching.

This author believes passionately in the value of high quality science learning in the classroom, but also believes it needs to be complemented by learning out of the classroom. This chapter explores what research has to say about learning science outside the classroom. The hope is to increase the amount of learning that takes place in science outside the classroom so as to help students learn science better, to enjoy it more and to make it more likely that they will continue studying it when it is no longer mandatory.

Science in the classroom

Whether science is taught in a specialised laboratory (as in many Secondary schools) or in a typical classroom with some specialist equipment (as in many Primary schools), the fundamental idea is that students are presented with a simplified version of reality in which it is easier for them to be introduced to key scientific ideas. Consider, for example, a typical piece of practical work (it might be a demonstration, an investigation or an experiment) in which students look at a range of substances to see which are magnets, which are magnetic materials and which are non-magnetic materials. All that is required are standard magnets (with North and South poles that can be distinguished) and a range of materials (such as a number of non-metals and metals including iron, steel, nickel, cobalt, copper and aluminium).

In a classroom or laboratory setting, the whole exercise need take no more than 15 minutes. And yet in nature, it would not only take far longer but make much greater demands on students in terms of the interpretations they would have to make to reach the same conclusions. This, above all, indicates the value of classroom learning in science.

The purified, controlled and simplified version of reality with which students are presented makes it much easier for a teacher to help students understand the conclusions of science.

And yet such a version of nature is indeed purified, controlled and simplified. Unless it is complemented by the richer, messier world outside of the classroom, students may fail to connect their classroom learning with the world beyond the classroom. One can envisage three categories of this outside-of-the-classroom world (Braund and Reiss, 2006):

1   the actual world (for example, as accessed by fieldtrips and other visits to see science in use)
2   the presented world (for example, in science museums, botanic gardens and zoos)
3   the virtual world (for example, through ICT simulations).

Learning in the actual, the presented and the virtual world can valuably complement learning about science that takes place within school. We need to remember that even during their school years students spend most of their waking hours outside of school. Indeed, much work in early years education shows the extent to which children come to school with a tremendous array of presumptions about the natural world. Sometimes science educators seem to deal with such presumptions as if they were mostly misconceptions that school science education needs to eradicate. In reality, much of this learning forms a valuable foundation on which schools science can build.

For example, Ruby et al. (2007) showed how families from a range of cultures passed on information about the growing of fruit and vegetables to their young children (between three and six years old) in East London. In the case of five-year-old Sumayah, who is British Bangladeshi, an interaction she had with her cousin (of the same age), mother and grandmother in their garden in Tower Hamlets was video-recorded. Using a blend of Bengali and English, Sumayah talked about various species of tree (apple, lemon) and other plants (potato, pumpkin, tomato). Both she and her cousin demonstrated that they understood the importance of watering and, indeed, competed with one another to use the watering can. Sumayah's mother reinforced the importance of water for plant growth by saying to Sumayah, 'Tell 'em to grow – tomorrow!'. Sumayah pointed out to her grandmother that there were new leaves growing at the tip of the lemon tree, and also indicated that she had learned from her family about colour changes in plants as they grow in size.

Learning in the actual world

Amos and Reiss (2006) evaluated the effects of residential fieldwork (of a few days in duration) on the learning of students of 11–14 years of age. A framework of questions was used that derived from Rickinson et al. (2004), who proposed four possible areas of impact that outdoor learning might have:

*   **cognitive impacts** – concerning knowledge, understanding and other academic outcomes
*   **affective impacts** – encompassing attitudes, values, beliefs and self-perceptions
*   **interpersonal/social impacts** – including communication skills, leadership and teamwork
*   **physical/behavioural impacts** – relating to physical fitness, physical skills, personal behaviours and social actions.

Amos and Reiss used a range of methods to collect data from over 400 students in ten London state schools: ethnography during the fieldtrips, student questionnaires and focus groups, and teacher interviews. While there was evidence of positive cognitive impacts, it was the affective, interpersonal/social and physical/behavioural impacts that stood out. Teachers and students reported that levels of student motivation and participation were very high. Many students surpassed their own expectations of achievement during the courses, and both students and teachers felt that the general levels of trust in others and the self-confidence shown by the students on the courses were higher than in school. Teachers were very impressed overall by the development of teamwork skills among the students and the majority of students maintained or built positive relationships with each other, with teachers and with staff in the centres where they were based for the fieldwork.

These findings are typical of studies that evaluate fieldwork. In a review of the literature on field trips to out-of-school settings, DeWitt and Storksdieck (2008) note that documented cognitive gains are often relatively small. They conclude:

> 'Field trips, however, are not ideal for teaching complex concepts or even isolated facts, they are not "better classroom setting"; instead, they serve best as opportunities for exploration, discovery, first-hand and original experiences.'

> DeWitt and Storksdieck (2008, p181)

The real value of fieldtrips may typically be in the social and affective domains. And yet the links between these and the cognitive domain should not be underestimated. Many environmentalists cite childhood experiences of the natural environment as being a key influence on their career choice (Palmer et al. 1999).

Biology teachers have something of a tradition of taking students on fieldtrips to 'unspoilt' areas of natural beauty. However, much can be gained from taking students on visits to see science in use in industry. The Children Challenging Industry project started in 2006 and is still running. It began after a Mori Poll indicated that perceptions of the chemistry industry had hit an all time low (Children Challenging Industry, 2010). Primary children undertake a series of scientific investigations in school before visiting a local industrial partner to see how the scientific concepts are applied. Internal evaluations have been positive (Porter, Parvin and Lee, 2010): 97% of students state that they have learned something new; 85% state that they enjoy the challenges of the classroom science; 92% state that they enjoy learning about industry; and 82% state that they now enjoy science more after taking part in the activities.

Learning in the presented world

There is a large literature on the contribution that science museums, botanic gardens, zoos, farms and other out-of-the-classroom presentations of science can make to learning in science (Braund and Reiss, 2004). While the issue of 'presentation' is important, of course, in the school classroom, and even in the 'actual' world, it is perhaps of particular importance in such sites as are considered in this section.

Think, for example, of the issue of 'evolution' and its treatment in museums (cf. Bennett, 2004; Scott, 2007). Even if we presume that a museum decides to concentrate on the mainstream scientific account of evolution, eschewing, for example, any debates with creationism or intelligent design, there are still myriad decisions (conscious or otherwise) that those putting together an exhibition or display have to make.

1   To what extent does one favour mammals and birds (beloved by visitors) over the less spectacular but sometimes more informative invertebrates and other species?

2   How much does one simplify (for example, over the story of the evolution of the horse)? Too little simplification and the typical visitor is going to learn almost nothing, overwhelmed by difficult detail. Oversimplification and what our visitor learns may be no better than a reinforcement of error.

3   To what extent should the curator(s) concentrate on scientific consensus and to what extent should they address scientific controversy (for example, over the importance of punctuated equilibria in evolution)?

4   To what extent should the social and cultural contexts of evolution be addressed (for example, the reception by Victorian society of Darwin's *On the Origin of Species* in 1859)?

Of course, comparable decisions are made by school teachers all the time but science museum exhibitions and other presentations of science cannot, unlike classroom teachers of science, rapidly alter their presentations to take account of the particular learners in front of them. We need a science education that enables students to interrogate such presentations.

More mundanely, the literature suggests that much could be done to improve the effectiveness of museums, botanic gardens, zoos and other out-of-the-classroom sites for learning in science (Braund, 2004, p.113). The onus is especially on the classroom teacher to make links between what children experience on their visit and what they experience in their science classrooms both before and after their visits.

Mention should perhaps also be made of the potential for museums to enable 'wonder'. Miles (2006) showed that visitors to the Natural History Museum in London quite often experience wonder, and Bell et al. (2009) list excitement, delight, awe and surprise among signs of visitor pleasure at interactive experiences. As with the childhood experiences in the natural environment considered in the previous section, it is such emotional responses to scientific presentations that may have particular long-lasting value, though the evidence for this is largely anecdotal to date (cf. Green, 1986; Royal Society, 2004).

Learning in the virtual world

The third way in which learning out of the classroom might contribute to science education is through the ever-growing importance of the virtual world. While virtual learning still seems to have had surprisingly little impact on mainstream school science education, it seems difficult to imagine that its potential will continue to be marginalised (see http://wise.berkeley.edu). For literally decades, advocates of IT in science education have written about the possibilities for IT to do more than provide data-loggers. For example, Yair, Mintz and Llitvak (2001) introduced a virtual environment intended to aid astronomy learning:

'It is based on powerful scientific visualization techniques and can be used as an effective aide in astronomy teaching. The learner "enters" a virtual model of the physical world, journeys through it, zooms in or out as he or she wishes, changes his or her view point and perspective, as the virtual world continues to "behave" and operate in its usual manner. The continual motion of the planets generates day and night, seasons, eclipses, and phases — topics that are customarily hard to grasp, especially at young age. The model allows for a powerful learning experience, and facilitates the mental construction of three-dimensional space, where objects are varied and different, but share common features and obey the same physical principles.

The new platform helps to overcome the inherent geocentric view and ensures the transition to a scientific, heliocentric view of the solar system.'

Yair et al. (2001, p. 293)

Such promises are increasingly common, though their realisation is all too frequently unresearched. More generally, a useful categorisation of the way in which learning through ICT compares to classroom learning and home learning is provided by Wellington and Britto (2004) and summarised in Table 1. Wellington and Britto's point is that in terms of such characteristics as learner autonomy, individualisation and empowerment, learning through ICT sits between conventional classroom and home learning.

Table 1 Comparing classroom learning, learning through ICT and home learning (from Wellington and Britto, 2004, p. 211).

Classroom learning	Learning through ICT	Home learning
conformity and order is central learning is compulsory and collective	personal empowerment is central learning is individualised (usually)	voluntary personal individual (often)
keeping people 'together', 'on track', on course directed, staged, sequenced, paced learning	exploring, having a free rein, going their own way free access to information	free range undirected haphazard unstructured unsequenced
measurable learning outcomes assessment driven extrinsically motivated	free-ranging learning outcomes	many unintended outcomes (outcomes more difficult to measure) not always assessment driven or extrinsically motivated
timetabled, 'forced' access teacher control	flexible access, when it suits them learner or teacher control	free access learner (or parent) control
clear boundaries and targets, e.g. times, deadlines, subject divisions	unclear boundaries and targets	few boundaries and limits open-ended
teacher-led, teacher-centred	learner-led, learner-centred	learner-centred
teacher-filtered, distilled, vetted	unfiltered, not always vetted or censored	often unfiltered or unvetted
legislated for, e.g. by National Curriculum or other statutes	not always governed by documents	not legislated for

Mention ought perhaps also to be made of the potential for the role of the imagination (with or without software) for virtual learning in science. Much of science fiction relies on imagined worlds in which one or more key physical parameters differ from those we experience in reality. Interestingly, science fiction generally seems to wrestle more with the social and ethical implications of such differences (for example, in the more recent *Star Trek* series, especially *Deep Space 9* and *Voyager*) but much can be achieved in school science lessons by getting students genuinely to wrestle with the implications of, for example, ice having a density greater than that of liquid water, of global temperatures rising by an average of 10°C and of the Earth having only half its present circumference (other things being equal in each case). There is a long history, especially in physics, of such 'thought experiments' (for example, Schrödinger's cat, Maxwell's demon and Einstein chasing a light beam).

Bringing it all together

Recent reviews of what is often termed the 'informal sector' in science education have stressed the need for it and school science to complement one another. Fenichel and Schweingruber (2010) point out that in the course of our daily lives, almost all of us engage in informal science education:

> *'Society must better understand and draw on informal experiences to improve science education and science learning broadly.'*

Fenichel and Schweingruber (2010, p. 1)

Stocklmayer, Rennie and Gilbert (2010) suggest that the informal sector can provide a 'third space' in which the competing discourses of the school system and the everyday world are reconciled:

> *'The third space, however, is not simply the undefined ethereal space of the world-wide web. It is the potential real space into which the informal sector can move, bridging the gap between school and community and hence blurring the boundaries between them. This space is presently quite empty, occupied here and there by an enthusiastic scientist; an outreach programme from a science centre or a university; or an enthusiastic after-school provide. We believe that the potential for use of this space is much greater than this sporadic and incoherent activity. To exploit it will require resources and careful planning and synthesis, plus a deal of goodwill from informal providers and from cooperating schools.'*

Stocklmayer *et al.* (2010, p. 30)

Unless the formal science sector takes up this challenge, there is a danger that school science will continue all too often to fail to engage most learners, and go on being perceived as irrelevant to them and their needs.

References

Amos, R. and Reiss, M. (2006) What contribution can residential field courses make to the education of 11–14 year-olds? *School Science Review* **88**(322) 37–44.

Bell, P., Lewenstein, B., Shouse, A.W. and Feder, M.A. (eds) (2009) *Learning Science in Informal Environments: People, places and pursuits.* Washington DC: National Academies Press.

Bennett, T. (2004) *Pasts Beyond Memory: Evolution, museums, colonialism.* London: Routledge.

Braund, M. (2004) Learning science at museums and hands-on centres. In Braund, M. and Reiss, M.J. (eds) *Learning Science Outside the Classroom* (pp. 113–128). London: Routledge Falmer.

Braund, M. and Reiss, M. (2006) Towards a more authentic science curriculum: the contribution of out-of-school learning, *International Journal of Science Education* **28**, 1373–1388.

Children Challenging Industry (2010) www.cciproject.org (accessed 15 July 2011).

DeWitt, J. and Storksdieck, M. (2008) A short review of school field trips: key findings from the past and implications for the future, *Visitor Studies* **11**, 181–197.

Fenichel, M. and Schweingruber, H.A. (2010) *Surrounded by Science: Learning science in informal environments*. Washington DC: National Academies Press.

Green, M. (1986) Stephen Jay Gould; driven by a hunger to learn and to write what he knows, an outspoken scientist fights back from life-threatening illness, *People* **25**(2 June), 109–114. Available at www.stephenjaygould.org/library/green_sjgould.html (accessed 15 July 2011).

Miles, S. (2006) *Reweaving the Rainbow: The development and use of an instrument to determine the extent of young children's sense of wonder at the Natural History Museum*, MA dissertation. London: Institute of Education, University of London.

Palmer, J.A., Suggate, J., Robottom, I. and Hart, P. (1999) Significant life experiences and formative influences on the development of adults' environmental awareness in the UK, Australia and Canada, *Environmental Education Research* **5**, 181–200.

Porter, C., Parvin J. and Lee, L. (2010) *Children Challenging Industry: All regions study of the effects of industry-based science activities on the views of primary school children and their teachers 2006–8*. York: Children Challenging Industry. Available at: www.cciproject.org/reports/documents/CCI_National06-08.pdf (accessed 15 July 2011).

Rickinson, M., Dillon, J., Teamey, K., Morris, M., Choi, M.Y., Sanders, D. and Benefield, P. (2004) *A Review of Research on Outdoor Learning*. Shrewsbury: National Foundation for Educational Research and King's College London.

Royal Society (2004) *Taking a Leading Role: A good practice guide for all those involved in role model schemes aiming to inspire young people about science, engineering and technology*, London: Royal Society. Available at: http://royalsociety.org/uploadedFiles/Royal_Society _Content/Education/2011-06-07-Taking_a_leading_role_guide.pdf (accessed 15 July 2011).

Ruby, M., Kenner, C., Jessel, J., Gregory, E. and Arju, T. (2007) Gardening with grandparents: an early engagement with the science curriculum, *Early Years* **27**, 131–144.

Scott, M. (2007) *Rethinking Evolution in the Museum*. Abingdon: Routledge.

Stocklmayer, S.M., Rennie. L.J. and Gilbert, J.K. (2010) The roles of the formal and informal sectors in the provision of effective science education. *Studies in Science Education* **46**, 1–44.

Wellington, J. and Britto, J. (2004) Learning science through ICT at home. In Braund, M. and Reiss, M.J. (eds) *Learning Science Outside the Classroom* (pp. 207–223). London: Routledge Falmer.

Yair, Y., Mintz, R. and Llitvak, S. (2001) 3D-virtual reality in science education: an implication for astronomy teaching. *Journal of Computers in Mathematics and Science Teaching* **20**, 293–305.

Chapter 12

Scientific inquiry

Wynne Harlen

Enquiry-based science education – or the synonymous term 'inquiry-based' which we will use here to reflect the wider use and spelling in the US and Europe, and in the acronym IBSE – is spreading rapidly throughout the world (InterAcademies Panel on International Issues, 2006). Examples of programmes devised to help teachers put it into practice include *Primary Connections* developed in Australia, *Learning by Doing* in China, *ECBI* (Spanish acronym) in Chile, *La main à la pâte* in France, and many programmes derived from *Science and Technology for Children* developed in the USA and adapted for use in Sweden and in several countries of South America. These programmes, and similar ones in the UK, share the aim of enabling students to develop and use inquiry and problem-solving skills in building their understanding of scientific aspects of the world around them. They are mainly for the education of children up to the age of about 12 years, in recognition not only of the fact that teachers of these children are likely to need a good deal of help in their own understanding of science and of the nature of scientific activity, but also of the importance of children developing positive attitudes towards science in their early education. This is not to say that inquiry is less relevant at the Secondary school level – indeed many programmes are being extended into the Secondary stage – but rather to establish the priority of ensuring that children reach Secondary school with essential skills and habits of mind to benefit from further science education.

Implementing IBSE programmes is likely to require a considerable change in teachers' practice, with implications for professional development, the curriculum and assessment. Not surprisingly, policy makers and practitioners alike need to know whether the considerable effort involved is worthwhile. Does inquiry-based practice 'work' in the sense of the providing the benefits that are claimed for it? In what ways is it better than other ways of learning and teaching science? What evidence is there to justify these claims? Before looking at some of the research addressing these questions, we need to be clear about what 'it' is and why it is considered important.

Learning and teaching science through inquiry

There are plenty of definitions and descriptions of scientific inquiry, most reflecting the activity of scientists in collecting and using evidence in developing models and theories that help understanding of how the natural and made world works. Box 1 gives a widely quoted definition, which emphasises the developing nature of scientific ideas and theories, which are changed if new evidence is found that conflicts with them. It also recognises that neither scientists nor children begin from a clean slate but from what they already know.

Box 1 A definition of inquiry (National Research Council, 1996, p. 23).

> Inquiry is a multifaceted activity that involves making observations; posing questions; examining books and other sources of information to see what is already known; planning investigations; reviewing what is already known in light of experimental evidence; using tools to gather, analyze, and interpret data; proposing answers, explanations, and predictions; and communicating the results. Inquiry requires identification of assumptions, use of critical and logical thinking, and consideration of alternative explanations.

However, unlike scientists, children do not already have well-developed skills of observing, collecting evidence, making predictions, testing possible explanations and interpreting findings. Thus a key aim of inquiry-based science education is to help learners to develop these skills. However, it is a mistake to see skill development as the only focus of inquiry-based learning. Rather, it also involves the development of scientific ideas, even for the youngest children. This combination of process and ideas is reflected in the actions in which learners are likely to be involved in inquiry (see Box 2).

Box 2 Actions involved in learning through inquiry.

- Raising questions and considering how answers may be found through investigation.
- Gathering evidence, which may be by observing and exploring real events or using other sources.
- Working in collaborative groups, sharing ideas and constructing understanding together.
- Proposing possible explanations of observations and using them to make predictions that can be tested or questions that can be answered through inquiry.
- Taking part in planning and carrying out investigations with appropriate controls to answer specific questions.
- Keeping notes and recording results in suitable ways using appropriate scientific vocabulary and representations.
- Relating results to the ideas being tested or question addressed and attempting to explain results.
- Thinking logically in interpreting evidence and in drawing conclusions.
- Communicating what they have done; listening to and sharing ideas with others.
- Reflecting self-critically on the process of the inquiry and on any change in ideas.

It is useful to note two further points in relation to defining inquiry. One is that not all learning in science involves inquiry. There are some things, such as conventions, names and the basic skills of using equipment, that are more efficiently learned by direct instruction, as and when they are needed. But while it is not expected that all learning in science will involve inquiry, it is important to ensure that inquiry is used where the aim is to develop understanding of events and phenomena in the world around us. The other is that not all inquiry in science will include all the ideas listed in Box 2. In particular, inquiry is not defined only by direct interaction with materials; the 'engagement' with events and objects can be through observation at a distance (as it must be in developing understanding of the apparent movements of the Sun and stars) or through secondary sources. Nor is inquiry the same as the broader view of 'practical work', which would include observation at a distance. Inquiry emphasises the mental activity in deciding what is relevant evidence and coming to conclusions about what it means. Thus in this chapter we do not consider the value and role of practical work, which is the subject of Chapter 8 in this book.

The rationale: why is learning science through inquiry important?

Briefly there are three main reasons:

1   Because learning through inquiry accords with modern views on how learning takes place – that is, through the active participation of the learner (Bransford, Brown and Cocking, 1999). In this view, learning is not a passive activity of acquiring ready-made ideas and skills, but the construction of knowledge (both propositional and procedural) through mental and physical activity. Inquiry learning also takes account of the existing ideas and skills of learners, using them as starting points for developing further.

2   Because it supports the development of scientific literacy, taking this to be not the detailed knowledge required by those involved in or aiming for a science-based career, but the general understanding of scientific ideas and the nature of science that is needed by everyone in making informed decisions about science-based aspects of life today (Bybee, 1997; Roberts, 2007; Harlen, 2009).

3   Because it helps to prepare young people for life in an increasingly technological, scientific and changing world. Today's school students will need to continue to develop new skills and concepts throughout life. Thus the ability to learn and the willingness to do so are acknowledged as important aims of education (Organisation for Economic Co-operation and Development, 1999, 2006). Reflection on what and how they have learned, as part of inquiry, has an important role here.

These reasons are based on value judgments of what education should provide; for instance, that we value learning with understanding rather than rote learning and consider a scientifically literate population to be a worthwhile goal. Many decisions in education are based on values and arguments. But while we may not have proof of the rationale for inquiry, we can find out whether it 'does what it says on the tin' – does learning through inquiry lead to better understanding, to scientific literacy and to continued learning? Is there evidence for the claim made in an influential report from the EU that:

'IBSE methods have been shown to have a positive impact on students' attainments with an even stronger impact on the students with lower levels of self-confidence and those from disadvantaged background.'

Rocard et al. (2007, p. 12)

Research evidence

Convincing evidence about the impact of an inquiry approach to teaching science would show that it leads to better learning compared with other approaches. But the aims of inquiry learning are broad, making it difficult in the first place to know when it is actually in operation (the independent variable) and what impact it has (the dependent variable). Comparing two groups, one experiencing learning science through inquiry and the other learning science in some other way (the control group) is an attractive 'scientific' method. The problem is how to ensure that the approach used is the only difference between the two groups, given that there are so many variables that could also affect their learning in science (for instance, home background, learning in other school subjects, personal interests, TV programmes and other media). Having large numbers of students in each group helps to ensure that these differences are likely to affect each group similarly. But large numbers make it more difficult to avoid another problem, which is to ensure that all in the inquiry group really do experience this way of learning. Close observation of classes supposedly using inquiry all too frequently shows that 'old habits die hard'. Randomly assigning students to the inquiry and control groups is another approach, but this is rarely done as it interferes with teaching groups and interactions among students.

In relation to the dependent variable (the outcome) there is a problem in deciding how to make a fair comparison of outcomes, given that the aims of inquiry and the other approach are different. For example, in the evaluation of *Primary Connections*, summarised in Box 3, the tasks used to assess performance were related particularly to the aims of inquiry. It would be reasonable to argue that, since the control classes did not experience inquiry, then they could hardly be expected to do as well on the inquiry tasks as the classes experiencing inquiry. What the research in Box 3 shows is that when students are taught through inquiry they do achieve the skills, provided we assume that they did not have the skills at the start – for there was no baseline (pre-test) measure of the students' performance before working with the inquiry units.

Box 3 Assessing the impact on students of working with the *Primary Connections* programme.

Equal numbers of students were recruited from schools where units of the *Primary Connections* project had been used during a year and from other schools where science had been taught in other ways. There were about 700 in each group. Special tasks were created to assess the learning goals of the *Primary Connections* units, which included observation, reasoning with data, identifying relationships between variables and planning fair investigations. For example, one task asked students to observe and produce a labelled drawing of their thumb; another provided data for interpretation. The tasks, and a seven-item 'attitude to science' scale, were given to both groups towards the end of the school year. There was no pre-test of the students at the start of the year but the two groups were carefully matched for age, gender, ethnic background, and type of school. The results of the assessment tasks showed that the performance of the *Primary Connections* classes was significantly above that of the control classes. This was true for all groups of students. The attitude scale results showed that both groups of students enjoyed school science, with differences in favour of the *Primary Connections* group on two items.

Based on Hackling and Prain, 2008

What we don't know from this evaluation is how the two groups would have fared had the tests reflected the aims of both groups or on a test that was more general, such as a national or international test (such as TIMSS – see Chapter 2). Researchers in the USA (Ruiz-Primo et al. 2002) investigated the extent to which similar results are found from tests in which the items are 'close' to the learning experiences and those which are more 'distant' from the actual science activities. Not surprisingly, they found that this 'distance' from particular experiences did matter; so whether or not an evaluation shows that students do learn more through inquiry (or any other approach) will depend on how closely the tests used to assess achievement resemble the learning experiences.

With all these obstacles to identifying the impact of inquiry-based science on students' learning, it is not surprising that reviews of research find only small differences. An extensive systematic review conducted by the Education Development Centre in the USA, begun in 2001, found that the most positive impact was found in relation to the physical sciences. Not all studies incorporated all aspects of inquiry, but it was found that the more aspects experienced, the better the understanding of science concepts (Minner, Levy and Century 2010).

Instead of attempting to study the impact of inquiry as a complex whole, some research studies have addressed specific components, usually in small-scale research studies. For example, White and Frederiksen (1998) compared two classes who were given regular time to reflect on what they were learning with two classes who were studying the same unit of work but used this time for discussing how the activities could be improved. They reported that the 'reflection' classes performed better on other projects and on the unit tests. Another study in which reflection was encouraged is summarised in Box 4.

Box 4

Herrenkohl and Guerra (1998) investigated the impact of reflection on learning by assigning roles to students corresponding to aspects of inquiry, such as making predictions or relating findings to initial questions. They reported that students aged 10 to 11 were able to take on these roles, progressively recognising the kind of questions that were appropriate. Classroom discussions became more focused and included more interactions between students rather than student-to-teacher interactions.

Using classroom observations

As we have seen, the aims of inquiry-based science are broad and complex. Consequently it is questionable as to whether it is possible to evaluate its impact adequately through outcome measures such as tests. A greater range of factors can be taken into account by observing how students work and what they produce in regular lessons rather than just at one time in a test. Teachers are in the best position to collect this evidence and so their perceptions of the value of inquiry are often used in evaluating the impact of inquiry-based work. These perceptions are usually collected by interview or questionnaire. For example, Sharp and Hopkin (2007) used a questionnaire to survey Primary teachers' experiences and views on teaching science and found that when asked which one area of science they enjoyed teaching, more chose scientific inquiry than any other area. Teachers invariably report positive student responses to inquiry, particularly of those students who in other circumstances seem to be low achievers, chiming with the EU claim quoted earlier.

Teachers' views on the impact of inquiry are supported by those of observers who are able to look across classes and so are in a better position to see patterns in learning experiences and performance. The Ofsted report *Success in Science* (2008) brought together evidence of this kind. In relation to Key Stage 2, it noted that:

> 'In this survey, the schools with the highest or the most rapidly improving standards were those where scientific inquiry was at the core of their work. Pupils in these schools were enthusiastic about the subject and had the confidence and skills to plan investigations and collect, present and evaluate evidence.'

Ofsted (2008, para 8)

At the Secondary level, inspectors noted that progress was seen when students:

1 understood clearly the standards they had achieved, knew what they needed to do to improve and were involved in self- and peer-evaluation
2 took part in decision making, discussion, research and scientific inquiry
3 were engaged in science that had relevance to their lives.

The inspectors' report was assembled before the Key Stage 3 national tests were abandoned, but it is still instructive to note their finding that:

> 'At times, preparation for national tests and examinations at the end of Key Stages 3 and 4 inhibited pupils' enjoyment of science, particularly when it led to fewer opportunities for practical work and discussion. From observing and interviewing pupils during the survey, it was clear that they had far greater interest and understanding when they continued to be involved in scientific inquiry and the exploration of "How Science Works". Such activities helped them understand scientific concepts and gave them a vehicle for testing their ideas in the context of practical work, research and debate.'

Ofsted (2008, para 40)

> 'The results of this survey show that schools are now placing greater emphasis on learning through investigative work and this is having a very positive impact on pupils' understanding and enjoyment of science. However, there is still some way to go before it is a regular part of every pupil's experience.'

Ofsted (2008, para 87)

Similar findings are reported by Scottish inspectors (HMIE, 2008), who emphasise the importance of practical investigation in developing successful learners. At the same time they point out that other factors than practical work, such as working on topics that are seen by students as relevant to real life and the development of thinking skills, are also important.

Main points

1 Learning science through inquiry means that students build their understanding of key science ideas by using evidence in developing and testing models and theories that help understanding of how the natural and made world works.

2   Inquiry may include but extends beyond 'hands on' practical work.

3   The reasons for adopting inquiry-based teaching and learning relate to the process of learning, the value of developing scientific literacy and the need to develop skills of lifelong learning.

4   The research evidence of the impact of inquiry shows that introducing some aspects of inquiry can be effective in raising achievement, but the more aspects the greater is the effect.

5   Classroom observations by teachers and inspectors confirm that inquiry helps students' conceptual understanding as well as developing thinking and investigative skills.

References

Bransford, J., Brown, A.L. and Cocking, R.R. (eds) (1999) *How People Learn*. Washington DC: National Academy Press.

Bybee, R.W. (1997) *Achieving Scientific Literacy: From purposes to practices*. Portsmouth, NH: Heinemann.

Hackling, M.W. and Prain, V. (2008) *Impact of Primary Connections on Students' Science Processes, Literacies of Science and Attitudes to Science*. A research report for the Australian Academy of Science. Australian DEWR and Australian Academy of Science. Available at: www.science.org.au/primaryconnections/research-and-evaluation/images/irr-15.pdf (accessed August 2011).

Harlen, W. (2009) Teaching and learning science for a better future. *School Science Review* **90**(333) 1–9.

Herrenkohl, L.R. and Guerra, M.R. (1998) Participation, scientific discourse and student engagement in fourth grade, *Cognition and Instruction* **16**(4) 431–473.

HMIE (2008) *Science: A portrait of current practice in Scottish Schools*, Edinburgh: HMIE. Available at: www.hmie.gov.uk/documents/publication/HMIePDFtoHTML.html (accessed 15 July 2011).

InterAcademies Panel on International Issues (2006) *Report of the Working Group on International Collaboration in the Evaluation of Inquiry-Based Science (IBSE) Progams*. Santiago, Chile: IAP.

Minner, D.D., Levy, A.J., and Century, J. (2010) Inquiry-based science instruction – what is it and does it matter? Results from a research synthesis years 1984–2002, *Journal of Research in Science Teaching* **47**(4) 474–496.

National Research Council (1996) *The National Science Education Standards*. Washington DC: National Academy Press.

Ofsted (2008) *Success in Science*. London: Ofsted.

Organisation for Economic Co-operation and Development (1999) *Measuring Student Knowledge and Skills*. OECD Programme for International Student Assessment (PISA) Paris: OECD.

Organisation for Economic Co-operation and Development (2006) *Assessing Scientific, Reading and Mathematical Literacy: A framework for PISA 2006*. Paris: OECD.

Roberts, D.A. (2007). Scientific literacy/science literacy. In Lederman, S.K. (ed) *Handbook of*

graduates could recite what photosynthesis is when asked the question directly, they could not relate this knowledge to the everyday context. Such failings expose the weakness of science education that has placed emphasis on what rather than why something should be believed. A further problem concerns the gaps between research, policy and practice. There are useful research findings on how to support student scientific reasoning, including using argumentation, but theses have not been implemented in the classroom.

Engaging students in argumentation is important because it places the students in the position where they can begin to collect, interpret and evaluate evidence for our claims. In this respect, science learning becomes aligned with how scientists themselves do science. Science is not about cookbooks where procedures are replicated mindlessly. Manipulation of variables for the sake of verifying already known outcomes is also not scientific in nature. Authentic scientific inquiries allow for the generation of evidence and justification of scientific knowledge in the classroom. They create room for students not only to generate and evaluate evidence but also to establish the criteria and standards by which to judge evidence in the social environment of the classroom. Authentic scientific inquiries have argument at their core (Erduran, 2007).

Another reason why argumentation is important for science education is that recent accounts from educational psychology have demonstrated the important role of talk and language in learning. Language contains the linguistic structures and patterns that define and shape an endeavour like science. Language has a lot to do with thinking as well. Indeed, some psychologists like Lev Vygotsky have claimed that thinking itself is shaped and formed by language. When we turn to talk and language in science classrooms, however, we witness that the predominant form of talk is what is typically called the **IRE** sequence: **I**nitiation, where the teacher asks a question; **R**esponse, where the student gives an answer; and **E**valuation where the teacher evaluates the students' response and then typically moves on to another theme. Although useful for certain purposes, this type of verbal interaction in the science classroom does not promote extended discussions where students' ideas can be projected to the public domain and where the teacher or other students can negotiate and resolve ideas. Strategies such as group discussions do help in breaking away from the constraints of IRE patterns and getting students engaged in more varied interactions in talk. Without a chance for students to talk to each other, without the space to debate and communicate their ideas, it is difficult to imagine how students could consolidate their learning.

The teaching of argument in the classroom does create tensions for teachers and students alike. As long as assessment of learning focuses on recall of scientific knowledge, the pressures on teachers to deliver such knowledge and on students to acquire it, will persist. Inclusion of themes such as argument and strategies such as group discussions will be problematic when teachers need to ensure that their students can master performance on recall. Argument will also lead to the emergence of ideas in the classroom that we may not always feel comfortable with. Consider, for instance, a child making a claim that it is the Sun that moves around the Earth, not the other way around because he has evidence from his observations that the Sun moves and the Earth does not seem to be moving anywhere! Mistaken theories, models and explanations will all surface. How teachers deal with these ideas is indeed at the core of teaching. Teachers could help students to coordinate ideas in the classroom such that ideas are held accountable to the force of evidence. The extent to which students can distinguish a well-reasoned and justified argument from one that is not is an important skill both for a scientist-to-be but also for a citizen who is well-equipped for informed decision-making strategies.

The rest of this chapter presents argumentation – the coordination of evidence and theory – as a central aspect of science teaching and learning, and describes how research ideas on argumentation are being infused in teachers' professional development. First, let us highlight some example definitions of argument that have been used by science educators who have been working in this area.

Models of argument

There is substantial research on argumentation (e.g. Perelman and Olbrechts-Tyteca, 1958; Kuhn, 1993; van Eemeren *et al.* 1996). However, research on argumentation in science education has typically concentrated on two main definitions of argument based on the work by Stephen Toulmin (e.g. Erduran, Simon and Osborne, 2004) and Douglas Walton (e.g. Walton, 1996; Duschl, 2008). While these two models have often been presented in contrast to each other, it is worthwhile to highlight that they actually address different aspects of argument and argumentation. Toulmin's framework, summarised in Figure 1, concentrates on the components of an argument (Toulmin, 1958), whereas Walton's schemes detail different types of arguments (Table 1, page 109).

Figure 1 Toulmin's framework.

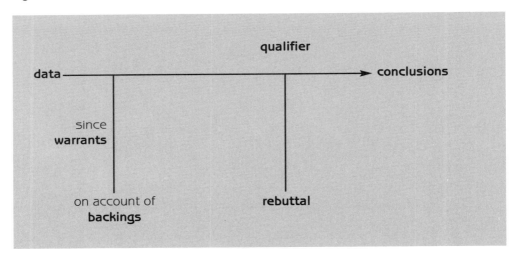

Table I Selected schemes from Walton's Presumptive Reasoning (Walton, 1996).

Argument from	Definition	Example
Argument from sign	Observation x is taken as evidence of event E.	Here are some bear tracks in the snow. Therefore, a bear passed this way.
Argument from example	If x has F then x will also have G.	If it is a solid matter, it must have a certain mass and a volume.
Argument from commitment	The proponent claims that the respondent is, or should be, committed to some particular position.	Ed, you are a communist, aren't you? Well, then you should be on the side of the union in this recent labour dispute.
Argument from evidence to a hypothesis	If a is true then b will be true.	If the Copernican system is correct, then Venus will show phases. Venus shows phases. Therefore, the Copernican system is correct.
Argument from cause to effect	If one type of event occurs, then it is predicted the other would also occur.	When nations do not remain consistent in their policies, their prestige drops. We do not remain consistent in our policies. Therefore, our prestige is likely to drop.

As an illustration of his framework of argument, Toulmin (1958) discusses the claim that Harry is a British subject. The claim can be supported by the datum that Harry was born in Bermuda. That there is a connection at all between datum and claim is expressed by the warrant that a man born in Bermuda will generally be a British subject. In turn, the warrant can be supported by the backing that there are certain statutes and other legal provisions to that effect. The warrant does not have total justifying force, so it follows that the claim that Harry is a British subject must be qualified. Moreover, there are possible rebuttals – for instance, if both his parents were aliens, or if he has become a naturalised American.

This framework was used in developing a resource for students to facilitate their writing of arguments (Osborne, Erduran and Simon, 2004). The writing frame had statements such as 'My idea is …', 'My reasons for my idea are …', 'I believe my reasons because …', which were derived from the features of Toulmin's model of an argument in terms of claims, data, warrants and so on. The *Mind the Gap* project, to be detailed later in this chapter, helps to develop our understanding of how science teachers engage in such writing frames (Erduran and Yan, 2009).

Bridging gaps between policy, research and practice

This section illustrates a case in which research findings have been transformed into the design of a professional development project.

Like many unfamiliar or relatively underemphasised strategies, the implementation of argumentation in real science classrooms will demand more than rhetoric at curriculum level. It will necessitate supportive professional development of science teachers in order to infuse argumentation at the level of the science classroom. In a professional development project called *Mind the Gap: learning, teaching and research in inquiry-based science teaching*, funded by the European Union FP7 Programme, teachers from schools in England explored the policy and research aspects of argumentation in their classrooms (Erduran and Yan, 2010). The components of the professional development programme that stemmed from this project are illustrated here, as well as some outcomes in terms of the resources produced by the teachers and the impact made on the teachers adopting the new approach.

The contemporary context for argumentation in England and Wales is the 'How Science Works' (HSW) component of the Science National Curriculum (DfES/QCA, 2006). The HSW agenda suggests the incorporation of evidence-based reasoning and argumentation in various aspects of science teaching and learning (Table 2). For instance, not only should students learn about coordination of evidence and explanation but they should also be communicating arguments. Similar calls have been made about argument internationally (Organisation for Economic Co-operation and Development, 2003) in other countries – for instance, in South Africa (Department of Education, 2003) and Chile (MEC, 2004).

Table 2 How Science Works in the Science National Curriculum and potential target skills in argument (from LaVelle and Erduran, 2007).

Curriculum descriptor	Argument skills
data, evidence, theories, explanations	understanding the nature of evidence and justifications in scientific knowledge
practical and inquiry skills	justifying procedures, and choices for experimental design generating and applying criteria for evaluation of evidence
communication skills	constructing and presenting a case to an audience either verbally or in writing
applications and implications of science	applying argument to everyday situations including active social, economic and political debates

While policy and research recommendations unite in promoting argumentation in science classrooms, significant gaps remain between educational policy, research and practice in the context of inquiry teaching and in argumentation in particular. For example, the professional development of science teachers in argumentation is rare (Zohar, 2008). The *Mind the Gap* project, funded by the European Union, aimed to transform research and policy findings for professional development purposes – six teachers from four schools in England were supported in exploring aspects of argumentation in their classrooms, in collaboration with researchers from the University of Bristol.

In infusing ideas about argumentation into the professional development of science teachers, the *Mind the Gap* project engaged not just in research on argumentation but also on professional development. There is a substantial body of research literature on professional development of science teachers. According to Supovitz and Turner (2000), a high-quality professional development programme should immerse participants in inquiry, questioning and experimentation in a collaborative manner. Our project was guided by the principles of teachers' collaborative exchanges with peers and reflective inquiries into their own teaching.

The teachers were recruited by writing to schools about potential involvement in the project and the participating teachers volunteered to join. They were primarily mid-career teachers who specialised in chemistry and physics. Each workshop had input from researchers, in terms of research evidence on the teaching of argument, and from teachers, in terms of classroom learning and teaching practices. A variety of activities and formats were employed including group discussions and presentations. The professional development aspects of the project are summarised in a DVD (Erduran and Yan, 2009). The clips range from how the teachers addressed the curriculum policy context to the strategies used to support professional development such as evaluating and reflecting on peer teaching (Box 1). The project teachers indicated a range of ways in which the project had facilitated their professional development, as exemplified in clips 9–13. The impact of the professional development agenda can be summarised by a set of themes as follows.

Exchange and communication

'Teaching, to some extent, is quite a lonely journey.'

Teacher

The teachers appreciated the opportunity to exchange experiences and communicate with teachers across different schools with different experiences and backgrounds. Furthermore, the friendly environment in the workshops encouraged the participants to critically and reflectively comment on each other's work.

Ownership and engagement

'It is like [what we need] to do with the students – this open project allows us to do what we are interested in.'

Teacher

The participants enjoyed this teacher-oriented programme that focused on their interests or issues. They felt supported to explore their interests in their own teaching situations. The sense of ownership motivated them to take on the initiatives.

Clarification and justification of curricular policy

'If teachers only see How Science Works as one of the policy changes in the curriculum, they won't bother to think seriously about it, never mind take on initiatives to teach differently in the classroom.'

Teacher

The teachers appreciated this programme for clarifying the justification of the policy initiative from the trainer's introduction and guided peer discussions.

During the workshops, the teachers had a better idea about the reason why How Science Works was introduced to the curriculum and what would be the benefits of teaching and learning science via argumentation. Through exploration of the gaps between the policy and teaching practice, the teachers' awareness of the issues was raised. They indicated that their understanding of How Science Works and argumentation was also improved through the dynamic discussions in the workshops. Furthermore, the teachers' discussion and sharing made the idea of How Science Works clear, explicit and practical in practice.

Awareness of role of argument in teaching science

'I realised that teachers need to model an argumentation structure that pupils will understand.'

Teacher

Teachers were appreciative of the infusion of research outcomes in the workshops. They indicated that a teacher's perception of the importance of argumentation might affect their motivation to teach it, and their lack of experience might be an obstacle as well. The resources shared by other teachers in the workshops extended their personal experiences and opened up reflective discussions.

Box 1 Video clips in the DVD of *Minding Gaps in Argument: Supporting the teaching of scientific inquiry* (Erduran and Yan, 2009).

Clip 1: Teachers' group discussion about policy

In the first workshop, the teachers discussed the How Science Works (HSW)* component of the curriculum. They were given some questions to prompt them to talk about how they got to know about HSW. They talked about such issues as insufficiency of teacher in-service training about this new initiative, the history of the curriculum change, and their perceptions of this new initiative in terms of its importance in the class and its relation to other components of the curriculum. They also addressed the issue of assessment and how it is not well unpacked for teaching HSW.

*(HSW was introduced in 2006 in the Science National Curriculum for England and Wales at Key Stage 3 (ages 11–13) and Key Stage 4 (ages 14–16). It aims to promote understanding of aspects of the nature of science including scientific inquiry, communication of science and science in context.)

Clip 2: Teachers' group discussion about challenges of teaching HSW

Teachers were asked to identify the challenges of teaching HSW based on their own experiences. They were asked to write down and prioritise these challenges in a table. In these clips, the teachers raised the challenges of:

- teaching HSW to students, particularly miscommunication in terms of the nature of science
- engaging students in scientific inquiry
- their own understanding of HSW
- difficulties involved in changes in teachers' roles
- time limitations in teaching HSW.

Clip 3: Model of professional development

The teachers brought examples from their teaching between the first and second workshops. They shared their experiences and resources in the group and got peers' feedback.

Davina had designed an open-ended experiment about dissolving in water and got her colleague, Catherine, to video-tape the students' work and interview the students. Davina and Catherine shared their experiences and reflected on their practice with the other teachers in the group.

Alex introduced a 'card game' as an activity to promote critical thinking skills involved in scientific inquiry.

In the third workshop, the teachers evaluated and reflected on Steve's Runny Honey lesson (see Clip 7, below), referring back to what they had discussed in the previous workshops.

Clip 4: Introducing a model of argument

During the workshops, the researchers drew from existing research evidence on argumentation to define argument. For example, in this clip from the first workshop, the researcher introduced the Toulmin's Argument Pattern as a model and the writing frame derived from it as a practical resource. The writing frame had statements such as 'My idea is …', 'My reasons for my idea are …', 'I believe my reasons because …', derived from the features of Toulmin's model of an argument in terms of claims, data, warrants and so on (see diagram on page 108).

Clip 5: Supporting written argument

In this series of clips, the teachers were:

- applying a writing frame to resources that they had brought from their own classrooms, to explore its relevance and applicability
- using the writing frame with a topic example proposed by themselves in order to explore the structure of argument
- evaluating and adapting the writing frame.

Clip 6: Evaluating assessment tools for HSW

The teachers used the internet to search for potential assessment tools for evaluating HSW in students' learning. The clip shows the teachers' discussion of the assessment tools they found online. The discussion centres around the application of assessment tools and the issue of differentiation of HSW skills.

Clip 7: Steve's Runny Honey lesson

This clip shows Steve's practical lesson with year 9 students on investigating the viscosity of honey. The clip includes:

- how Steve introduced the aim of the lesson with a real-life context and demonstration to the class
- students planning and carrying out various practical work in order to address the question of viscosity
- Steve reflecting on how and why he implemented HSW.

Clip 8: Catherine's starters

This clip illustrates Catherine's use of 'starters' in order to promote understanding of variables in different contexts. In the first part, Catherine introduces the purpose of the starters to the rest of the teachers. In the second part, a lesson scenario of the implementation of the starters is included.

Clip 9: Catherine on the impact of the project on her teaching practice

Catherine talks about how the project helped her to clarify teaching goals and students' needs on HSW.

Clip 10: Alex on the impact of the project on his understanding of the difficulties and gaps in HSW

Alex talks about how the project helped him to realise the difficulties of teaching argumentation as a high-level skill and motivating students. He also discusses how it has improved his awareness of the gaps between the curriculum and teaching, as well as the gaps in teachers' knowledge and understanding, of HSW.

Clip 11: Grace on impact in terms of exchanges among peers

Grace appreciated the opportunity offered by the project to share skills, experiences and resources among her peers.

Clip 12: Steve on features of professional development

Steve talks about how the project inspired his reflections on the identity of a science teacher, how he appreciated the teacher-orientated design of the CPD to allow the teachers to pursue their own interests, and how he enjoyed the platform provided by the project to develop a network of professionals.

Clip 13: Craig's experience

Craig, who joined in the project in the last workshop, talks about his experience as a new participant.

Conclusions and implications

In this chapter, the rationale for and research on argumentation in science teaching and learning has been reviewed, and a professional development project described that aims to bridge policy, research and practice of argumentation in the context of the How Science Works curriculum agenda in England. The programme of work with the teachers highlights the need to infuse research and policy ideas into teachers' practices in the context of collaborative and reflective inquiries on their own teaching and that of their peers. It is through such transformations of research findings for professional development purposes that, eventually, claims made in science classrooms will begin to rest on evidence from students' perspectives.

References

Department of Education, South Africa (2003) *National Curriculum Statement Grades 10– 12* (General). Physical sciences. Pretoria: Department of Education, South Africa.

DfES/QCA (2006) *Science: the National Curriculum for England and Wales.* London: HMSO.

Duschl, R. (2008) Quality argumentation and epistemic criteria. In Erduran, S. and Jimenez-Aleixandre, M.P. (eds) *Argumentation in Science Education: Perspectives from classroom-based research* (pp. 59–175). Dordrecht: Springer Academic Publishers.

Erduran, S. (ed) (2007) Editorial: special issue on argument, discourse and interactivity. *School Science Review* **88**(324) 31–40.

Erduran, S. and Jimenez-Aleixandre, M.P. (eds) (2008) *Argumentation in Science Education: Perspectives from classroom-based research.* Dordrecht: Springer Academic Publishers.

Erduran, S. and Yan, X. (eds) (2009) *Minding Gaps in Argument: Supporting the teaching of scientific inquiry.* Booklet and DVD. Bristol: University of Bristol.

Erduran, S. and Yan, X. (2010) Salvar las brechas en la argumentacion: el desarrollo profesional en la ensenanza de la indagacion cientifica. *Alambique* **63**, 76–87.

Erduran, S., Simon, S. and Osborne, J. (2004) TAPping into argumentation: developments in the use of Toulmin's Argument Pattern for studying science discourse. *Science Education* **88**(6) 915–933.

Kaya, E., Erduran, S. and Cetin, P. (2010) *Assessing Understanding of Argument: investigating high school students' arguments and implications for classroom practice.* Paper presented at the annual conference of the National Association for Research in Science Teaching, Philadelphia, USA.

Kuhn, D. (1993) Science as argument. *Science Education* **77**(3) 319–337.

LaVelle, B.L. and Erduran, S. (2007) Argument and developments in the science curriculum. *School Science Review* **88**(324) 31–40.

Ministerio de Educación y Ciencia, Republic of Chile (MEC) (2004) *Estudio y comprensión de la naturaleza.* Santiago de Chile: Ministerio de Educación y Ciencia, Republic of Chile.

Organisation for Economic Co-operation and Development (2003) PISA Assessment Framework – *Mathematics, Reading, Science, and Problem Solving Knowledge and Skills.* Paris: OECD.

Osborne, J., Erduran, S. and Simon, S. (2004) *Ideas, Evidence and Argument in Science Education*, CPD Pack. London: King's College London.

Perelman, C. and Olbrechts-Tyteca, L. (1958) *Traité de l'Argumentation. La nouvelle rhétorique*. Bruxelles: Éditions de l'Université de Bruxelles. (*The New Rhetoric: A treatise on argumentation*. Notre Dame: University of Notre Dame Press, 1969.)

Supovitz, J.A. and Turner, H.M. (2000) The effects of professional development on science teaching practices and classroom cultures. *Journal of Research in Science Teaching* **37**(9) 963–980.

Toulmin, S. (1958) *The Uses of Argument*. Cambridge: Cambridge University Press.

van Eemeren, F.H., Grootendorst, R., Henkemans, F.S., Blair, J.A., Johnson, R.H., Krabbe, E.C.W., Plantin, C., Walton, D.N., Willard, C.A., Woods, J.M. and Zarefsky, D. (1996) *Fundamentals of Argumentation Theory: A handbook of historical backgrounds and contemporary developments*. Mahwah, NJ: Lawrence Erlbaum Associates.

Walton, D.N. (1996) *Argumentation Schemes for Presumptive Reasoning*. Mahwah, NJ: Lawrence Erlbaum Associates.

Zohar, A. (2008) Science teacher education and professional development in argumentation. In Erduran, S. and Jimenez-Aleixandre, M.P. (eds) *Argumentation in Science Education: Perspectives from classroom-based research* (pp. 245–268). Dordrecht: Springer Academic Publishers.

Chapter 14

Modelling as a part of scientific investigation

John Oversby

Modelling is a pervasive activity for scientists, who often model intuitively. However, the intellectual effort that goes into the active modelling process of creating, refining and using models is rarely paralleled by an understanding of what the modelling process is by those involved in science education. In science education, modelling has long been a subject for inquiry and research. Chang (2008) reports:

'In the process of learning and teaching science, models are important representations and tools... Scientific models and modelling processes could also make students develop higher order scientific thinking such as developing meta-cognition to understand the inquiry process in scientific community, getting familiar with the development and construction of knowledge and individually reflecting on the understanding of scientific knowledge...'

These are major claims, which will be explored in this chapter.

What is modelling in science education?

Gilbert (1993) characterised a scientific model as a representation of a system, event, idea, process or object. Gilbert and Boulter (1998a, 1998b) made it clear that models have specific purposes in explaining science, and that the role of models is determined by the explanatory requirements and the audience. They had in mind, particularly, explanations that are influenced by the prior knowledge of the reader or listener and that focus on aspects of phenomena that are selected for importance at the time. In a development of this, Treagust, Chittleborough and Mamiala (2001) pointed out the role of the student in understanding the nature of models and modelling, in order to make sense of the explanation that is being provided.

In modelling, the scientist draws on the need to explain something, the target, and something that is already known about, the source. The picture below shows a representation of an atomic structure. Such diagrams abound in textbooks, including those aimed at the general public. It seems to be modelled on similar depictions of the solar system. The orbits of electrons are not as clear as the orbits of planets (especially if using the cloud model), so this could be seen as a point of non-correspondence.

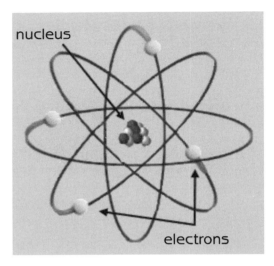

Of course, there is the question of whether atomic structure (the target) or the solar system (the source) are well-enough understood by those attempting to make sense of atomic structure. The point being made here is that there are points of correspondence and non-correspondence between the source and the target. Understanding of the corresponding points is thought to help fix salient features of the target. Rarely, though, does it seem that attention is paid to making explicit at least some of the points of non-correspondence that may mislead the learner. In the research on modelling, this aspect of dealing with non-corresponding points waits to be investigated. For the atomic structure model, some points of correspondence and of non-correspondence are indicated in Table 1.

Table 1 Points of correspondence and non-correspondence for a model of atomic structure drawing upon an understanding of the solar system.

Points of correspondence	Points of non-correspondence
Both systems have a central point about which things orbit.	The scale of the atomic structure model and the solar system are very different.
There are different orbits for planets in the solar system, and for electrons in the atom.	There is no indication of the direction of travel of the orbiting electrons in the atomic structure.
	The nucleus in the atom has parts that are distinguished while in the solar system there is only one thing in the centre, the Sun.

Researchers in modelling often stress the importance of noticing points of correspondence and of non-correspondence in the explanatory process to avoid misunderstandings. While it may well be true that models only exist for the process of modelling in explanation, this point seems to be rarely mentioned by authors.

Classification of modelling types and an evaluation

Harrison and Treagust (2000) proposed ten types of model:

1 scale models
2 pedagogical analogical models
3 maps
4 diagrams and tables
5 iconic and symbolic models
6 mathematical models
7 simulations
8 mental models
9 concept-process models
10 synthetic models.

All of these are expressed, tangible models, available for all to see, except for mental models, which are private. Gobert and Clement (1994) used a classification of 'structural', 'functional' and 'spatial' for the models they discussed. Buckley, Boulter and Gilbert (1997) used the attributes of 'static versus dynamic', 'deterministic versus stochastic' and 'material versus symbolic', while Gilbert, Boulter and Rutherford (1998) used the ideas of tested and agreed consensus models, teaching models, expressed models and mental models.

Clearly, the authors found each of these frameworks useful in terms of the models they used as examples but there does not seem to be, yet, an overarching framework that has been adopted by most science education researchers.

While the researchers focus on models as existing in themselves, it is a relatively recent interest to look at how they are used in explanations – that is, the *process* of modelling.

Views of models in science

Treagust *et al.* (2001) focused, in their chemistry education research, on student views of models and constructed what they described as *My Views of Models in Science (VOMS)*. This was based on a statement bank, from which they asked students to choose alternative statements. Table 2 gives the quantitative data for six statements in the VOMS instrument. The researchers claim that the responses show:

> 'that a large majority of students (>70%) view models as a representation of ideas or how things work (item 1)
>
> that there could be many other models to explain ideas (item 2)
>
> that models are used to explain scientific phenomena (item 3)
>
> that a model is based on facts that support the theory (item 4)
>
> that a model is accepted when it can be used successfully to explain results (item 5)
>
> that a model may change in future years (item 6).'

They go on to examine the detail in the data, and to explore gender and age issues.

Table 2 Students' responses to six statements about models in science (Treagust *et al.* 2001).

Statement	Total % (n = 248)	% for each year group			
		11 (n = 74)	10 (n = 90)	9 (n = 32)	8 (n = 52)
1 Models and modelling in science are important in understanding science. Models are: **a** representations of ideas or how things work	79	91	77	66	75
b accurate duplicates of reality	21	9	23	34	25
2 Scientific ideas can be explained by: **a** one model only – any other model would simply be wrong	12	3	8	16	31
b one model – but there could be many other models to explain the ideas	88	97	92	84	70
3 When scientists use models and modelling in science to investigate a phenomenon, they may: **a** use only one model to explain scientific phenomena	11	9	12	6	13
b use many models to explain scientific phenomena	89	91	88	94	87
4 When a new model is proposed for a new scientific theory, scientists must decide whether or not to accept it. Their decision is: **a** based on the facts that support the model and the theory	73	77	79	69	60
b influenced by their personal feelings or motives	27	23	21	31	40
5 The acceptance of a new scientific model: **a** requires support by a large majority of scientists	14	6	15	21	15
b occurs when it can be used successfully to explain results	86	94	85	79	84
6 Scientific models are built up over a long period of time through the work of many scientists in their attempts to understand scientific phenomena. Because of this scientific model: **a** will not change in future years	17	15	12	19	29
b may change in future years	83	85	87	81	71

It seems from this research that the majority of students are clear that models are representations and not the real thing.

Specific issues of modelling in science

In this section, we explore issues around some examples of modelling for learning, from the sciences. Inevitably, some of the research quoted has only implicit modelling embedded in the reports. Nevertheless, the research points the way to what has been done and what could be done in the next stage of research. Where there are blanks, it is generally because there is little published research.

Modelling in biology

Biological themes	Issues in modelling	Research about modelling for learning	Further research needed
super-macroscopic: ecology	• visualising networks • food chains and food webs (example of moving from simple models to complex models) • understanding Sankey energy diagrams	e.g. Griffiths and Brandt (1985) on food webs	• use of 2D and 3D models • perceptions of biomass and energy pyramids • perceptions of energy and mass flows
macroscopic	• sectional diagrams, colours, e.g. in blood circulation		• perceptions of the use of colour and symbols in depicting organs • converting 3D into 2D for sectional diagrams
microscopic	• being 3D aware when viewing a 2D section	e.g. Dreyfus and Jungwirth (1988) on cells	• converting 3D into 2D for sectional diagrams • the role of symbols and conventions in diagrams
sub-microscopic	• symbols and conventions in biochemical processes		*this is dealt with in more detail in chemical modelling below*

Modelling in chemistry

Chemical themes	Issues in modelling	Research about modelling for learning	Further research needed
macroscopic	• drawings of equipment, taking on a specific and agreed convention		• perceptions of the symbolic quasi-sectional drawings of apparatus
sub-microscopic	• diagrams of atoms and molecules • spacing of particles in solids, liquids and gases	e.g. Ben-Zvi, Eylon and Silberstein (1986) about thinking about atoms	• mixing of macroscopic and sub-microscopic/symbolic, e.g. particles in a solution in a beaker
symbolic	• interpretation of dot-and-cross, stick and cloud models of bonds		• teacher interpretation of chemical models

Modelling in physics

Physical themes	Issues in modelling	Research about modelling for learning	Further research needed
super-macroscopic: astronomy	• diagrams that have two perspectives at the same time		• challenge of imagining two positions simultaneously
macroscopic: electrical diagrams	• understanding conventional diagrams and symbols	e.g. Joshua (1984) on electrical diagrams	• understanding of convention and symbolism
sub-microscopic	• scale	e.g. Black and Solomon (1987) on electric current	
mathematical	• processes of idealisation • representation by algebraic notation		• how concepts are represented by algebraic forms

Modelling in earth sciences

Biological themes	Issues in modelling	Research about modelling for learning	Further research needed
super-macroscopic: plate tectonics	• plates are a construct created to make sense of a wide variety of data, such as seismology, earthquakes, volcanoes, trenches and valleys, and continental shelves – may be too challenging for learners in schools	none available	• whether teachers and learners manage a wide variety of data to understand how models are built, or simply accept models as scientific fact
macroscopic: rock formation	• practical tangible modelling, e.g. laying down and deforming layers of coloured modelling clay or sand	none available	• extent to which teachers and learners see the connection between the modelling and the 'real' process that happens with the target
sub-microscopic: rock structure	• dangers of overlooking non-correspondences between source and target – e.g. using circles and spheres to *represent* sub-microscopic rock particles involves risk of learners coming to believe that the particles *are* circles and spheres, i.e. a move from modelling to realist perspective	none available	• whether teachers and learners adopt a realist position, or are actively moving from source to target in a modelling process
mathematical modelling	• in earth sciences, such modelling often involves calculus and complex geometry, and parameters such as Young's Modulus for stress and deformations – may be too challenging for learners in schools	none available	• teachers' understandings of mathematical modelling – might unearth valuable insights into difficulties of learning though mathematical modelling

Conclusion

Modelling as an explicit process in science education to aid learning has so far been underused as a pedagogical method. Possible ways forward are to:

- provide teachers with an understanding of the nature of the modelling process, as has been attempted in this chapter
- with teachers, create exemplary lessons in which the modelling process is made explicit to the learners, and their reactions and achievements, in conceptual understanding and in understanding the process itself, are recorded
- conduct more research on teaching and learning the modelling process, especially in terms of levels of understanding and matching them to learners of different ages
- extend and exemplify the broad overviews of each science discipline provided above.

References

Ben-Zvi, R., Eylon, B. and Silberstein, J. (1986) Is an atom of copper malleable? *Journal of Chemical Education* **63**(1) 64–66.

Black, D. and Solomon, J. (1987) Can pupils use taught analogies for electric current? *School Science Review* **69**, 249–254.

Buckley, B., Boulter, C. and Gilbert, J. (1997) Towards a typology of models for science education. In Gilbert, J. (ed) *Exploring Models and Modelling in Science and Technology Education.* Reading: University of Reading New Bulmershe Papers.

Chang, S.N. (2008) The learning effect of modeling ability instruction. *Asian Pacific Forum on Science Learning and Teaching* **9**(2), Article 3 (Dec 2008). Available at: www.ied.edu.hk /apfslt/v9_issue2/changsn/index.htm#con

Dreyfus, A. and Jungwirth, E. (1988) The cell concept of 10th graders: curricular expectations and reality. *International Journal of Science Education* **10**(2) 221–229.

Gilbert, J.K. (ed) (1993) *Models and Modelling in Science Education.* Hatfield, UK: Association for Science Education.

Gilbert, J.K. and Boulter, C. (1998a) Models in explanation, part 1: horses for courses? *International Journal of Science Education* **20**(1) 83–97.

Gilbert, J.K. and Boulter, C. (1998b) Models in explanation, part 2: whose voice? Whose ears? *International Journal of Science Education* **20**(2) 187–203.

Griffiths, A.K. and Brandt, B.A.C. (1985) High school students' understanding of food webs: identification of a learning hierarchy and related misconceptions. *Journal of Research in Science Teaching* **22**(5) 421–436 (May 1985).

Gobert, J. and Clement, J. (1994) *Promoting Causal Model Construction in Science Through Student-generated Diagrams.* Presented at the annual meeting of the American Educational Research Association, New Orleans.

Harrison, A.G. and Treagust, D.F. (2000) A typology of school science models. *International Journal of Science Education* **22**(9) 1011–1026.

Hoese, W.J. and Casem, M.L. (2007) *Drawing Out Misconceptions: Assessing student mental models in biology.* Fullerton, CA: Department of Biological Science, California State University. Available at:
http://bioliteracy.colorado.edu/Readings/papersSubmittedPDF/Hoese and Casem.pdf

Joshua, S. (1984) Students' interpretation of simple electrical diagrams. *European Journal of Science Education* **6**(3) 271–275.

Treagust, D.F., Chittleborough, G. and Mamiala, T.L. (2001) *Students' concept of models: an epistemological and ontological perspective.* Proceedings Western Australian Institute for Educational Research 2000. Available at: www.waier.org.au/forums/2001/treagust.html

Chapter 15

Formative assessment and learning

Paul Black

Formative assessment has been prominent since the late 1990s, although the concept had been discussed in the literature for over 20 years before the Task Group on Assessment and Testing (TGAT) report (DES, 1988) stated that it should be central to any assessment policy. Ten years later the Black and Wiliam publications (1998a, 1998b) drew attention to evidence of its positive effects on learning and there followed a project to develop such innovations. This produced evidence of successful implementation, but also made clear that it would call for radical and difficult changes (Black *et al.* 2003; Wiliam *et al.* 2004). The varied menu of practices that were developed reflected the research findings; it included classroom questioning, comment-only marking, peer- and self-assessment, and the formative use of tests.

What follows is a discussion of how understanding of these activities has developed over the past few years, drawing on research studies that have enriched this understanding. The second main section sets out the underlying rationale that interrelates these activities and which helps to locate them in a broader context of teaching and learning. The third and final section discusses the three main obstacles to progress, namely the misrepresentation that reduces formative work to frequent testing, the tensions between formative and summative assessment practices, and the tough challenges that teachers face when adopting a formative approach in their daily teaching.

While the phrases 'assessment for learning (AfL)' and 'formative assessment' are used interchangeably, there is a note of caution about terminology in the third section.

The main practices – progress in understanding

From questioning to classroom dialogue

The following definition of formative assessment sets the scene:

> 'An assessment activity can help learning if it provides information to be used as feedback by teachers, and by their pupils in assessing themselves and each other, to modify the teaching and learning activities in which they are engaged. Such assessment becomes "formative assessment" when the evidence is actually used to adapt the teaching work to meet learning needs.'
>
> Black and Wiliam (1998b, p. 2)

Application of this to classroom teaching implies that activities should 'provide information' in the light of which teachers might choose how best to adapt their next step. The starting point is to frame a question or task that can both engage the interest of the class and evoke important aspects of their understanding. A detailed study by Cowie et al. (2008), with teachers of science and technology at junior levels, showed that many teachers do not produce such effective starting points, because they do not think through in detail the learning aims that they are trying to serve. Their report gives detailed advice and tools to help this planning: they also stress the importance of using a variety of ways to stimulate interest and discussion, such as pictures, recordings, artefacts and experiments.

Given effective presentation of a well-designed task, teachers then have to make best use of the students' responses. A very common pattern of classroom discussion is for a teacher to Initiate with a question, a student to Respond, and the teacher to then Evaluate the response, declaring it correct or incorrect, before moving on to the next question. Any strategy in which a teacher is anxious to attain a predetermined target and to keep up a fast 'pace' will mean that students do not have time to think, so that the only questions that can 'work' are those looking for knowledge of a right answer. The students' contributions will then be limited to words or short phrases, which is all that is needed if you are only expected to show that you know the 'answer', while students will see each question as a test so that those who lack confidence or think slowly will learn to keep quiet. Research into classroom dialogue shows that this **IRE** sequence is a very common pattern of classroom discourse (e.g. Smith et al. 2004).

In a dialogic classroom, the teacher initiates discussion, gives students time to think about and discuss the issue, and then steers the dialogue, noting the ideas that students express, and bouncing them back, to stimulate other ideas, and to summarise the different ideas that are being suggested. The aim is to avoid, at this stage, passing judgment, but rather to use each student's contributions to help all to develop their thinking. One consequence ought to be that the students express themselves in sentences, and that they use such terms as 'because' and 'we thought'. Examples of dialogue in science lessons given by Black et al. (2003, p. 37), and by Scott and Ametller (2007) show how this phase of dialogic intervention both engages the class in thinking about the topic and provides the basis from which the teacher can plan a way to take the issue further. A study by Furtak and Ruiz-Primo (2007) has shown that science students scored more highly in tests if they were learning with more richly developed classroom dialogue. The value of engaging in talk about learning has often been emphasised; Alexander (2006) expresses this forcibly:

> 'Children, we now know, need to talk, and to experience a rich diet of spoken language, in order to think and to learn. Reading, writing and number may be acknowledged curriculum "basics", but talk is arguably the true foundation of learning.' (p9)

Most teachers who have worked on improving their classroom dialogue have found it a slow and difficult matter. Since it requires that students are given time to think, privately or in peer-discussion, and that several responses be called for so that the teacher can decide how best to serve the needs of the class as a whole, it can seem to threaten loss of control and to be risky in spending a long time on specific tasks.

A deeper problem is that, as students are encouraged to express their own ideas, the teacher will face unexpected challenges. A classic example comes from a Primary class where students had been drawing pictures of daffodils. The teacher asked one child 'What *is this flower called?'* and the child's answer was *'I think it's called Betty'* (Fisher, 2005). One response to this unexpected answer would be to ask others until the word daffodil was produced. Apart from harming the first student, this would also miss a learning opportunity. What the student understood by the expression 'is called' in the question was not the meaning that the teacher had in mind. It is commonplace that what is 'heard' in any discussion is not what the speaker intended. However, the teacher would have to pause and reflect on why the student might have given that answer before deciding how to use it to open up a discussion of the difference between generic and individual names.

In general, the teacher faces a formidable problem in trying to discern the thinking that may lie behind any response (Black and Wiliam, 2009). It helps of course to ask the student to explain an answer, and to ask others to comment on this, or to add their own ideas. Without such clarification, the eventual response may not actually deal with the source of the students' difficulties.

Many of the criteria for effective oral dialogue also apply to consideration of dialogue in writing. Consider the following reflection by a teacher about her work in developing dialogue:

> '… because they have to explain their answers each time orally this has carried through to their written work and now they set out their answers fully without being prompted.'
>
> Black *et al.* (2003, p. 40)

This relates oral dialogue to dialogue in writing. A teacher's return of written work to a student can be formative if the response is designed both to help the student to understand the strengths and weaknesses of the work, and to give guidance about how to improve. Thus a comment such as 'Good work, this shows you have tried hard' is of little value compared with one which guides improvement, such as 'Richard – clear method, results table and graph, but what does this tell you about the relationship?' The challenges, to carefully design the task and to interpret the student's thinking, arise here as they do in oral work, only here the teacher has more time to frame a response. The student also has more time: a study comparing students' responses in class discussion with their written responses showed that a wider and more thoughtful range of responses was found in the written work, suggesting that it would be valuable to follow up the one with the other (Furtak and Ruiz-Primo, 2008).

When a teacher returns written work to students with a mark or grade and a few comments, there is hardly any formative interaction, not least because it has been shown that students usually ignore the comments, looking only at the marks and thereby missing the opportunity to further improve understanding. There is also evidence that interactions highlighting marks and grades promote a comparative and competitive attitude in which feedback is seen as a judgment of one's 'ability'. Dweck (2000) and others have shown that both high and low attainers are disadvantaged by such feedback. Comments that are about how to improve focus on the task in hand and can help learners to believe that they can improve by their own effort.

Whole-class dialogue and group work

Many science lessons alternate between whole-class discussion and discussion between students in pairs or small groups. It is important to note that the quality of such discussions depends on the quality of the teacher's conduct of classroom dialogue. By listening carefully to what others say, by giving emphasis to reasoned understanding rather than to formulaic answers, and by trying to help the class to arrive at consensus in a shared understanding rather than by imposing a conclusion arbitrarily, a teacher can make whole-class dialogue a model for students' group discussions. In both contexts, students are experiencing engagement in reasoned discourse; this may be a unique opportunity for many of them. An empirical study of this linking has shown that interventions to improve group discussions do not work where the whole-class discussion is in the IRE mode – the students still focus in their groups on spotting the right answer, rather than on achieving consensus or on exploring reasons to support assertions. The teacher's classroom style is their model (Webb, 2009; Webb and Jones, 2009).

The combination of good-quality feedback in both oral and written modes and students' engagement in both whole-class and small-group discussions sets up the basis for peer-assessments. The aim here is for each student to develop the habit of self-assessment, which is an essential basis for becoming an independent learner. Peer assessment can help such development. This topic is discussed in more detail in Chapter 17.

AfL and the role of assessment in teaching and learning

Two principles underlying all of the practices are the constructivist theory, that learning has to start from and build upon the learner's initial understanding, and the idea that learning proceeds through engagement in dialogue. Through such dialogue students can be helped to understand the aims of their learning, and can come to understand the criteria for success – both essential requirements for growth in self-assessment and independent learning. At the same time, a focus on improving one's work, rather than on competitive ranking alongside others, helps learners to believe in the value of their own efforts to improve.

These principles are the unifying rationale, but the picture they present needs to be complemented by a different scheme, which looks at the work of teaching and learning as a whole. The following is a simplified attempt to meet this need. It presents the task of treating a particular topic as developing through four main stages, as follows.

A **Clear aims** – These may give priority to developing conceptual understanding, or specific procedural skills, or improving students' general skills. The priority here is to be clear and specific about which aim or aims are to be served.

B **Planning activities** – The potential of any activity to elicit responses that help clarify the student's understanding will depend on the level of cognitive demand that a task makes, its relation to previous learning experiences, and its potential to generate interest and engagement.

C **Interaction** – The way in which a plan is implemented in the classroom is crucial. If students are engaged, then the teacher can elicit responses and work with these to help advance students' learning. This may be described as 'interactive regulation', a way of describing formative interaction that stresses the need to build on the students' contributions.

D **Review of the learning** – At the end of the learning episode, there should be a review, to check before moving on. It is here that tests, with formative use of their outcomes, can play a useful part.

On a longer timescale, and therefore at less frequent intervals, there is a need to plan for a fifth stage, as follows.

E   **Summing up** – This is a more formal summative assessment and might use the outcomes of the 'review' work from several preceding topics. Here the results may be used to make decisions about a student's future work or career, to report progress to other teachers, school managements and parents, and to report the overall achievements more widely to satisfy the need for accountability. Consideration of this issue lies outside the scope of this chapter (see chapter 16), except insofar as summative requirements are in tension with formative practice.

Obstacles and challenges

Misunderstanding and misappropriation

It is the interaction, as set out in step C above, which is the core activity of AfL, yet many appear to have understood it as no more than frequent summative testing. The following extract from a statement, drawn up by an international group of leading researchers in assessment, analyses this difficulty:

> 'Some of these misunderstandings and challenges derive from residual ambiguity in the definitions. Others have stemmed from a desire to be seen to be embracing the concept – but in reality implementing a set of practices that are mechanical or superficial without the teacher's, and, most importantly, the students', active engagement with learning as the focal point. While observing the letter of AfL, this does violence to its spirit. Yet others have arisen from deliberate appropriation, for political ends, of principles that have won significant support from educators.'
>
> Klenowski (2009, p. 263)

The ambiguity referred to arises from a serious misinterpretation of 'Assessment for Learning'. For example, an implementation based on a valid definition, that AfL involves 'deciding where the learners are in their learning, where they need to go and how best to get there', can go wrong by focusing on only the first two of the three components – that is, on testing students to know where they are, and on giving them detailed statements of learning targets. AfL can then be equated to frequent testing and to telling students the next target that they must aim to achieve. What is ignored is the third component – 'how to get there'. In the USA, some publishers provide AfL materials that are no more than sets of progress tests, while in England the DCSF (2008) statement of AfL emphasised a similar misinterpretation. The emphasis is on judgment of learning achievement and not on helping the learning itself, whereas the whole point of AfL is to enhance the quality of those formative interactions that help learners to grasp what they are finding hard to understand. Indeed, the 'frequent testing' approach is deeply flawed for three reasons. It seems to rest on the evidence that AfL can improve learning, whereas in fact the balance of research evidence on frequent testing is that on its own it produces very little gain (Hattie and Temperley, 2007); it diverts teachers' attention away from the AfL activities which actually help students to learn; and it can damage the learners' attitude to their own learning (Harlen and Deakin Crick, 2003).

The formative–summative tension

If AfL is (mis)understood as the use of frequent testing, then the sequence set out in steps A to E above is reversed. Step E, driven by pressures of accountability, sets the scene for step D, in which the topic-by-topic work of the teachers is framed by working to the high-stakes testing, to the detriment of the link between the review of learning and its continuation of the formative emphasis in step C. Where teachers are freed from such pressures, which is the case in the UK, in the Primary phase (apart from year 6 in England) and in the Secondary phase (apart from the years immediately before school-leaving examinations), then teachers and schools are free to design their own summative assessments. The task of building positive links between formative and summative practices can more readily be tackled where there is such freedom: teachers can prepare students in a formative way and lead them in to producing the pieces of individual work on which assessment will be based, confident that they will thereby understand the task and will show their full potential (Black *et al.* 2010, 2011).

The formidable challenge

Studies of the ways in which teachers have changed practice when engaged in training to develop their classroom assessments have shown that it is a slow development, taking between one and two years for change to be achieved. Studies of Primary teachers (Webb and Jones, 2009) and of Secondary teachers (Black *et al.* 2003; Lee and Wiliam, 2005) have illustrated the diverse problems that arise. While such studies show that different teachers change in their own individual ways, they do show that one condition is essential: teachers must have sustained support, including regular provision of time to reflect on and exchange experiences and findings with colleagues and with experienced advisers. To the extent that national policies are not so framed that they support such an approach, the task is made more difficult. The evidence is that the rewards repay the effort involved (Yeh, 2009).

References

Alexander, R. (2006) *Towards Dialogic Thinking: Rethinking classroom talk*. York: Dialogos.

Black, P. and Wiliam, D. (1998a) Assessment and classroom learning. *Assessment in Education* **5**(1) 7–73.

Black, P. and Wiliam, D. (1998b) *Inside the Black Box: Raising standards through classroom assessment*. London: GL Assessment.

Black, P. and Wiliam, D. (2009) Developing the theory of formative assessment. *Educational Assessment, Evaluation and Accountability* **21**(1) 5–31.

Black, P., Harrison, C., Lee, C., Marshall, B. and Wiliam, D. (2003) *Assessment for Learning: Putting it into practice*. Buckingham: Open University Press.

Black, P., Harrison, C., Hodgen, D. Marshall, B. and Serret, N. (2010) Validity in teachers' summative assessments. *Assessment in Education* **17**(2) 215–230.

Black, P., Harrison, C., Hodgen, J., Marshall, B. amd Serret, N. (2011) Can teachers' summative assessments produce dependable results and also enhance learning? *Assessment in Education* **18**(4) 457–469.

Cowie, B., Moreland, J., Jones, A. and Otrel-Cass K. (2008) *The Classroom InSiTE Project: Understanding classroom interactions to enhance teaching and learning in science and technology in Years 1–8.* Wellington, NZ: Ministry of Education. Available at: www.tlri.org.nz/school-sector (accessed 15 July 2011).

DCSF (2008) *National Strategies. Assessment for Learning.* Details available on: http://nationalstrategies.standards.dcsf.gov.uk/node/182275 (accessed October 2011).

DES (1988) *National Curriculum Task Group on Assessment and Testing: A report.* London: Department of Education and Science. Available at: www.kcl.ac.uk/content/1/c6/01/54/36/TGATreport.pdf (accessed 15 July 2011).

Dweck, C.S. (2000) *Self-Theories: Their role in motivation, personality and development.* Philadelphia, PA: Psychology Press.

Fisher, R. (2005) *Teaching Children to Learn* (second edition). London: Nelson Thornes.

Furtak, E.M. and Ruiz-Primo, M.A. (2007) Exploring teachers' informal formative assessment practices and student understanding in the context of scientific inquiry. *Journal of Research in Science Teaching* **44**(1) 57–84.

Furtak, E.M. and Ruiz-Primo, M.A. (2008) Making students' thinking explicit in writing and discussion: an analysis of formative assessment prompts. *Science Education* **92**(5) 799–824.

Harlen, W. and Deakin Crick R. (2003) Testing and motivation for learning. *Assessment in Education* **10**(2) 169–208.

Hattie, J. and Temperley, H. (2007) The power of feedback. *Review of Educational Research* **77**(1) 81–112.

Klenowski, V. (2009) Assessment for learning re-visited: an AsiaPacific perspective. *Assessment in Education* **16**(3) 263–268.

Lee, C. and Wiliam, D. (2005) Studying changes in the practice of two teachers developing assessment for learning. *Teacher Development* **9**, 265–283.

Scott, P. and Ametller, J. (2007) Teaching science in a meaningful way: striking a balance between 'opening up' and 'closing down' classroom talk. *School Science Review* **88**(324) 77–83.

Smith, F., Hardman, F., Wall, K. and Mroz, M. (2004) Interactive whole class teaching in the National Literacy and Numeracy strategies. *British Educational Research Journal* **30**(3) 395–411.

Webb, M. and Jones, J. (2009) Exploring tensions in developing assessment for learning. *Assessment in Education* **16**(2) 165–184.

Webb, N.W. (2009) The teacher's role in promoting collaborative dialogue in the classroom. *British Journal of Educational Psychology* **79**, 1–28.

Wiliam, D., Lee, C., Harrison, C. and Black, P. (2004) Teachers developing assessment for learning: impact on student achievement. *Assessment in Education* **11**(1) 49–65.

Yeh, S.H. (2009) The cost-effectiveness of raising teacher quality. *Educational Research Review* **4**(3) 220–232.

Chapter 16

What research tells us about summative assessment

Wynne Harlen

Compared with formative assessment, or assessment *for* learning, with its justified image of a positive impact on learning, the image of summative assessment, or assessment *of* learning, is rather less favourable. But if we subscribe to the view that all assessment should help learning (Gardner *et al.* 2009), then summative assessment can take its place as a necessary and constructive component of education. Unlike formative assessment, using assessment to summarise, record and report learning has always been part of education; it is not a matter of choice. What we can choose, however, is how to conduct it to suit the various purposes it serves. This chapter draws on research evidence about the dependability and impact of summative assessment when carried out by testing or by using teachers' judgments. But decisions about how to assess are affected by the use being made of the results. So we begin with these and end with a summary of pros and cons emerging from research.

Uses and abuses of summative assessment

Assessment is a process of making judgments about students' learning, attributes and accomplishments. It involves decisions about what evidence to use, how to collect that evidence in a systematic and planned way, how to interpret it, and how to communicate the judgment. The decisions depend on the use to be made of the information. In the case of formative assessment, there is one use only – to help learning. In the case of summative assessment, however, there are several uses. These can be grouped under two main headings: use of results for individual students, and use of results for groups of students (classes, year groups, national populations).

Results for individual students are used within the school for monitoring their progress, record keeping, reporting to parents, the students and other teachers, and perhaps for grouping or setting and for career guidance. The results may also be used by agencies outside the school to select students or to award qualifications. Both of these uses directly affect the individual student to some degree and have the potential to help their future learning.

When the decisions based on the results are of importance for the students' future, they are described as being 'high stakes' for the student.

In addition, the aggregated results of summative assessments for groups of students are used both within and outside the school. Within the school they may be used for school self-evaluation, to monitor trends in performance of classes or year groups or perhaps to evaluate the impact of changes in procedures or materials. These uses affect students more indirectly through the decisions made about, for instance, policies, programmes and use of resources. More controversially, aggregated results may also be used by agencies and authorities outside the school for accountability – for evaluation of teachers, schools and local authorities against targets – and for monitoring achievements within and across schools in particular areas and across a whole system for year-on-year comparison. Both of these external uses are problematic, particularly when the only information used is derived from test scores (Tymms, 2004; Assessment Reform Group, 2006). When the results of tests and examinations are used to set targets for teachers and schools, this makes them 'high stakes' for the teachers even though (as in the case of national tests at Key Stage 2 in England) they may not have high stakes for the students.

Dependable summative assessment

To be useful, any assessment needs to be as reliable and valid as is necessary for the purpose for which it is being used. Also to be considered in deciding how best to conduct assessment for a certain purpose are the cost, in terms of time and other resources, and the impact on teaching and learning. We look at impact and resources later, but consider here the key properties of *validity*, taken to mean how well what is assessed corresponds with the behaviours or learning outcomes that are intended to be assessed, and *reliability*, meaning the consistency or accuracy of the results, often measured by the extent to which the assessment gives the same results if repeated.

A key factor concerning validity and reliability in assessment is that in practice these properties are not independent of each other. Rather, they interact in a way that makes it impossible to change one without affecting the other. For instance, efforts to increase the reliability of a test mean that the sample of items included will favour those that can be most consistently marked. This is likely to mean more items requiring factual knowledge and using a closed format (multiple choice or short answer), and the exclusion of more open-ended tasks and those requiring application of knowledge. The consequent limitation on what is covered in a test affects its validity; increasing reliability decreases validity. Attempts to increase validity by widening the range of items, say by including more open-response items where more judgment is needed in marking, will mean that the reliability is reduced. The higher the stakes, the more the emphasis on accuracy at the expense of validity.

Research on methods of assessment

In theory anything that a student does provides evidence of some ability or attribute that is required in doing it. So the regular work that students do in school is a rich source of evidence for assessment, which is used to advantage in formative assessment. For the purpose of summative assessment, which must be a summary of what has been achieved at a certain point in time, this evidence is too detailed, unstructured and variable. There have to be procedures for summing up this evidence in a way that provides dependable

judgments and ensures that different but equivalent work is judged in the same way. Such procedures exist and are effective, but a way to avoid this problem entirely is to create the same conditions and tasks for all students – that is, to use tests. In this section, we look at the research evidence about the dependability and impact of tests and of the alternatives to testing using teachers' judgments.

Pros and cons of tests

Testing is a method of assessment in which procedures, such as the task to be undertaken and often the conditions and timing, are specified. Usually tests are marked according to a prescribed scheme either by the students' teacher or by external markers, who are often teachers from other schools. The reason for the uniform procedures is to allow comparability between the results of students, who may take the tests in different places. Tests are described as 'performance', 'practical', 'paper-and-pencil', 'multiple choice', 'open book', and so on, according to the nature of the tasks that are prescribed. Teachers regularly create their own tests for internal school use; in other cases, they are created by an agency external to the school.

The reason for using tests, as already noted, is that they are considered to be fair and accurate in giving the same opportunities to all students and that they are judged and marked in the same way. But both these claims are in doubt. As for any measurement, there are unavoidable errors and because these measurements involve human beings and not inanimate objects, there are additional sources of error:

- a test can only include a small sample of all items that would thoroughly cover the areas of achievement being assessed and inevitably the particular sample in any test will suit some students more than others
- a test takes place at a fixed time and some students will perform worse on some days than they would on others
- errors in marking or even in marking schemes cannot be completely eliminated.

The error due to first of these (due to sampling) is much larger than is generally realised. For example, estimates by Wiliam (2001) and Black and Wiliam (2006) of the reliability of the levels awarded in National Curriculum tests in England suggest as many as one third of Key Stage 2 students may be awarded incorrect levels. The longer the test, the better the sample of possible items, but Black and Wiliam (2006, p. 126) calculated that to reduce the error so that only 10% of students were given the incorrect level, the test for each subject would need to be over 30 hours.

In relation to validity, the main issue is the extent to which the test includes a representative range of all types of learning goals. High validity is essential, since what is assessed contains strong messages about what is valued. When the stakes are high, however, as in England where the results of national tests are used for evaluation and accountability of teachers and schools, the requirement of high validity tends to be compromised by the need for high reliability of the results in the interests of fairness. What this means is that what is included in the test is restricted to those learning outcomes where performance can be most easily marked as correct or incorrect.

In the case of the national tests at Key Stage 2 in science, this restriction was one of the reasons given for ending these tests (in 2010) and replacing them with teachers' assessment.

Other strong reasons were the impact of the tests, due to their high stakes use for accountability, on teaching and on students' liking and motivation for learning science. There was ample research evidence of this collected in a review of research by Harlen and Deakin Crick (2003). Bringing together results from research studies in all parts of the world where high-stakes testing was prevalent, the review found evidence of teaching focused on the content of the tests (Crooks, 1988; Gordon and Reese, 1997), use of repeated practice tests and a particularly negative impact on the lower achieving students who were constantly faced with evidence of their low-achievement (Black and Wiliam, 1998). There was evidence of tests dominating the ethos of the classroom (Pollard et al. 2000), little use of formative assessment (Broadfoot and Pollard, 2000) and students being judged and judging themselves by their test performance. Thus those whose achievements lie outside the range of what is tested develop a low opinion of themselves and lack motivation for further learning (Reay and Wiliam, 1999).

One of the studies is summarised in Box 1. This concerned the impact of the 11+ examination, still in place at the time in Northern Ireland but likely to be replaced by more widely based criteria for entrance to grammar schools. However, the same story also emerges from research into the impact of Key Stage 2 tests in England – and Wales too, until the end of national tests there in 2004.

Box 1

A study by Johnston and McLune (2000), conducted in Northern Ireland, indicated how the impact of high-stakes tests on teachers' teaching style can affect students' feeling of themselves as learners. These researchers used several instruments to measure students' learning dispositions, self-esteem, locus of control and attitude to science and related these to the transfer grades obtained by the students in the 11+ examination. From the measures of how students preferred to learn in science, they grouped students according to their learning dispositions. These showed a strong preference for learning through first-hand exploration and problem solving. The researchers also observed in classrooms to identify the teaching style of the teachers. They found a high proportion of teaching through highly structured activities and transmission of information and very little opportunity for students to learn 'hands-on'. In interviews the teachers indicated that they felt constrained to teach in this way on account of the nature of the tests. This meant that many students were not able to learn in the way they were disposed to learn and as a result felt inadequate and demoralised as learners.

Teacher-made tests are useful for checking up on learning in specific topics, when they are not intended to cover a large part of a subject and so their limited range is not a problem. Even then it is important to avoid the anxiety that accompanies tests for many students. This can be done by involving students in decisions about testing (Little, 1994; Leonard and Davey, 2001), ensuring that the demands of the test are consistent with the capabilities of the students (Duckworth, Fielding and Shaughnessy, 1986), developing students' self-assessment skills so that they are aware of what they are able to do (Schunk, 1996; Pollard et al. 2000) and developing a supportive ethos in relation to tests so that the results are used to help students direct their effort in learning (Roderick and Engel, 2001).

Assessment by teachers

Just as there is a variety of different kinds of tests, so there is no single approach to teachers' assessment. The different procedures vary according to two independent dimensions: the extent to which the tasks that students are undertaking when assessed are prescribed, and the detail in which criteria for judging are specified (Harlen, 2005). Tasks can vary from being solely those of regular work to special tasks, integrated to varying extents into normal work. Criteria can vary from those implied in the learning goals or syllabus to detailed descriptions of performance typical of particular grades or levels. The combination of these various approaches to specifying the type of evidence and the criteria produce a plethora of different procedures. For example, portfolio assessments can be of many different kinds, depending on how the contents of the portfolio are chosen and whether the criteria are very general or linked to particular types of product.

The chief arguments in favour of using teachers' assessment relate to the opportunity to use information from the full range of learning activities and all goals. Some special tasks may be useful to fill in gaps in teachers' observation but these ought to be seen as part of the programme of learning and not the only basis for assessment. An example of such tasks is the material devised by the Science Teaching Action Research (STAR) project (Schilling *et al.* 1990). The Primary school students were introduced to various features in an imaginary walled garden: water, walls, wood, minibeasts, leaves, bark and a sundial. For each of these, there was a poster giving suggestions for activities and posing some questions mainly relating to inquiry skills. The children worked on the posters in any sequence and across the whole set. These activities provided opportunities for the teachers to assess the use inquiry skills in a variety of contexts. However, using special tasks should be seen as providing a supplement to evidence gathered over a longer time, otherwise one of the advantages of assessment by teachers – of removing the anxiety associated with performance at a particular time – can be lost.

Evidence that changing teachers' assessment can encourage a richer curriculum experience for students was reported by Flexer *et al.* (1995). When teachers of third grade students in a school district in the USA were introduced to assessment methods using evidence from students' classroom performance instead of using tests, the researchers reported several effects on teachers and students after a year of using these methods. Teachers were using more hands-on activities, problem solving and asking students for explanations. They were also trying to use more systematic observations for assessment. Similar indications emerged from the research by Collins *et al.* (2010). The research, funded by the Wellcome Trust, took advantage of the end of national testing in Wales from 2004, to explore the impact of testing in science on the teachers of year 6 students (end of Primary school, aged 11) in England and in Wales in 2007. Using a combination of telephone surveys and focus groups to give quantitative and qualitative data, the research confirmed that teachers in England focused on those aspects of science likely to be included in paper-and-pencil tests with few science investigations in year 6. In Wales, year 6 teachers reported working to develop effective teacher assessment strategies although many continued to use the optional test material to support their judgments. Practical science activities, including investigations, were reported as becoming an important feature of science lessons in year 6 in Wales.

There is also research evidence that using teacher assessment is compatible with formative assessment and there is a potential saving in resources, both of time and cost. The build-up to national tests and examinations takes up days, if not weeks, of potential learning and teaching time through preparation, practice tests and organising and invigilating mock examinations. Costs of test development, trials, postage, marking and so on, run into hundreds of millions (Harlen, 2007). The costs of assessment by teachers although not negligible are small by comparison and, as noted later, involve practices that are of benefit to education.

While summative assessment by teachers has several important advantages over tests, it is in relation to reliability that it is perceived as being inferior to more controlled and formal methods. A review of research into the reliability of teachers' judgments and how it can be improved (Harlen, 2004) confirmed that there was evidence of low reliability in certain circumstances but at the same time showed how the reliability can be improved and lead to fair and dependable results. Higher reliability was found in approaches where there were detailed, but generic, criteria which could be applied across a range of work. Studies by Frederiksen and White (2004) and Shavelson, Baxter and Pine (1992) in relation to science inquiry, and Hargreaves, Galton and Robinson (1996) in relation to creative arts, all suggest that when criteria are well specified and understood, teachers are able to make judgments that are at least as reliable as tests.

Examples of criteria that can be used in this way are included in the Assessing Pupil Performance materials, already published for Key Stage 3 (DCSF, 2009) and being developed for Key Stage 2 in science. Criteria for judging the level at which students are working are provided in the form of 'assessment focuses', which unpick level descriptions of the National Curriculum. There is guidance as to how to use these criteria periodically in making 'best fit' judgments. The published materials for Key Stage 3 are reported as contributing to improved learning and more responsive teaching. The evidence for this comes from teachers' use of the on-going summative assessment to indicate how they might adjust their programmes through identifying the needs of individual students or groups, or the gaps in evidence they can gather.

Other factors that have been found to be important for increasing both the validity and reliability of teachers' assessment are:

1 professional development to ensure understanding of procedures and particularly to address known sources of error and bias
2 involving teachers in the process of identifying criteria so as to develop ownership over them
3 some form of moderation to ensure comparability of judgments among teachers
4 time for teachers to meet and collaborate with each other and with assessment advisers.

The experience of using assessment by teachers in Queensland for the end of high school certificate reflects these features. In particular, the use of collaborative moderation, in which teachers meet together to discuss examples of student work, is described as *'the most powerful means for developing professional competence in assessment'* (Maxwell, 2004, p. 7). Working in England with teachers at the other end of the age range, Hall and Harding (2002) noted a difference between Key Stage 1 teachers who worked collaboratively on their assessment and those who worked individually. The former shared their understandings of the criteria (level descriptions), helped each other plan the collection of evidence, saw assessment as useful and integral to teaching and went to greater length to make assessment meaningful to parents. However, when funds were not available for meeting and attention was focused on other priorities (the National Literacy strategy) there was *'a decline overall in the level of collaboration'* (Hall and Harding, 2002, p. 8).

Conclusions

What has been learned from research about the properties of summative assessment conducted in different ways is summarised in Table 1 (which uses some material from Harlen, 2007, p. 63). The points in Table 1 reflect the assessment system in which the research was carried out. In the case of England, this is one where individual student results are used for high-stakes judgments about schools. It is this use rather than the nature of tests *per se* that leads to the intense focus on what is tested. Nevertheless not all the 'cons' of tests can be explained in this way.

Table 1 Main pros and cons of different summative assessment practices.

Pros	Cons
Tests	
• Ensures that all students are judged on the same items or tasks. • Possible bias due to teachers' knowledge of students eliminated by external marking. • Schools ensure that students are taught what is required by the tests or examination bodies' specifications. • Testing can motivate if results are used to help students direct their efforts.	• Can include only some goals and only a sample of these. • Errors due to sampling of possible items means that a large proportion of students may be misclassified. • Leads to coaching what is tested, frequent practice tests and an emphasis on scores and levels rather than understanding. • Tends to occlude attention to formative assessment. • Preparation and practising can occupy a large proportion of teaching and learning time.
Assessment by teachers	
• Potential for the full range of goals to be included. • Freedom from test anxiety enables students to show what they can do in normal conditions. • With training and moderation reliability is comparable to tests, without the error due to sampling. • Reflects and reinforces what is taught. • Encourages formative assessment by summarising evidence collected and used as part of teaching. • Provides opportunities for student self-assessment. • Releases teacher time from test preparation, organisation and marking. • Increases student learning time.	• Depends on the full range of goals being included in the classroom programme. • Data collected during regular work may need to be supplemented by special tasks to fill gaps in teachers' observations. • Perceived as being unreliable and biased. • Judgments require moderation to raise reliability. • Requires more time to be spent on reflecting on students' learning and applying criteria. • Ideally requires that teachers be given time to meet together for moderation and discussion of procedures.

References

Assessment Reform Group (2006) *The Role of Teachers in the Assessment of Learning.* London: ARG. Available at: www.assessment-reform-group.org/ASF%20booklet%20English.pdf (accessed 15 July 2011) and from the CPA office of the Institute of Education, University of London.

Black, P. and Wiliam, D. (1998) Assessment and classroom learning. *Assessment in Education* **5**(1) 7–74.

Black, P. and Wiliam, D. (2006) The reliability of assessment. In Gardner, J. (ed) *Assessment and Learning.* London: Sage.

Broadfoot, P. and Pollard, A. (2000) The changing discourse of assessment policy: the case of English Primary education. In Filer, A. (ed) *Assessment: Social practice and social product.* London: Falmer Press.

Collins, S., Reiss, M. and Stobart, G. (2010) What happens when high-stakes testing stops? Teachers' perceptions of the impact of compulsory national testing of science of 11 year olds in England and its abolition in Wales. *Assessment in Education* **17**(3) 273–286.

Crooks, T. (1988) The impact of classroom evaluation practices on students. *Review of Educational Research* **58**, 438–481.

DCSF (2009) *New Focus Area for Assessment of Pupil Progress.* Department for Children Schools and Families. Available at: http://nationalstrategies.standards.dcsf.gov.uk/secondary

Duckworth, K., Fielding, G. and Shaughnessy, J. (1986) *The Relationship of High School Teachers' Class Testing Practices to Pupils' Feelings of Efficacy and Efforts to Study.* Oregon: Oregon University.

Flexer, R.J., Cumbo, K., Borko, H., Mayfield, V. and Marion, S.F. (1995) How 'messing about' with performance assessment in mathematics affects what happens in classrooms. Technical Report 396. Los Angeles: Centre for Research on Evaluation, Standards and Student Assessment (CRESST). Available at: http://crest96.cse.ucla.edu/reports/tech396.pd

Frederiksen, J. and White, B. (2004) Designing assessment for instruction and accountability: an application of validity theory to assessing scientific inquiry. In Wilson, M. (ed) *Towards Coherence between Classroom Assessment and Accountability, 103rd Yearbook of the National Society for the Study of Education part II* (pp. 74–104). Chicago: National Society for the Study of Education.

Gardner, J., Harlen, W., Hayward, L. and Stobart, G. with Montgomery, M. (2010) *Developing Teacher Assessment.* London: McGraw Hill

Gordon, S. and Reese, M. (1997) High stakes testing: worth the price? *Journal of School Leadership* **7**, 345–368.

Hall, K. and Harding, A. (2002) Level descriptions and teacher assessment in England: towards a community of assessment practice, *Educational Research* **44**, 1–15.

Hargreaves, D. J., Galton, M. J. and Robinson, S. (1996) Teachers' assessments of primary children's classroom work in the creative arts. *Educational Research* **38**, 199–211.

Harlen, W. (2004) A systematic review of the reliability and validity of assessment by teachers used for summative purposes. In *Research Evidence in Education Library,* Issue 1, London: EPPI-Centre, Social Sciences Research Unit, Institute of Education.

Harlen, W. (2005) Trusting teachers' judgment: research evidence of the reliability and validity of teachers' assessment used for summative purposes. *Research Papers in Education* **20**(3) 245–270.

Harlen, W. (2007) *Assessment of Learning*. London: Sage.

Harlen, W. and Deakin Crick, R. (2003) Testing and motivation for learning. *Assessment in Education* **10**(2) 169–208.

Johnston, J. and McClune, W. (2000) Selection project sel 5.1: Pupil motivation and attitudes – self-esteem, locus of control, learning disposition and the impact of selection on teaching and learning. In *The Effects of the Selective System of Secondary Education in Northern Ireland* (pp. 1–37) Research Papers, 2. Bangor Co Down: Department of Education.

Leonard, M. and Davey, C. (2001) *Thoughts on the 11 plus*. Belfast: Save the Children Fund.

Little, A. (1994) Types of assessment and interest in learning: variation in the south of England in the 1980s. *Assessment in Education* **1**, 201–222.

Maxwell, G.S. (2004) *Progressive Assessment for Learning and Certification: some lessons from school-based assessment in Queensland*. Paper presented at the third conference of the Association of Commonwealth Examination and Assessment Boards, redefining the roles of educational assessment, March, Nadi, Fiji.

Pollard, A., Triggs, P., Broadfoot, P., Mcness, E. and Osborn, M. (2000) *What Pupils Say: changing policy and practice in primary education* (Chapters 7 and 10). London: Continuum.

Reay, D. and Wiliam, D. (1999) 'I'll be a nothing': structure, agency and the construction of identity through assessment. *British Educational Research Journal* **25**, 343–354.

Roderick, M. and Engel, M. (2001) The grasshopper and the ant: motivational responses of low achieving pupils to high stakes testing. *Educational Evaluation and Policy Analysis* **23**, 197–228.

Schilling, M., Hargreaves, L. and Harlen, W., with Russell, T. (1990) *Assessing Science in the Primary Classroom: written tasks*. London: Paul Chapman Publishing.

Schunk, D. (1996) Goal and self-evaluative influences during children's cognitive skill learning. *American Educational Research Journal* **33**, 359–382

Shavelson, R.J., Baxter, G.P. and Pine, J. (1992) Performance assessments: political rhetoric and measurement reality. *Educational Researcher* **21**, 22–27.

Tymms, P. (2004) Are standards rising in English primary schools? *British Educational Research Journal* **30**(4) 477–494.

Wiliam, D. (2001) Reliability, validity and all that jazz. *Education 3–13* **29**(3) 17–21.

Chapter 17

Assessment for Learning: classroom practices that engage a formative approach

Chris Harrison

Assessment for Learning (AfL) is a group of classroom practices that are utilised to help students in their learning and so bring about improvement in their achievement. The seminal review paper by Black and Wiliam (1998a) laid out the premise for such practices and over the last decade or so, this work has encouraged several groups in many countries to put AfL into action. Some of this has been successful (Bell and Cowie, 2001; Wiliam *et al.* 2004), while some was informative (Black *et al.* 2003; Black *et al.* 2006) but also made it clear that AfL calls for radical change in classroom practice. It is therefore not surprising that some studies have raised concerns about the degree to which AfL is working in classrooms (Smith and Gorard, 2005; Brooks and Tough, 2006: DCSF, 2007; Ofsted, 2010) and these studies highlight the need for extensive and focused professional development (Black and Wiliam, 1998b; Black *et al.* 2004; Harrison and Howard, 2009) that has as its central pillar support for learning and not judgment of learning achievement (Klenowski, 2009).

Black and Wiliam also packaged their thinking on formative assessment into a short booklet for teachers entitled *Inside the Black Box* (1998b). Following the publication of this, a research group was formed and the first long-term study of formative practice was set up – the King's Medway Oxfordshire Formative Assessment Project (KMOFAP). This study raised the attainment and also documented what AfL practices looked like in classrooms (Black and Wiliam, 2003, 2004). The project began to explore and understand how the interactions and formative feedback between teachers and students provided guidance for improvement. It is the process by which teachers tune into the thinking of their learners, diagnose where they are in their learning and then use this data to decide on the next steps in learning. At the same time, learners have an important role to play in this process.

What is Assessment for Learning?

Sadler (1989) conceptualised formative assessment as the way in which judgments about student performance could be used to hone and improve their competence by short-circuiting the randomness and inefficiency of trial-and-error learning. This approach can still enable teachers to make *'programmatic decisions with respect to readiness, diagnosis and remediation'* (p. 120). Formative assessment provides teachers and learners with data on learning so that future learning experiences can be matched to the learner's needs. Teachers, therefore, are able to feed back information from assessments into the teaching process and take decisions about the next step needed to support the development of individual student learning (Gipps, 1995; Black, 1998). This is a two-fold process in that teachers have to make a judgment about the next learning step for the student and the appropriateness of the next task, so that an effective match can be achieved. In the choice of task, there is an implicit understanding of the progression within the subject domain, which enables decisions to be made about the learning goal that the teacher considers is attainable by each student. This process supports teachers in matching the pace of learning and amount of challenge to their students.

In formative assessment, the goal is to find out what students know, what they partly know and what they do not know (Black and Harrison, 2004). This awareness comes out of activities that encourage students to talk about their learning, and to apply whatever knowledge they have, from which teachers can gauge their level of understanding. The idea is to try to elicit knowledge of student understanding, and so teachers need to explore the ways in which their students are making sense of their learning experiences. At the same time, students will be able to compare their developing understandings and ideas with those of their peers (Stiggins, 2007). Listening to another student trying to explain how something works or what they believe are the advantages and disadvantages of a particular process, can help students question their own learning as they try to make sense of their own ideas in relation to those of others.

Shifting the balance of classroom talk

Many studies have mapped the type of talk that happens in classrooms (Barnes and Todd, 1995; Mercer, 2000; Alexander, 2004). It seems that in most British classrooms, the teacher is responsible for most of what is said and the type of talk involves:

> *'… closed rather than open questions, very brief responses and a "dialogue" which is a sequence of teacher-student-teacher-student interactions.'*
>
> Black (2009, p. 4)

This is not a recent phenomenon and teachers can find it difficult to break away from dominating classroom talk and generally require some professional development and coaching to enable them to make such changes. In the King's Medway Oxfordshire Formative Assessment Project (KMOFAP) (Black et al. 2003), which involved science, mathematics and English Secondary school practitioners, the teachers often began their lessons with question-and-answer sessions intended to link the lesson with previous learning experiences. At the start of the project, teachers dominated most of the lesson starters by a factor of 10:1. When teachers did try to engage learners, by asking questions, the answers tended to be limited to one-word or one-sentence responses and the focus was on recall; such questions are not useful in tapping understanding. This approach restricts learners' opportunities to express their ideas and creates difficulties for teachers in collecting evidence of strengths and weaknesses in student understanding.

With support from the research team, teachers began to address this imbalance in classroom talk. By the end of the project, most of the teachers had introduced techniques that reduced the dominance of teacher talk. This result was achieved by helping students to find a voice (Black *et al.* 2002, 2003) through working on strategies to help them raise their own ideas. This process began by extending 'wait time' (Rowe, 1974) – the time a teacher takes between asking a question and accepting an answer. It was also enhanced by many teachers allowing students to rehearse and construct answers in groups, prior to a whole-class discussion, and working on techniques that encouraged the continuation of themes and ideas within the talk. This strategy involved teachers planning scenarios and situations that the class could talk about, instead of using classroom talk as a series of questions to check whether some students knew the answers or not.

Opening up the dialogue

A helpful way of understanding the dynamics of the classroom, and the constraints and possibilities it offers for dialogue and feedback, is through Perrenoud's (1998) concept of the regulation of learning. He describes two different types of classroom – the 'traditional' and the 'discursive or negotiated' classroom. In traditional classrooms, lessons are highly regulated with activities tightly defined and, consequently, learning is prescribed. The outcomes tend to be content driven and predetermined, with little opportunity for the students to play an active role in their own learning. From these types of lessons, teachers can only glean what students cannot do, according to the narrowly defined terms of reference (Marshall and Wiliam, 2006).

In a discursive, or negotiated, classroom, the tasks are more open-ended. The scope for students to be active in their learning, and to govern their own thinking, is greater. This creates a classroom environment in which teachers can more readily gauge understanding and provide meaningful feedback for learners. Learners co-construct knowledge through such learning experiences, and the teacher's role is both instigatory and facilitatory. A starting point in this process is formulating questions that make students think and which motivate them to want to discuss ideas – for example, questions such as, 'Is it always true that green organisms photosynthesise?' are better at generating talk than, 'Which types of organisms photosynthesise?'

Sometimes playing on the ambiguities that puzzle learners can be a good starting point for discussion. For example:

'Which one of these statements is true?

- a) *0.33 is bigger than 1/3*
- b) *0.33 is smaller than 1/3*
- c) *0.33 is equal to 1/3*
- d) *You need more information to be sure.'*

Hodgen and Wiliam (2006, p. 6)

This question would be unacceptable in a summative test, because there are several possible answers that depend on the way the question is approached. The question is not designed to check on a specific understanding, but rather to generate talk to explore a number of different understandings. Learning can benefit greatly from the talk that is generated from good questions, and teachers need to put planning time aside to generate questions and to share effective questions with colleagues (Harrison, 2006).

Formative feedback

Improving the communication between students and teachers requires teachers to facilitate student–student talk so that both teacher and learners can locate where the students are in their learning in order that decisions can be made about next steps. Feedback from learners to teachers underpins this approach.

More direct feedback is given to learners when teachers give oral or written responses to the work that has been produced in class or for homework. The key here is in providing descriptive comments about what has been achieved and guidance on what needs to be done next to improve the work or develop it further.

Effective feedback requires the teacher to provide guidance for improvement by indicating where the student needs to focus their efforts, through pointing out a problem with a strategy or process, asking a question, making a suggestion for action or offering a reminder or link to previous work. It is not about correcting work and providing exemplars. Instead, formative feedback should enable the student to think and possibly discuss what they need to do to move their work forward and, crucially, the responsibility for action lies with the student (Harrison, 2011). This approach helps students move their partial understanding to a fuller appreciation of a skill, idea or concept and so provide a positive model for improving learning in the future. The ultimate aim of formative assessment is to help students develop a self-regulated approach to learning (Harrison and Howard, 2009) where students use assessment to look honestly at where they are at, and utilise the assessment process to help them move forward in their learning.

Conclusion

Teachers need support in making the changes in classroom practice that AfL demands. This is not an easy task, particularly when there are also problems in overcoming the habits of their students who have had several years of approaching learning and assessment with a performance rather than learning orientation. This can only be overcome by teachers and senior leaders in schools committing regular, extensive and exclusive time to making these changes work (Harrison, 2009).

References

Alexander, R. (2004) *Towards Dialogic Teaching: Rethinking classroom talk*. Cambridge: Dialogos.

Barnes, D. and Todd, F. (1995) *Communication and Learning Revisited*. London: Heinemann.

Bell, B. and Cowie, B. (2001) *Formative Assessment and Science Education*. Dordrecht: Kluwer

Black, P. (1998) *Testing: Friend or Foe? The theory and practice of assessment and testing*. London: Falmer.

Black, P. (2009) Looking again at formative assessment. *Learning and Teaching Update 30*. London: Optimus.

Black, P. and Harrison, C. (2004) *Science Inside the Black Box: Assessment for Learning in the science classroom*. London: GLAssessent.

Black, P., McCormick, R., James, M. and Pedder, D. (2006) Learning How to Learn and Assessment for Learning: a theoretical inquiry. *Research Papers in Education, 21*(2) 119-132.

Black, P. and Wiliam, D. (1998a) Assessment and classroom learning, *Assessment in Education* **5**(1) 7–74.

Black, P. and Wiliam, D. (1998b) *Inside the Black Box*. London: GLAssessment.

Black, P. and Wiliam, D. (2003) "In Praise of Educational Research": formative assessment. *British Educational Research Journal* **29** (5) 623-37.

Black, P. and Wiliam, D. (2004) Classroom Assessment is not (Necessarily) Formative Assessment (and Vice-Versa) *Towards Coherence Between Classroom Assessment and Accountability - 103rd Yearbook of the National Society for the Study of Education* (ed. M. Wilson), p.183-188 Chicago: University of Chicago Press for the NSSE.

Black, P. and Wiliam, D. (2009) Developing the theory of formative assessment. *Educational Assessment, Evaluation and Accountability* **21**(1) 5–31.

Black, P., Harrison, C., Osborne, J. and Duschl, R. (2004) *Assessment of Science 14–16: A report prepared for the Royal Society*. London: Royal Society.

Black, P., Harrison, C., Lee, C., Marshall, B. and Wiliam, D. (2002) *Working Inside the Black Box: Assessment for Learning in the classroom*. London: NFER Nelson.

Black, P., Harrison, C., Lee, C., Marshall, B. and Wiliam, D. (2003) *Assessment for Learning: Putting it into practice*. Maidenhead: Open University Press.

Brooks, R. and Tough, S. (2006) *Assessment and Testing: Making space for teaching and learning*. London: IPPR.

DCSF (2007) Assessment for Learning (AfL) 8 Schools Project. Available at: http://national strategies.standards.dcsf.gov.uk/node/97897 (accessed August 2011.)

Gipps, C. (1995) *Beyond Testing: Towards a theory of educational assessment*. London: Falmer.

Harrison, C. (2006) Banishing the quiet classroom. *Education Review* **19**(2) 67–77.

Harrison, C. (2009) Assessing the impact of Assessment for Learning 10 years on. *Learning and Teaching* Update 31, pp. 1–10. London: Optimus.

Harrison, C. (2011) Classroom assessment. In Dillon, J. and Maguire, M. (eds) *Becoming a Teacher: Issues in Secondary teaching* (fourth edition). London: Open University Press.

Harrison, C. and Howard, S. (2009) *Inside the Primary Black Box: Assessment for Learning in primary and early years classrooms.* London: GLAssessent.

Hodgen, J. and Wiliam, D. (2006) *Mathematics Inside the Black Box: Assessment for Learning in the mathematics classroom.* London: GLAssessent.

Klenowski, V. (2009) Assessment for learning re-visited: an AsiaPacific perspective. *Assessment in Education* **16**(3) 263–268.

Marshall, B. and Wiliam, D. (2006) *English Inside the Black Box: Assessment for Learning in the English classroom.* London: nferNelson.

Mercer, N. (2000) *Words and Minds.* London: Routledge.

Ofsted (2010) *Standards and Quality 2009/10. The Annual Report of Her Majesty's Chief Inspector of Schools.* London: The Stationery Office.

Perrenoud, P. (1998) From formative evaluation to a controlled regulation of learning processes: towards a wider conceptual field. *Assessment in Education: Principles, Policy and Practice* **5**(1) 85–102.

Rowe, M.B. (1974) Wait time and rewards as instructional variables, their influence on language, logic and fate control. *Journal of Research in Science Teaching* **11**, 81–94.

Sadler, R. (1989) Formative assessment and the design of instructional systems. *Instructional Science* **18**(2) 119–144.

Smith, E. and Gorard, S. (2005) 'They don't give us our marks': the role of formative feedback in student progress. *Assessment in Education: Principles, Policy and Practice* **12**(1) 21–38.

Stiggins, R. (2007) Assessment through the student's eyes. *Educational Leadership* **64**(8) 22–26. Available at: www.assessmentinst.com/wpcontent/uploads/2010/01/Asssessment -Through-the-Students-Eyes.pdf (accessed 15 July 2011).

Wiliam, D., Lee, C., Harrison, C. and Black, P. (2004) Teachers developing assessment for learning: impact on student achievement. *Assessment in Education: Principles, Policy and Practice* **11**(1) 49–65.

Chapter 18

Teaching science in ICT-rich environments

Anna Cleaves and Rob Toplis

In the 21st century, the governments of many countries have facilitated the provision of a variety of Information and Communication Technology (ICT) tools in classrooms in Australia, New Zealand, USA, England and Hong Kong (Eadie, 2001). The UK has the highest levels of embedded classroom technology in the European Union – there is one computer for every three students, and almost every single school has broadband (Ofsted, 2008). For many school students in the UK, a technology-rich environment within and beyond the home (in public libraries and museums, for example) is the norm. Over three decades, it has been anticipated that ICT would transform education. It is not surprising therefore that attention has been paid to the contribution that ICT makes to science teaching.

A new science curriculum for the 21st century was introduced into the UK in 2004 with a change in emphasis from content to skills, a development that aimed to provide the means to evaluate the evidence base of scientific ideas. The changes have come about as the result of research into the views of employers about which skills students should acquire for science-based employment (Coles, 1998), students' views about the curriculum (Osborne and Collins, 2000), students' views about practical work (Cleaves and Toplis, 2008) and Government inspections (Ofsted, 2004). Inevitably, teaching practices have had to change to meet new curriculum requirements and to incorporate ICT.

The potential for the enrichment and improvement of students' experiences, particularly in the light of changes in science curricula since 2004, has been a matter for professional discussion and continuing professional development (CPD). Research into the extent, use and pedagogical purposes of ICT in science has examined the teaching strategies that utilise available hardware and software (and more recently emerging technologies) in relation to student engagement.

Potential of ICT for teaching science

In order to use ICT effectively, teachers need to have an understanding of the role that ICT can play in supporting, inspiring and extending students in science lessons. The variety of ICT available can help to motivate students, explore models, develop understanding of key concepts, communicate ideas and collect and analyse data. In 1997, Scrimshaw urged teachers to see the computer:

'… not as an exotic extra, but as a responsive and integral element in a classroom curriculum that has been rethought to include a view of what computers might do.'

Scrimshaw (1997, p. 100)

The purchase of Interactive White Boards (IWBs), projectors and digital cameras and access to the internet has continued to rise sharply with over half the purchases destined for subject-specific spaces (British Educational Communications and Technology Agency, BECTA, 2006). Custom-designed materials directly related to science curricula are being increasingly purchased, both in Primary and Secondary schools. The internet offers information, interactive sites, live experiments and models, which can be used for presentation, discussion, evaluation and comparison, both national and international, on a wide variety of science topics. Some examples of the ways in which ICT tools have been used is depicted in Table 1.

Table 1 ICT tools and their uses (adapted from Cleaves and Toplis, 2008).

ICT tool	Examples of applications
computer and projector	• displaying lesson objectives • showing presentations
computer, internet connection and projector	• displaying animations and video clips, e.g. beating heart, sodium reacting with water, formation of a rainbow
computer and internet	• researching topics • advertising science programmes • advertising local science week events
computer, internet connection and email	• exchanging of data within school groups and in the 'Science Across the World' project
digital camera	• capturing images of experimental set up, records from the field etc.
video camera	• recording students conducting experiments, drama presentations, topic presentations
remote data-loggers	• collecting data in the field, e.g. light level, sound level, temperature
fixed data-loggers	• collecting continuous or intermittent data (automatic short or long time intervals) such as pH, temperature, light level, voltage

The ImpaCT2 project (Harrison *et al.* 2003) and the British Educational Communications and Technology Agency (BECTA, 2003) report the benefits of using ICT in science education in the UK and aim to encourage schools to capitalise on the large investment that the government has made in ICT and on the excellent examples of ICT use in learning and teaching. A further BECTA report (Crook *et al.* 2010) updates this initial report. Examples of ICT use in science lessons, from these reports, include:

1 use of video, sometimes with mobile phones, to record practical activity and field trips
2 use of photography to capture critical events for future discussion
3 use of a variety of innovative recording and discussion techniques such as blogs for student–student and teacher–student interactions
4 use of the internet to search for information,
5 use of 'clickers' to transmit responses to questions in real time
6 use of wikis to provide a collaborative workspace for files, discussions, sources, and so on.

Teaching strategies using ICT

Newton and Rogers (2001) comment that, despite increase in ICT resource provision, it is:

> '… probably true that the widespread and routine use of new technology in science teaching remains a goal still to be achieved.'

> Newton and Rogers (2001, p. 15)

In similar vein, several years later, Ofsted (2008) describe ICT use across the curriculum as underdeveloped, even though Information and Communication Technology as a subject is considered to perform well.

Science teachers, who were interviewed about their use of spreadsheets, data-logging and presentations, justified the use of ICT in terms of increasing efficiency, saving time and improving pace (Osborne and Hennessy, 2003). Most widespread was the use of presentations to provide projected information onto an IWB, usually without student interaction, and to accentuate the important points of a topic, a use that helps to provide each lesson starter and plenary. Similarly, trainees used ICT, again often presentations, as tools to structure lessons (Cleaves and Toplis, 2008). Teachers reasoned that technology improved the currency and widened the scope of reference and experience that could be brought into the classroom, thereby improving student motivation and engagement (Osborne and Hennessy, 2003). There was some idea of fostering self-regulation and collaborative learning, although Ruthven, Hennessy and Brindley (2004a) found little evidence that experienced teachers promoted independence or collaboration.

The Bristol InterActive project identified features of teachers' integration of ICT in a range of subjects in Secondary and Primary schools (Sutherland, 2004; Sutherland *et al.* 2004; John and Sutherland, 2005). They found that teachers used ICT tools to:

- transform their own knowledge of their curriculum areas
- expand, develop and adjust their teaching repertoire
- scaffold work in the classroom
- capitalise on the potential of ICT to give rapid feedback
- support students' engagement for sustained periods of time.

BECTA (2005) audited teachers' use of interactive materials in class and found that teachers delivered learning outcomes with more pace, freeing up time for focused interaction and consolidation.

When teachers and trainees used ICT tools for conceptual understanding, they were used for teacher explanation rather than by the students for modelling or trying to answer conjectural questions (Osborne and Hennessy, 2003; Cleaves and Toplis, 2008). Although there is a danger that unguided use of interactive simulations by students may lead to the acquisition or reinforcement of misconceptions, the main reasons for little uptake of ICT for conceptual understanding may be the limitations imposed by access, availability – or awareness of the availability – of appropriate ICT resources, or the teachers' confidence to incorporate these into their teaching.

Among trainees, active student collaboration, albeit rare, was facilitated with ICT tools. For example, students used digital cameras to create animations and compared energy from light bulbs using data from temperature probes (Cleaves and Toplis, 2008). Over a decade ago, Rogers and Wild (1996) found that students quickly became adept with the technology. Ruthven et al. (2004a) report considerable student confidence and expertise with using ICT. Clearly, out-of-school use of ICT by students has an effect on their expertise within school where they are able to draw on both sets of experiences (Sutherland et al. 2004). Most students frequently encounter ICT in their daily lives outside school and the use of ICT provides a form of continuity with their home environment.

Data-logging equipment is used mainly in science (including sports science) departments in schools, and when students use it they avoid the drudgery of data collection and processing to enable progression to higher-order skills (Wellington, 2005). The earliest of the ICT hardware in science apart from computers themselves were the data-loggers, which could detect temperature, light, sound and pH. Rogers and Wild (1996) made observations of practical science tasks with and without the use of data-loggers and identified the potential for a shift in pedagogy, with the teacher as the key figure in promoting student independence and collaboration. Data-logging equipment was seen to be useful for supporting exploration and experimentation because it could bypass the need for students to collect, record and process data. Data could be collected over large timescales with high frequency, errors were reduced and the time saved could be used for student discussion about, and deeper analysis of, the data. However, although Frost (2001) suggested many activities using data-loggers that could be incorporated into science lessons, the equipment was quite cumbersome and unreliable and teachers were anxious about using it. More recently, schools have prioritised in favour of other hardware despite vast improvements in data-logger reliability and portability. Most science teaching is carried out with little use of data-loggers and Cleaves and Toplis (2008) found that trainee teachers seldom used data collection hardware, although some experienced teachers who were early adopters were adept in their use.

The vast majority of science trainees considered a number of applications to be potentially useful in developing their use of ICT, although some comments were negative (Barton and Haydn, 2005). Mutton, Mills and McNicholl (2006) formed the opinion that, when trainees are in school, difficulties arise frequently because mentors often have less skill in using ICT than their trainees.

Multimedia simulations of investigations were thought to be useful as they always produce perfect or 'sanitised' data, which students can interpret and analyse (Baggott la Velle, McFarlane and Brawn, 2003, p. 196). Ruthven, Hennessy and Deaney (2004b) found that when students manipulated data on the IWB it proved to be beneficial in terms of motivation and involvement in constructing graphical representations, with a related increase in understanding.

Sorenson *et al.* (2007) carried out a longitudinal study using mixed methods: interviews, focus groups, questionnaires and case studies. They found that attitudes and confidence in the use of the internet improved over several years, although teachers are still concerned about planning time requirement in selecting suitable sites, limited pedagogical guidance and lack of role models in schools. Half of teachers still used the internet infrequently or never. The study identifies a need to change the emphasis to pedagogy rather than technology.

The research seems to show that both experienced and trainee teachers have considered pedagogic justifications for using a variety of ICT tools, particularly to achieve pace, engage in whole-class teaching, and to use starters and plenary sessions as recommended in the *National Strategy* (Department for Education and Skills, 2003). However, an emphasis on whole-class teaching encourages teacher control of ICT resources and mitigates, to some extent, against teaching styles that use ICT to promote student independence and collaboration.

Emergent technologies

Emerging technologies should encourage students to share and build knowledge, track achievement and engage others to support their learning. The ideal situation envisaged by Ofsted (2008) was that all those involved in students' education should have the opportunity to interact through dynamic environments such as project sites, blogs, wikis and real-time communication. BECTA (2006) reported that such provision was patchy in both Primary and Secondary schools.

Schools started to use Virtual Learning Environments (VLEs) in 2000, and it was envisaged that all schools should have had a VLE by 2010 so that teachers could, for example, return coursework, provide notes for students who have missed lessons and post mock exam questions. The best VLEs allow learners to reinforce their routine work, or catch up on missed lessons with material that is both fun and helpful. However, Ofsted described school development of VLE as more of a cottage industry than a national technological revolution:

> 'Schools have established virtual learning environments, in which pupils and teachers are able to access computer files created in school from home, although their rollout nationally has been slow. A few schools allow parents to post comments on their websites. The use of school websites for consultation with parents, pupils and the community is generally underdeveloped.'
>
> Ofsted (2008, p. 84)

The authors note that, during their work in schools, versions of VLEs in schools amounted to 'mini-internets', restricting rather than expanding the students' horizons. Particularly in Primary schools, teachers could not spare the time to keep the VLE up to date and post materials on it. Ofsted (2008) partly attributed the slow uptake of VLEs to managers who may not have given sufficient encouragement or arranged training to enable teachers to use the online classrooms.

Tension exists between students' digital learning outside and what goes on inside school. BECTA (2008) identify emerging technologies in which young people use ICT in ways that are rarely adopted in schools. Ito (2005) describes today's students as the 'millennials' – the generation that has grown up in the digital age and who use ICT in their everyday routines. For example, they habitually use embedded cameras on their mobile phones, annotate photographs they have taken, communicate via text messaging, and play electronic games. Their internet use includes downloading music, looking up events, online social networking, online translation programmes and role-playing social sites. Students could equally well download science animations, role play a record of events such as the discovery of smallpox vaccination, and be involved in Science Across the World.

Technology, student learning and pedagogy

Teachers of science, whether Primary or Secondary, inevitably link science with technology even though Ofsted (2008) failed to establish a direct link between using ICT and achievement, because other factors may be pertinent. However, research findings show that science teachers often use ICT in a way that is pedagogically neutral in the sense that they tend to adopt a teacher-centred approach involving demonstration and instruction and it is this which accounts for similar achievement pre- and post-ICT adoption. Little attention is paid to improving the underlying pedagogy to allow more student collaboration or independence and few teachers or trainee respondents in research studies take into account the world of instant communication and data capture in which our students now live.

For the information age we not only need technological skills, but competence in ways to access knowledge. The current UK science curriculum demands that students access and process knowledge to understand How Science Works. Current technologies, such as Flickr and Wikipedia, encourage sharing, collective intelligence and collective capacity. Schools constitute communities of practice in which participants share and contribute knowledge and skills (Lave and Wenger, 1991). Although there is some debate about the nature of communities of practice (Wubbels, 2007), it is generally accepted that they are social organisations with varied forms of membership (Lave and Wenger, 1991). The concept of collective intelligence recognises that not everyone knows everything, but that most people know something. The approach in which participants, experienced teachers, trainee teachers and students actively contribute to a community of practice is more appropriate in ICT-rich environments than other teaching models.

BECTA was formed in 1988 and recognised that no matter how fast educators develop their own ICT skills, learners will be there first. Research indicates that there were deficiencies in the policy that put computer hardware such as data-logging equipment and IWBs into schools in the 1990s before the associated changes in pedagogy had been thought through. Some excellent examples of implementation have most often been practitioner-led (BECTA, 2006), which seems to point to the need for an infrastructure that can support peer tutoring.

In order to embed ICT in Primary schools BECTA encouraged all teachers to log on to the Hands On Support Matrix, which consisted of a series of questions relating to teachers' confidence and competence in ICT, both professionally and personally. Websites like Teachernet gave guidance about how the matrix could be used to identify staff needs, from those who needed more basic skills training to those who might have benefited from some support. Developments in ICT tend to be practitioner-led rather than institution-led and this initiative gave Senior Management Teams the opportunity to combine the two approaches by inviting teachers who themselves were able to give support to be involved in the CPD programme.

As Ofsted (2005) report, schools are increasing the use of ICT tools, although ICT provision and the extent to which it is embedded into practice is variable, depending on the commitment of school management to implement the necessary changes. There are indications that the use of ICT in science is being used more effectively, especially so in 'outstanding' schools (Ofsted, 2011). It is well established that teachers prefer to learn from colleagues who have already adopted the technology than from courses (BECTA, 2006). Recognition of different levels of experience in learning communities may develop new approaches both to ICT use in science and to the development of teachers' professional skills.

References

Baggott la Velle, L., McFarlane, A. and Brawn, R. (2003) Knowledge transformation through ICT in science education: a case study in teacher-driven curriculum development. *British Journal of Educational Technology* **34**(2) 183–199.

Barton, R. and Haydn, T. (2005) *Trainee Teachers and 'Impact' Learning: a study of trainees' views on what helps them to use ICT effectively in their subject teaching.* Coventry: BECTA.

British Educational Communications and Technology Agency (2003) *What the Research Says About Using ICT in Science.* Available at: https://www.education.gov.uk/publications/standard/publicationdetail/page1/15015

British Educational Communications and Technology Agency (2005) The *BECTA Review 2005.* Coventry: BECTA.

British Educational Communications and Technology Agency (2006) *The BECTA Review 2006.* Coventry: BECTA.

British Educational Communications and Technology Agency (2008) *ICT Mark, a Guide for School Leaders.* Coventry: BECTA.

Cleaves, A. and Toplis, R. (2008) Pre-service science teachers and ICT: communities of practice? *Research in Science and Technological Education* **26**(2) July 2008, 203–212.

Coles, M. (1998) Science for employment and higher education. *International Journal of Science Education* **20**(5).

Crook C., Harrison C., Farrington-Fleet L., Tomàs, C. and Underwood, J. (2010) *The Impact of Technology: value-added classroom practice. Final report.* BECTA. Available at: http://webarchive.nationalarchives.gov.uk/20101102103713/http:/schools.becta.org.uk/upload-dir/downloads/page_documents/research/reports/the_impact_of_technology.pdf

Department for Education and Skills (2003) *Key Stage 3 National Strategy – Key messages: pedagogy and practice.* London: DfES. Available at: www.sgfl.org.uk/ICT/File/.../Leadership/Pedagogy%20and%20Practice.pdf

Eadie, G. (2001) *The Impact of ICT on Schools: classroom design and curriculum delivery.* A report for the Winston Churchill Memorial Fellowship, 2000. New Zealand.

Frost, R. (2001) *Data-logging in Practice.* Hatfield, UK: ASE Publications.

Harrison, C., Comber, C., Fisher, T., Haw, K., Lewin, C., Lunzer, E., McFarlane, A., Mavers, D., Scrimshaw, P., Somekh, B. and Watling, R. (2003) *ImpaCT2 The Impact of Information and Communication Technologies on Pupil Learning and Attainment.* Available at: https://www.education.gov.uk/publications/eOrderingDownload/dfes-0696-2002.pdf

Ito, M. (2005) Technologies of the childhood Imagination: Yugioh, media mixes, and everyday cultural production. In Karaganis, J. (ed) *Structures of Participation in Digital Culture.* Durham, NC: Duke University Press.

John, P. and Sutherland, R. (2005) Affordance, opportunity and the pedagogical implications of ICT. *Educational Review* **57**(4) 405–413.

Lave, J. and Wenger, E. (1991) *Situated Learning. Legitimate peripheral participation.* Cambridge: Cambridge University Press.

Mutton, T., Mills, G. and McNicholl, J. (2006) Mentor skills in a new context: Working with trainee teachers to develop the use of information technology in their subject teaching. *Technology, Pedagogy and Education* **15**(3) 337–352.

Newton, L. R. and Rogers, L. (2001) *Teaching science with ICT.* London: Continuum.

Ofsted (2004) *ICT and Schools: The impact of government initiatives five years on.* Ofsted. Available at: www.ofsted.gov.uk/resources/ict-schools-2004-impact-of-government-initiatives-five-years

Ofsted (2005) *Embedding ICT in Schools. A dual evaluation exercise.* Ofsted. Available at: http://www.ofsted.gov.uk/resources/embedding-ict-schools-dual-evaluation-exercise

Ofsted (2008) *The Annual Report of Her Majesty's Chief Inspector of Education, Children's Services and Skills 2007/08.* Norwich: The Stationery Office.

Ofsted (2011) Successful science An evaluation of science education in England 2007–2010. Available at: www.ofsted.gov.uk/resources/successful-science.

Osborne, J. and Hennessy, S. (2003) *Report 6: Literature Review in Science Education and the Role of ICT: Promise, problems and future directions.* Bristol: NESTA Futurelab.

Osborne, J. and Collins, S. (2000) *Pupil's Views of the School Science Curriculum.* London: Wellcome Trust, Kings College, London.

Rogers, L. and Wild, P. (1996) Data-logging: effects on practical science. *Journal of Computer Assisted Learning* **12**, 130–145.

Ruthven, K., Hennessy, S. and Brindley S. (2004a) Teacher representations of successful use of computer-based tools and resources in secondary-school English, mathematics and science. *Teaching and Teacher Education* **20**(3) 259–275.

Ruthven, K., Hennessy, S. and Deaney, R. (2004b) *Eliciting Situated Expertise in ICT-integrated Mathematics and Science Teaching.* Final Report to ESRC 2004. Cambridge: University of Cambridge Faculty of Education.

Scrimshaw, P. (1997) Computers and the teacher's role. In Somekh, B. and Davis, N. (eds) *Using Information Technology Effectively in Teaching and Learning* (pp. 100–113). London: Routledge.

Sorenson, P., Twidle, J., Childs, A. and Godwin, J. (2007) The use of the internet in science teaching: a longitudinal study of developments in use by student teachers in England. *International Journal of Science Education* **29**(13) 1605–1627.

Sutherland, R. with the InterActive Project Team (2004) Designs for learning: ICT and knowledge in the classroom. *Computers and Education* **43**, 5–16.

Sutherland, R., Armstrong, V., Barnes, S., Brawn, R., Breeze, N., Gall, N., Matthewman, S., Olivero, F., Taylor, A., Triggs, P., Wishart, J. and John, P. (2004) Transforming teaching and learning: embedding ICT into everyday classroom practices. *Journal of Computer Assisted Learning* **20**, 413–425.

Wellington, J. (2005) Has ICT come of age? Recurring debates on the role of ICT in education, 1982–2004. *Research in Science and Technological Education* **23**(1) 25–39.

Wubbels, T. (2007) Do we know a community of practice when we see one? *Technology, Pedagogy and Education* **16**(2) 225–233.

Section 2

Doing research

Chapter 19

Planning for research

Jane Johnston

Being reflective before setting out on the journey of research

This section was written to promote the notion of the reflective practitioner. Being reflective about research is not simply thinking about what the practitioner is doing. Having a body of knowledge, such as what relevant previous research has been accomplished and what theories of learning pertain to the investigation, is necessary. Having procedural skills, such as how to frame research questions, how to design an investigation, how to collect and record data, how to analyse and interpret data, and how to frame a conclusion, is an essential requirement before setting out on the journey of research. Of course, the journey itself develops many of the necessary skills and makes accessible the body of knowledge. Being reflective involves all of these aspects, and progression in being reflective requires progression in each of them.

The kind of research envisaged in this section – that is, practitioner research – is focused on the actions of the teacher, with data collected from the learning process to illuminate those actions. It is therefore focused on practice and is, as a result, a powerful tool for linking research and practice. The research is valuable for the learner researcher as an improvement tool, for developing personal capacity in carrying out research, in raising the level of critical thinking about teaching and learning, and, in its publication, in sharing valuable outcomes with others.

Metacognition

Understanding personal and professional understandings and skills and learning (metacognition) is an important part of all research. Metacognition often precedes or follows cognition; realisation of cognitive challenges stimulates the need for metacognitive strategies (Roberts and Erdos, 1993). However, the relationship between cognition and metacognition, which is that metacognition is explicit thinking about cognition, is a deepening process, so that during the research process individual researchers may identify that understandings are underdeveloped and undertake reading to both develop that understanding (cognition), while monitoring the strategies to improve understanding (metacognition).

Winn and Snyder (1996) identify two aspects of metacognition in relation to research in particular: monitoring progression, and adjusting strategies as appropriate. These often, but not always, occur symbiotically and simultaneously and involve the researcher in being self-reflective and reflexive, taking initiative and responsibility for their own learning. A researcher who has a high level of metacognition is able to take conscious control of their own learning through research, plan appropriate learning strategies, monitor progress, analyse effectiveness and make any necessary changes to their learning pathway (Ridey et al. 1992). A learner researcher who is operating as a novice (Ertmer and Newby, 1996) may well not take time to evaluate their learning or understand their learning needs or set targets for themselves. They may expect that knowledge is imparted to them and not see their part in the learning process. They might also be unable to see the relevance of, or be able to make links between, what they read or experience and their own practice. A learner researcher who is beginning to be metacognitive will identify links between issues raised through discussions, reflections or reading, and practice. They will be able not only to describe workplace data but to begin to critically analyse and evaluate those data. An expert learner researcher will question personal assumptions and current practices and clearly identify specific and pertinent issues for personal development. They will identify the relevance of the area of research to their own professional context as well as to the broader educational context. They may be aware of the need to monitor, correct and redirect their focus of research. As Livingstone (1997) has identified, metacognitive learners/researchers will be able to:

- be clear about their current task and targets
- allocate the necessary resources (time, texts and so on) to the task
- plan appropriate steps to achieve tasks and targets
- monitor and evaluate progress, adjusting pace as appropriate
- predict outcomes based on their personal knowledge.

Research understandings and skills

There are many research understandings and skills that develop through school and undergraduate study. Table 1 shows how these understandings and skills develop through undergraduate (Level 4) to postgraduate M level (Masters Level 7) work.

Table 1 (See page 160) Research skill development from undergraduate (Level 4) to postgraduate (Masters Level 7). The vertical format of the table, for ease of reading, is to have the higher level to the right. Note this is different from the normal practice where hierarchical structures are usually vertical.

Research skill development	Level			
	4	**5**	**6**	**7**
Methodology	Begin to understand the difference between research and scholarship.	Understand one or two types of methodology and be able to use with support.	Begin to understand different types of methodology and identify suitable methodology for specific purpose (with support).	Understand and choose appropriate methodology for research, providing a clear rationale for choice. Understand and apply the difference between methodology and methods.
Research questions	Be able to answer given research questions.	Identify and clearly articulate researchable questions with support.	Identify researchable research questions.	Identify researchable research questions that link to a coherent and focused study.
Key research issues	Begin to understand the need for research to be replicable and truthful.	Begin to show understanding of reliability and validity.	Show understanding of reliability and validity and ability to apply these to research, with support.	Show clear understanding of reliability and validity and ability to apply these to research in terms of both data collection and analysis techniques.
Primary data collection	Be able to collect primary data using given methods. Be able to design a research instrument.	Be able to choose appropriate research methods. Be able to devise a research instrument fit for purpose.	Provide triangulation of primary data using different methods.	Show a clear coherence between primary methods and research questions. Provide effective triangulation, using quantitative and qualitative data where appropriate.
Secondary data collection	Be able to find relevant secondary data from a variety of sources (books, journals, internet).	Be able to use reading with support to formulate an argument and answer research questions.	Be able to use reading to support arguments and extend questions.	Be able to use reading to provide justified persuasive arguments to answer and extend research and pose new questions.
Research ethics	Identify own bias and the influence it has on work/ideas; identify objective stance in reading. Gain appropriate consent for research and ensure anonymity.	Recognise bias in reading and practice. Understand the ethics of research and be able to apply with support to own work.	Apply objectivity and ethics in research and writing.	Show clear understanding and application of research ethics, challenging assumptions in reading and own research.
Analysis	Answer analytical questions posed.	Generate analytical questions. Provide triangulation of analysis using critical friends.	Consider and use layers of analysis	Effectively use several layers such as chronology/history, questions, patterns, groups of collected data, new ideas, emerging issues, factors.
Synthesis	Be able to summarise research and reach some conclusions.	Be able to discuss research findings with support.	Be able to critically discuss research findings.	Deep and critical discussion of findings. Development of new ideas or models.
Communicating research	Be able to describe process to others.	Communicate to critical friends.	Use PowerPoint communication of research. Generate written research report.	Write up research using appropriate format to match methodology.

Box 1 Reflective task – identifying your ability to critically reflect on, and set targets for, your personal and professional development.

Use Table 1 to highlight the level of your skills, identifying the evidence that supports your decision. What have you done in that area that illustrates your competence?

Set yourself targets (to help you progress) in each area and prioritise these to identify what targets are the most important.

Identify the action that you will need to take to achieve your targets, and the expected timeline, the resources needed and how and when you will evaluate/review your progress.

Table 2 reorganises these understandings and skills using the Economic and Social Research Council's (ESRC, 2005, pp. 103–104) Joint Statement of the Research Council's/AHRB's Skills Training Requirements For Research Students. The advantage of this is that it shows how Masters level (M) understanding and skills can progress to Doctoral level (D). The same exercise as shown in Box 1 can be undertaken here so that you can identify your level in each of these areas.

Table 2 (page 162) M level study and research skills, understandings and attributes. The vertical format of the table, for ease of reading, is to have the higher level to the right. Note this is different from the normal practice where hierarchical structures are usually vertical.

Study and research skills, understandings and attributes		Masters level	Doctoral level
A Research skills and techniques	The ability to recognise and validate problems	Craft researchable questions that drive coherent and focused study.	Problematise an area of interest to establish a cogent and compelling area of inquiry that justifies clearly articulated research questions.
	Original, independent and critical thinking, and the ability to develop theoretical concepts	Engage in sustained independent thinking. Show a clear coherence between methods and research questions, providing effective triangulation, using quantitative and qualitative data where appropriate. Show an awareness of alternative models.	Theorise the area of inquiry, modelling ideas and developing them further.
	A knowledge of recent advances within one's field and in related areas	Show awareness of the interplay between policy, practice and research in developing one's field of inquiry.	Understand the symbiotic tensions and challenges between policy, practice and research and use these ambiguities to develop the leading edge of the field of inquiry.
	An understanding of relevant research methodologies and techniques and their appropriate application within one's research field	Show knowledge of selected research methodologies and explore a range of methods (techniques). Provide a clear rationale for the choice of methodology and methods and critique their application to the area of inquiry.	Show insight and acumen in developing methodology and methods appropriate for the area of inquiry.
	The ability to critically analyse and evaluate one's findings and those of others	Present data in a variety of forms deliberately exploring alternatives such as utilising tables, diagrams, images and text etc. as appropriate. Effectively use several layers of interpretation such as chronology, categorisation, individual perspectives etc. Critically analyse and evaluate a range of sources of ambiguous or contradictory evidence, concerning complex educational contexts and practice.	Build on the above to move from playful exploration to assured and nuanced decisions in framing and evaluating research.
	An ability to summarise, document, report and reflect on progress	Summarise, document, report and reflect on progress constructing cogent and compelling arguments.	Synthesise ideas and information in critical and innovative ways that create new and challenging presentations. This will involve deep and critical discussion of findings leading to the development of new ideas or models.
B Research environment	A broad understanding of the context, at the national and international level, in which research takes place	Engage in the learning and research culture by showing an informed interest in educational initiatives and issues and being interested and curious enough to want to investigate issues and develop personal understandings and skills.	Embed one's research in a widening research community. Engage in local, national and international debate through deliberate networking.
	Awareness of issues relating to the rights of other researchers, of research subjects, and of others who may be affected by the research	Show clear understanding and application of research ethics, challenging assumptions in reading and one's own research.	Articulate ethical considerations and their impact on the design, development and dissemination of research.

162

Study and research skills, understandings and attributes

		Masters level	Doctoral level
B **Research environment**	Appreciation of standards of good research practice in their institution and/or discipline	Be able to be reflexive as a result of practitioner research, showing understanding of the impact of educational research on professional practice.	Demonstrate confidence in the practitioner researcher role throughout study and professional life.
	Understanding of relevant health and safety issues and demonstrate working practices	Be aware of health and safety issues and adapt research design appropriately.	Anticipate health and safety issues for all concerned, undertake appropriate risk assessments throughout the research period and work proactively to ensure risks are appropriate.
	Understanding of the processes for funding and evaluation of research	Show awareness of the processes for funding research and evaluation and be alert to potential bias.	Be prepared to apply for funding streams where appropriate. Be alert to potential for bias and vested interests in research, reporting and evaluation.
	Ability to justify the principles and experimental techniques used in one's own research	Be able to provide a cogent rationale for the approaches used in one's own research design and articulate the strengths and weaknesses of the outcomes.	Articulate a sophisticated and nuanced justification of one's research philosophy, design and presentation. Show comprehensive understanding of related studies and demonstrate awareness of personal assumptions and potential bias.
	Understanding of the process of academic or commercial exploitation of research results	Be able to speculate tentatively as to possible explanations of findings and applications of educational research.	Show a proactive approach towards disseminating research findings appropriately to influence policy and practice in the workplace and further afield.
C **Research management**	Ability to apply effective project management through the setting of research goals, intermediate milestones and prioritisation of activities	Establish effective action plans for undertaking research and meeting deadlines. Maintain effective contact with tutors.	Sustain a reflexive action plan that is readily adapted in the light of events emerging within and beyond the research. Maintain focused and intellectually challenging dialogue with supervisors.
	Ability to design and execute systems for the acquisition and collation of information through the effective use of appropriate resources and equipment	Show knowledge and understanding of particular research methods applied to educational contexts and in applications with young and vulnerable people. Show clear understanding of key issues of reliability and validity and apply these to both data collection and analysis techniques	Develop an effective data collection framework making informed choices of appropriate tools. Establish the credibility of outcomes through robust application of issues of reliability and validity.
	Ability to identify and access appropriate bibliographical resources, archives and other sources of relevant information	Access an appropriate range of bibliographical sources and other written information. Show an ability to find and evaluate appropriate e-resources. Show critical understanding of specific research strategies to support reflection, critical analysis and synthesis of ideas and information.	Show confident expertise in accessing, evaluating and collating a broad range of appropriate written sources which can together provide a thorough overview of the area of inquiry.
D **Personal effectiveness**	Willingness and ability to learn and acquire knowledge	Audit personal knowledge base and plan proactively to maintain and extend this.	Sustain self-motivated study seeking deliberately to challenge one's preconceptions. Be prepared to read beyond what is advised.

Study and research skills, understandings and attributes		Masters level	Doctoral level
D Personal effectiveness	Ability to be creative, innovative and original in one's approach to research	Explore and adapt research methods presented in different modules to one's own situation.	Develop personal expertise in creative application of appropriate research methods to particular contexts.
	Flexibility and open-mindedness	Consider alternative interpretations, explore ambiguities and incongruous results. Show awareness of assumptions, bias, polemic, generalisation, in one's own and others' work.	Read and respond to research deliberately exploring different theoretical perspectives. Challenge assumptions, both one's own and others', both in discussion and in writing.
	Self-awareness and the ability to identify own training needs	Show an understanding of the process of personal learning. Take personal responsibility for further developing and monitoring one's own learning using a full range of learning resources.	Thoroughly audit current skills, knowledge and understanding. Be proactive, resourceful, responsive and helpful in meeting personal training needs and those of others.
	Self-discipline, motivation and thoroughness	Take responsibility for blending research and practice within one's professional life. Endeavour to meet deadlines and to enhance performance on each subsequent module.	Take responsibility for developing practice through researching within one's professional life. Show a disciplined approach to sustaining self study, and supporting others in their study in order to achieve milestones as well as final goals.
	Ability to recognise boundaries and draw upon/use sources of support as appropriate	Seek appropriate advice and send in interim work for feedback. Be able to see advice as constructive. Make an informed decision as a result of advice given and act on it as appropriate.	Demonstrate a proactive approach to working with your supervisors. Act as a critical friend to others in the cohort. Show a sensitive awareness of the different roles one plays as expert and novice, student and tutor, insider and researcher etc.
	Ability to show initiative, work independently and be self-reliant	Be able to persevere with MA study through the challenges of personal and professional commitments and achieve a reasonable work/life balance.	Maintain momentum of research and writing throughout an extended and complex project.
E Communication skills	Ability to write clearly and in a style appropriate to purpose	Communicate ideas in a dissertation of up to 20000 words, being able to match writing structure to research methodology, enabling structure to support expression, develop argument and extend understanding. Maintain 100% accuracy in all referencing.	Be aware that writing is research. Develop a compelling personal style of communication with an ability to use a variety of genres appropriately.
	Ability to construct coherent arguments and articulate ideas clearly to a range of audiences formally and informally through a variety of techniques	Be able to use reading to construct persuasive arguments that answer and extend research and pose new questions. Justify arguments explicitly using reading in a coherent and critical way. Develop new lines of reasoning, substantiated by wide reading.	Explore a variety of forums for dissemination – for example, present findings to colleagues, client groups and research conferences; write papers and case studies for newsletters; professional journals, peer-reviewed journals etc.
	Ability to constructively defend research outcomes at seminars and viva examination	Communicate research findings coherently, succinctly and persuasively in a variety of contexts (individual, small or large group presentations) and be able to answer questions posed by other participants. Respond to cold reader comments with the intention of enhancing the final dissertation.	Present own research and provide a powerful yet respectful critique of others through blogs, papers and presentations, as appropriate. Respond to comments by different readers/listeners through constructive, exploratory and open-minded defence.
	Ability to contribute to promoting public understanding of one's field	Contribute to the development of practice in one's own setting through disseminating research process and results.	Contribute to the development of policy, practice and understanding in one's field through disseminating research process and results in local, national and international forums, as appropriate.

Study and research skills, understandings and attributes

		Masters level	Doctoral level
E Communication skills	Effective support of the learning of others when involved in teaching, mentoring or demonstrating activities	Engage in critical discussion with peers, offering supportive and constructive advice eliciting ambiguities and challenging assumptions with clarity and respect.	Elicit the ideas and opinions of others and encourage clear articulation and development of both theory and practice. Engage fully with action learning sets, critical friend groups and the VLE. Constructively criticise others through robust and respectful challenge.
F Teamwork and networking skills	Development and maintenance of cooperative networks and working relationships with supervisors, colleagues and peers, within the institution and the wider research community	Be able to work effectively as a group leader or member with professional colleagues, participants, peer groups and tutors. Handle conflict with confidence and provide constructive support for other learners.	
	Understanding of one's behaviours and impact on others when working in and contributing to the success of formal and informal teams	Be able to use ICT networks (VLE (Virtual Learning Environment) Blogs etc.) to communicate with and support critical friends and extend one's own understandings and skills.	Integrate ICT, networks, learning sets etc. into one's learning patterns. Be responsible and responsive in working with others.
	Ability to listen, give and receive feedback and respond perceptively to others	Engage in critical listening in a range of contexts to support own and peer understandings and skills.	In addition, engage fully in critical discussion that responds sympathetically and perceptively to the needs of others in developing a line of research.
G Career management	Appreciation of the need for and show commitment to continued professional development	Audit experience, skills and understanding perceptively and use this to plan and review development as a practitioner researcher.	
	Ability to take ownership for and manage one's career progression, set realistic and achievable career goals, and identify and develop ways to improve employability	Articulate understanding of how research impacts on personal and professional development (personal, institution, colleagues and learners). Identify how engagement in researching practice can lead to new career avenues.	
	Insight into the transferable nature of research skills to other work environments and the range of career opportunities within and outside academia	Be able to articulate, extend and deploy research in a variety of professional contexts.	
	Ability to present one's skills, personal attributes and experiences through effective CVs, applications and interviews	Be able to use new skills and understandings achieved through research and scholarship to support career advancement. Let us know the outcomes!	

Phases of research

Researching is a complex process and has a number of phases, some of which are more comfortable and likely to be favoured than others. Understanding your own learning and the phases that you may engage with at particular points in your study will prove challenging, but it is an important aspect in developing and monitoring your personal research plan. The phases identified below (Johnston, 2005) are indicative of the research process and were developed in conjunction with research students who had well-developed metacognitive skills.

1 Sheep phase

In this phase of research you wander around grazing on interesting titbits but are not quite sure where you are going and why you are going there. You may find interesting bits of information, but they do not form a coherent whole and may not inspire you. The focus of your research appears as a distant speck on the horizon; one that you are wandering towards but not by any defined pathway. It can be a rather frustrating phase, although this frustration can be a motivating force to move towards a more defined focus.

2 Chick phase

In the chick phase, you need nurture and guidance. You rely on tutors for support but care needs to be taken that you do not become over-reliant and dependent on others. A healthy chick researcher will take advice, but become increasingly self-sufficient, thus moving from the comfort zone into new and more frightening territory. Less healthy chicks may need constant feeding, thus not achieving any independence, while cuckoo chicks expect that someone else will provide for all their needs at the expense of others. Yet other chicks (ducklings) may follow the lead without question and independent or original thought.

3 Squirrel phase

This is the phase where you know what you are doing and you read and collect information, which you squirrel away for future reference and use. It is a very comforting phase as you can collect a vast amount of information and feel very reassured by the reading which confirms your initial ideas. This comfort, however, can encourage you to stay in this phase for too long and keep hoarding information, which may not see the light of day unless you move on.

4 Lemming phase

This is one of the most frightening phases, which is the reason why some researchers try to avoid it. The lemming researcher needs to make a giant leap into the unknown; to take a big risk and voice new ideas, question assumptions and challenge perceptions. You may also have to leave behind preconceived ideas or lines of thinking or inquiry that you had previously though were important. Researching involves taking risks, but in this phase it is important to remember that you are not alone. There are other lemmings out there, who are just as frightened as you and will support you when you make the leap and may leap with you.

5 Sheepdog phase

The penultimate research phase (assuming you avoid the ostrich phase, below) is the sheepdog phase, in which you need to round up your research, collecting all the stray bits of information together and making a coherent whole of it. This is a very organised phase and can be very structured, which is of comfort to some researchers. However, a good sheepdog researcher will make decisions and act upon them and so will not just follow guidelines but reinterpret them to ensure the best possible outcome. So, the sheepdog researcher synthesises the data, draws conclusions, identifies implications and packages the research up in a final written form, making decisions for him/herself.

6 Ostrich phase

This phase is to be avoided at all costs. The ostrich phase occurs when you are struggling with the research, maybe thinking that you are not able to do the work. This can happen at any stage, although it is usually towards the end of the research. At this stage, you avoid all discussion of your research, finding excuses not to attend tutorials and seminars. It is important to talk to your supervisor and other students before your head gets buried so deep that all your senses have gone. Other students will have similar experiences and your supervisor will have been there themselves as a student and as a supervisor. Talking to others will help you to realise that the research journey is not always a perfect or smooth one and there are times when you do need to ask for help.

7 Songbird phase

This final phase is another frightening one, where you disseminate your research to a wider audience. You may present your research findings at appropriate conferences and write articles for further and wider dissemination or contribute to, or author, books.

Box 2 Reflective task – research terminology.

Write a definition for each of the following terms:			
action research	analysis	argument	case study
correlation	covariate	critical listening	deductive
dependability	design flexibility	deviation	discussion
empirical research	epistemology	ethics	ethnography
experiment	factor analysis	generalisability	grounded theory
hypothesis	illuminative evaluation	inductive analysis	interviews
narrative inquiry	naturalistic inquiry	ontology	paradigm
phenomenology	practitioner research	qualitative research	quantitative research
quasi-experiment	random sampling	reflection-in-action	reflection-on-action
reflective journal	survey	synthesis	validity

Sort the terms into those that relate to research understandings and research skills. Pick out those that are specific research methodologies (types of research) and methods (data collection tools).

Once you have completed the task, you may wish to look at the Glossary of key research terms on page 239 to check your definitions.

The research proposal

Successful research is dependent upon the quality of planning and the first step is to prepare a research proposal. Deb McGregor has suggested five steps to guide the development of a practitioner/researcher inquiry proposal. She also provides an outline planning sheet (Figure 1) and an example of a Gantt chart (Figure 2), which is a useful tool to plan ahead when mapping out a timeline for a research study.

Figure 1 An outline planning sheet.

Developing your Inquiry Plan

What are key professional issues (relating to your inquiry)?

What is your research focus?

What are your research questions?

What is your methodological stance (justifications/literature)?

What is the context of your study?	Who are the participants in your project?

What data/evidence/observations will be collected? Why?	How will the data/evidence/ observations be collected? When?

What do you anticipate will be an ethical issue(s)?

What is your analytical framework (justifications)?

What are your anticipated outcomes of the inquiry?

Figure 2 A Gantt chart.

Activity / Week															
1															
2															
3															
4															
5															
6															
7															
8															
9															
10															
11															
12															
13															
14															
15															
16															
17															
18															
19															
20															
21															
22															
23															
24															
25															
26															
27															
28															

Week	Jan				Feb			Mar				Apr					May			Jun				Jul		Aug/Sep		
Activity	1	2	3	4	5	6	7	8	9	10	11	12	13	14	15	16	17	18	19	20	21	22	23	24	25	26	27	28
Launch project. Ensure participants clear about aims.						X																						
Set up observation and interview dates							X																					
Design observation framework								X	X																			
Carry out observations										X	X																	
Analyse observational data											X	X																
Design interview tool													X	X														
Develop interview schedule															X	X												
Conduct interviews																	X	X	X									
Analyse data																				X	X							
Draft findings																						X	X					
Draft full report																								X	X	X		
Finalise report																											X	

Doing research

1 Identifying and defining the focus for research

Your research proposal should:

- have a clear focus that is guided by research questions (three is sufficient usually, more than five is often too much)
- consider likely outcomes, which can be communicated to and used by practitioners and/or participants to inform their practice
- consider how you might explore why and how things do and don't work in different situations and for different groups of practitioners or learners
- consider how to realistically balance the amount of effort required by the researcher and others to conduct the inquiry, with the potential benefit of the outcomes.

2 Building on what is already known about the focus for the research

Your research proposal should:

- be justified by building upon existing evidence:
    - i   from published research
    - ii   other documented information (reliable internet and intranet sources, archived data, and so on)
    - iii   from practice (in your own or other workplaces) about the area of focus
- indicate how you will contribute to what is already known around the focus of inquiry.

3 Gathering the evidence

Your research proposal should:

- consider how to use and/or increase use of relevant evidence that has already been collected
- ensure, as far as possible, that the process of collecting any new evidence is useful and pertinent to the research focus and meets the inquiry needs
- collect evidence that responds to the research questions
- be clear about the appropriate use of methods adopted (interviews, focus group discussions, observations, questionnaires, textual analysis, reflective journals, statistical analysis, and so on)
- have clear strategies for triangulating data (multiple perspectives of same incident(s) or events, collecting evidence over time, sampling comparable populations, analysing the data set in different ways, collecting evidence in more than one context – for example, in another class, department, group, phase, as well as your own), ensuring that evidence about processes and outcomes are consistent and that perceptions are complemented by observations
- ensure you follow ethical guidelines – for example, those developed by the British Educational Research Association (BERA, 2004)
- record and store evidence carefully (clearly labelled, organised, systematically anonymised if required).

4 Analysing and interpreting evidence

Your research proposal should:

- ensure that the analysis and interpretation of evidence are guided by a consistent logic
- check with the literature for similar methodological approaches to verify the proposed strategy
- consider issues that might arise from the collection of evidence, including contradictory messages, as well as those anticipated in the original research question
- consider what will be the practical arrangements to verify and validate your study (for example, meeting with supervisor, participants checking your interview notes, a second viewer of your video recordings and so on).

5 Communicating data and evidence

Your research proposal should plan for writing a report that:

- will deepen your understanding as well as presenting the outcomes in a way that other researchers and practitioners can learn from
- explains why you did what you did, how you did it, what you found out by doing it and reflectively what were the key messages (methodologically and content wise)
- explains how the evidence builds on what is already known and how it is useful to other practitioners
- substantiates your methodological stance, justifies your methods, presents your findings and indicates how the study answers your research questions
- describes how verifiability and validity are achieved
- acknowledges the ethical issues.

An example

A research proposal should identify the focus of the study, together with a rationale, research questions, brief details of the design of the research and an indication of the literature that informs the research. The proposal below is an example, which can also be found on the ASE website (www.ase.org.uk).

Focus of research

This should be a brief statement about the focus of the research (maybe with a title or an overarching research question).

My interest in observation in very young children arose out of previous research which looked at children aged between 4 and 11 years of age (Johnston, 2009). While presenting the research findings at a conference, I was asked why I had started at 4 years of age and my only reason was, because they were the youngest children in the school I conducted the research in. I therefore decided to conduct similar research with younger children to attempt to understand what observation looks like in young children and how we can support its development.

Doing research

Research questions

Identify about three questions that will help you to explore the area or answer your over-arching research question. These questions need to be SMART – that is, questions that can be answered through the chosen data collection methods and in the given the timescale. They should also not be so complex that each one poses multiple questions. Analytical questions ('why?', 'how?' and 'so what?') that give scope for deep answers are preferable to descriptive questions ('what?', 'who?', 'when?', 'where?'), which add to superficial understanding of the area, but do not look deeply at underlying reasons.

> *My current research with children under 4 years of age attempts to answer the following questions:*
>
> *1 What does the skill of observation look like in young children?*
> *2 How can we support the development of the scientific skill of observation?*

Methodology

This should be a brief statement about the type of research you are conducting. You can also identify research literature that is informing your choice of methodology and methods and annotate to identify how it supports your choices.

> *I usually prefer qualitative research methodologies as these provide depth of data which helps you understand so you can develop practice. This research falls into the interpretative sociocultural paradigm in that it attempts to understand both observation as a skill and the part played by social interaction on the development of the skill. In this research, the individual, peer and adult/teacher interaction has been analysed in an attempt to understand the skill of observation from both child and adult perspectives and the part played by different types of interaction. Objectivity can be a problem with this paradigm, especially where the researcher has strong views which may influence the interpretation. I have such views about the importance of practical learning approaches and so must take this into consideration when analysing the data.*
>
> *Literature that has influenced this choice is:*
>
> > Fleer, M. (2007) Young Children: Thinking about the scientific world. *Watson, ACT: Early Childhood Australia.*
> >
> > *Fleer has used the interpretative sociocultural paradigm in early years science educational research.*
> >
> > Lemke, J. L. (2001) Articulating communities: Sociocultural perspectives on science education. Journal of Research in Science Teaching, *38(3) 296–316.*
> >
> > *Lemke successfully used the interpretative sociocultural paradigm in science education.*
> >
> > Robbins, J. (2005) 'Brown paper packages'? A sociocultural perspective on young children's ideas in science. Research in Science Education, *35(2) 151–172.*
> >
> > *Robbins used the interpretative sociocultural paradigm in early years science educational research.*
> >
> > Rogoff, B. (1995) Observing sociocultural activity on three planes: Participatory appropriation, guided participation, and apprenticeship. In Wertsch, J. V., Del Rio, P. and Alvarex, A. (eds) Sociocultural studies of mind *(pp. 139–164). Cambridge, UK: Cambridge University Press.*

Rogoff identified the complexity of social interaction in her three 'inseparable, mutually constituting planes' (1995, p. 139); the personal, interpersonal and community/contextual. Fleer (2007) and Robbins (2005) have found these to be useful in analysing early scientific development.

Sample

Here you should identify how you chose the participants. This could be random sampling or theoretical sampling (the sample chosen to test out a theory).

The sample involved two groups of children aged between 15 months and 4 years of age engaged in a play activity, where they looked at a range of toys. The children attended a private day nursery in a rural location, who had agreed to support the research. All children at the nursery, whose parents had given permission, were included (see below).

Methods

This should be a list of methods to be used to collect evidence to answer your questions. Identify also how you can ensure your research methods are reliable and the data collected will be valid. Linking the methods to the research questions is also helpful to ensure that all the questions are answerable.

For each group of children, a collection of toys was placed on the floor and left for the children to play with. The toys included:

- *moving toys, such as a battery-operated hen, which danced while singing, wind-up toys and pull-back cars*

- *aural toys that made sounds, such as a rattle, a battery-operated chick, which cheeped, a megaphone that children could speak through in alien/robot/spacemen voices and a jack-in-the-box*

- *operated toys that involved some operation by the child, such as a ball and hammer set, a wooden frog that makes a frog noise when a stick is pulled across its back, a helicopter (whose propellers move when pushed) and colour-change ducks (which change colour when warm)*

- *soft toys, such as a large dog, a sheep rug (that can be worn)*

- *other toys, such as a large multifaceted mirror, a magnetic elephant and a wooden person (with moveable limbs).*

The toys were placed on a floor and left for the children to play with independently. The play was videoed and although the camera was in full view of the children, none took any notice of it during the play and it did not appear to have any effect on the results. The activity was structured into two parts: independent play and play with adult interaction. The independent play allowed the children to play freely with the toys for ten minutes without any intervention from the professionals and researcher. Although during this time some children came to familiar professionals in the room to interact with them, the majority of the play was completely independent. The second part of the activity involved the adults interacting with the children, playing with a toy, pointing out things the toys did to children and asking them questions about the toy, such as 'Why do you think that happens?'

The video of the interactions was transcribed with support of Transana (a computer programme that allows researchers to transcribe and analyse large collections of video and audio data). Analytical induction (Erickson, 1998) was used to identify the types of initial observations made by the children, and the number and types of observations made in the different parts of the activity. The initial observations were grouped into four categories:

- **affective**, *showing interest and motivation, such as expressions of glee, 'wow', squeals of delight and giggles*
- **functional**, *observing how the toys work*
- **social**, *involving interactions between children and the adult, such as negotiation for the use of a toy, playing with, or helping another child*
- **exploratory**, *leading to further scientific exploration and inquiry, such as questions that can lead to further exploration or inquiry.*

The two parts of the activity were analysed to ascertain the effect that personal, adult participatory and peer participatory interaction had on the scientific skill of observation.

Ethical statement

This should include a brief statement to explain how you have ensured your research adheres to ethical guidelines.

All parents were informed about the research and consent forms completed. To ensure that the children were disrupted as little as possible, the toys were introduced during a normal play session and their familiar professionals were present and interacted with them throughout.

All children and the nursery remained anonymous.

Literature

NB This list is shortened to provide an exemplar and is not indicative of the number of texts that should be used in the literature.

This should be an alphabetical list of reading, which will underpin your research and provide the basis for the literature review. Annotations or headings can explain the relevance to your research.

Observation

Covill, M. and Pattie, I. (2002) *Science skills – the building blocks. Investigating* **18**(4) 27–30.

Driver, R. (1983) *The pupil as a scientist.* Milton Keynes: Open University Press.

Early years pedagogies

BERA (2003) *Early Year's Research: Pedagogy, curriculum and adult roles, training and professionalism.* Southwell, Notts: BERA.

de Bóo, M. (2006) Science in the early years. In Harlen, W. (ed) *ASE Guide to Primary Science Education* (pp. 124–132). Hatfield: ASE.

Methodological

Erickson, F. (1998) Qualitative research methods for science education. In B.J. Fraser and K.G. Tobin (eds). *International Handbook of Science Education* (pp. 1155–1173). Dordrecht, The Netherlands: Kluwer Academic Publishers.

Lemke, J.L. (2001) Articulating communities: sociocultural perspectives on science education. *Journal of Research in Science Teaching* **38**(3) 296–316.

Robbins, J. (2005) 'Brown paper packages'? A sociocultural perspective on young children's ideas in science. *Research in Science Education, ***35**(2), 151–172

Acknowledgement

Many thanks to Ashley Compton and Lindy Nahmad-Williams of Bishop Grosseteste University College Lincoln, and Fiona Woodhouse of Huddersfield University, for their help with the section on *Phases of research*.

References

BERA (2004) *Revised Ethical Guidelines for Educational Research (2004).* Available at: www.bera.ac.uk/files/guidelines/ethica1.pdf (accessed 15 July 2011).

Economic and Social Research Council (ESRC) (2005) Postgraduate Training Guidelines. *ESRC Recognition of Research Training Programmes: a guide to provision for postgraduate advanced course and research students in the social sciences.* Fourth Edition. Available at: www.esrcsocietytoday.ac.uk/funding-andguidance/guidance/postgraduates/ptguide lines.aspx (accessed 15 July 2011).

Ertmer, P.A. and Newby, T.J. (1996) The expert learner: strategic, self-regulated, and reflective. *Instructional Science* **24**, 1–24. The Netherlands: Kluwer Academic Publishers.

Johnston, J. (2005) Research phases. *Newsletter of the Leicester Doctor of Education* Issue No. 13, February 2005.

Johnston, J.S. (2009) How does the skill of observation develop in young children? *International Journal of Science Education* **31**(18) 2511–2525.

Livingston, J. (1997) *Metacognition: An overview.* State University of New York at Buffalo. Available at: http://gse.buffalo.edu/fas/shuell/cep564/metacog.htm (accessed 15 July 2011).

Ridley, D.S., Schutz, P.A., Glanz, R.S. and Weinstein, C.E. (1992) Self-regulated learning: the interactive influence of metacognitive awareness and goal-setting. *Journal of Experimental Education* **60**(4) 293–306.

Roberts, M.J. and Erdos, G. (1993) Strategy selection and metacognition. *Educational Psychology* **13**, 259–266.

Winn, W. and Snyder, D. (1996) Cognitive perspectives in psychology. In Jonassen, D.H. (ed) *Handbook of Research for Educational Communications and Technology* (pp. 112–142). New York: Simon and Schuster Macmillan.

Chapter 20

Writing a
literature review

Jane Johnston

A literature review is an important part of beginning your research. It should contribute to 'setting the scene' and enlighten the reader about what has been done in the area of your study.

There are a number of different kinds of reviews that should be mentioned here.

- A **systematic review** is a rigorous approach based on a protocol for identifying, appraising and synthesising individual studies to produce novel information. It aims to minimise the risk of bias, and provide a highly transparent method capable of replication.

- A **best-evidence review** adopts a systematic, quantitative approach, often using rational methods in study selection and effectiveness of treatment (such as effect size), using statements of criteria for inclusion that are consistent and well-justified.

- A **narrative review** operates best on primary studies that differ in their methodology, yet focus on a consistent theme. It is holistic and influenced by the reviewers' views and experiences.

- A **meta-analysis** review is quantitative, taking only comparable studies producing data with a similar form, yielding a more powerful analysis than each individual study by a combination of the data.

- A **methodological review** surveys employed research designs, methods and procedures.

The literature review should discuss, in an informed way, the published materials in the area of your research. It should be more than just a simple summary of the sources. It should provide an overview of the area of research, identify key concepts and critique what the research says in answer to your research questions. The critical aspect of your review might draw strands of argument or evidence from several sources as well as indicate how or why you have rejected other perspectives, views or data, using the literature sources. The review should summarise (recapitulate important information) *and* synthesise (reorganise information) to create persuasive arguments and justifications for your study. A review may consider policy, research and practice in the area and give a new interpretation. It will show understanding of the depth, breadth and scope of the research area, define and discuss key concepts in the area and situate your research in the existing area of knowledge. It will not simply describe the literature or even just summarise the research in the area of study. It will compare and contrast the literature to provide a critical commentary on it. Golden-Biddle and Locke (1997) identify that a literature review will *not* simply:

- show that nothing has been written on the topic
- show your awareness of the publications in the area
- summarise the literature or introduce the reader to the area of research.

Reviewing the literature should be an iterative process that continues throughout the research. It should be written to be used as a reference point for your interpretations and research design. You will continue to uncover new work during the course of your research, and to refer back to it at the end of the study in discussing the implications of findings.

This chapter will consider the selection of appropriate literature, so that there is a combination of books, journals, policy documents and web-based sources, with no over-reliance on one type of source. It will also discuss how to read for understanding to develop persuasive arguments, as well as how to keep effective records of sources used so that referencing is accurate.

Selecting and sorting literature

In order to select and use reading effectively, as a researcher, you need to be very clear what the reading is being used for. Usually, this means having clear questions that need to be answered (see Chapter 19, Planning for research). Analytical questions that ask 'how?', 'why?' and 'so what?', will lead to deeper discussions in the literature review rather than descriptive questions that ask 'what?', 'when?', 'who?'. There also needs to be a clear timescale for selecting and sorting the reading. It is easy to allocate too much or too little time to this important part of your research. Machi and McEvoy (2009) identify that:

'A methodical approach to searching the literature and reflective deliberation on the impact of the literature on your topic will provide a sound foundation for your literature review.'

Machi and McEvoy (2009, p. 37)

The steps in their methodical approach involve deciding what you want a source for and why, followed then by collecting, selecting and organising the literature. Thody (2006) suggests a process of recording, summarising, integrating, analysing and then criticising.

Literature needs to be previewed, so that its value in the research can be ascertained. Your sources need to be a balance of policy, professional books and journals and research books and journals. This will enable you, the researcher, to discuss the tensions that exist between policy, practice and research, theory and practice, rhetoric and reality. While it is important to include older seminal texts and theories, it is also important to include more recent professional texts and research. In this way, using web search engines and online databases is essential.

It is important to remember that the purpose of sifting through the literature is not only to collect insightful quotations but also to read it for understanding. It is very easy to spend a significant proportion of the time available in reading and in collecting good snippets of information, as this is comforting and reassuring, but it is necessary to move on and use the reading too. Reading for understanding may require reading, reflecting and re-reading, or an **SQ3R** approach (Survey → Question → Read → Recall → Review). While reading it is important to make notes or record the reading in some way. One way to do this is to prepare a 'critical evaluation sheet', or a proforma for interrogating the literature being read (see Box 1). Another is to keep an electronic or card database with all the information on. These will help you to go back to literature and check ideas, references and so on, throughout your research.

Box 1 An example of a critical evaluation record sheet (*Starting to Write*, H. Marland, Bishop Groseteste University College, Lincoln).

Critical evaluation sheet

In order to **critically evaluate** a set of research articles it can be helpful to set up a proforma for interrogating the article. Here is an example which you may use or adapt. As you read your articles you may want to collate the key points onto one data collection matrix.

Author(s)	
Date	
Title	
Source	
Purpose of article	
Methodology	
Research tools - Design - Data collection - Analysis - Interpretation and conclusion	*Critically evaluate credibility of each stage. Consider validity, reliability, bias, ethics etc.*
Additional points	

While reading articles it is sensible to collate the key points onto one data collection matrix or spreadsheet, using headings such as:

- author
- methodology
- sample methods
- trustworthiness
- questions
- conclusions

or groupings connected to ideas and arguments emerging from the literature.

Box 2 Reflective task to test your skills of analysis and synthesis (by H. Marland, Bishop Groseteste University College, Lincoln).

Read some of the chapters in Section 1 of this book and identify passages that:

- **describe** or **retell** the content of other texts or key ideas
- **analyse** meanings, **contrast** texts, **critique** assumptions, **evaluate** claims
- **synthesise** ideas and **develop** arguments, **construct** models, **propose** interpretations.

If you have photocopied an extract, you could use highlighters to identify the different parts as above.

Starting to write (by H. Marland, Bishop Groseteste University College, Lincoln)

The literature review should set the theoretical framework for the discussion of your research. Through demonstrating an awareness of the ideas, issues and research that have gone before, you will be able to develop your own analytical critique and argument, showing how your work can make a significant contribution to on-going research. Rather than quoting extensively from reading, it is generally more appropriate to summarise and juxtapose key points. This will ensure that an argument is developed that proffers justification(s) for a view, direction of study or scrutiny of pertinent issues or dilemmas rather than just recounting others' work. Table 1 shows some examples.

Table 1 Examples of ways of analysing the landscape of current research, and positioning your own research within it.

General pattern identified	Example of wording to express this analysis
emerging consensus	*A, B and C have written about … from a variety of different perspectives: … However, they all agree on one point … This study seeks to establish a similar trend among …*
conflict	*A, B and C suggest that … However, a separate group of writers, D, E and F, from a different perspective based on …, outline a theory that conflicts: … By studying … this report seeks to explore which influences have affected …*
gap in the field	*A, B and C have studied … and concluded …, while D, E and F have applied this work to … and found that … Yet it appears that no one has focused on … This study seeks to address that gap.*
overlap	*A, B and C, writing about …, found that … However, the work of D, based on a study of …, might have implications for this earlier work … My own study looks directly at this area by …*

Once the literature has been previewed and noted, it can then be categorised according to the contribution it makes to the research (Thody, 2006). This may be an annotated list, which briefly summarises and evaluates the literature in the area. Machi and McEvoy (2009) suggest mapping according to the core idea of your proposed study or by author contribution.

Mapping by the core idea identifies what has been written and what is known about certain key ideas that relate to the core theme of the research. The key areas may well become the subheadings of the literature review, although some researchers believe that this breaks up the flow of the review (Thody, 2006). However, subheadings can provide clear indication of the main themes, helping the reader navigate the ideas and glimpse the writer's train of thought and arguments.

Mapping by author contribution can be a good way of filtering literature, but has the disadvantage that it can lead to constructing the literature review sequentially, by author or date of research. This has the tendency to describe or summarise (Thody, 2006) the research in the area, rather than analysing and discussing the emerging themes.

Using reading in developing arguments (or justifications)

Hart (1998) identifies that in a literature review the researcher should identify and discuss the key studies in the focus area, including as much as possible that is recent as well as relevant, and trying to be as objective as possible. As already noted, this should be more than just a summary of the literature (Thody, 2006) and should also indicate the links between different ideas, between theory, practice and research, between rhetoric and reality, between historical ideas and current ideas. Differences between research findings, analysis of findings and suggestions, implications or recommendations can be critically examined. It should be noted that critical examination does not mean criticism, even though that is the expression used by some authors. A critical examination involves an in-depth reflection on the meaning of the evidence from literature, the objectivity of the author and the implications for the research study in progress. In order to do this effectively, the author of a literature review needs to be able to provide a clear and persuasive argument.

The first step to critical examination and the development of arguments involves being clear what the nature of an argument is. An argument is an evidence-based belief or idea based on reflection and analysis of reading and experience, the validity of which can be rigorously tested or defended based on evidence. An opinion is a subjective belief or idea based on experience or anecdote which cannot be rigorously tested (Petty, 2008). According to Toulmin (1958), arguments consist of:

- **claims**, or assertions about what exists, or values that people hold
- **data**, or statements that are used as evidence to support assertion
- **warrants**, or statements that explain the relationship of the data to the claim
- **qualifiers**, or specified conditions under which claims hold true
- **backings**, or underlying assumptions that are often not made explicit
- **rebuttals**, or statements that contradict either the data, warrant, backing or qualifier of an argument
- **counter claims**, or opposing assertions.

A good argument therefore contains reasons (justifications) with evidence to support them and is enhanced by persuasive language as well as consideration of the counter argument. Osborne, Erduran and Simon (2004) identify five levels of argument, which can also be applied to any piece of argued reading.

- **Level 1** arguments are a simple claim versus a counter claim, or a claim versus a claim – for example, *'A human is a mammal but not a reptile.'*
- **Level 2** arguments consist of claims with data, warrants or backings, but do not contain any rebuttals – for example, *'All the metals I have tested conduct electricity, so metals are electrical conductors.'*
- **Level 3** arguments consist of a series of claims or counter claims with either data, warrants or backings, with the occasional weak rebuttals – for example, *'A penguin is a bird because it has feathers, even though it cannot fly.'*
- **Level 4** arguments consist of a claim with a clearly identifiable rebuttal; they may have several claims and counter claims – for example, *'Summer is caused by the Earth's tilt making that part of the Earth closer to the Sun at that time although it is both summer and winter at different places on the Earth on the same day.'*
- **Level 5** arguments are extended arguments with claims, supported by data and warrants with more than one rebuttal – for example, *'The surface of the Earth is made of plates of solid rock, moving independently on the mobile mantle underneath. Mountains are formed through underlying rocks being pushed up over a long time. Catastrophic movement of the plates relative to one another causes earthquakes, although earthquakes can happen in the centre of a plate and not only where they meet at the edges.'*

When undertaking writing, you, the researcher, can frame questions to develop your argument, such as 'Why do you think that?', 'What are your reasons for that assertion?', 'Can you think of another argument for your view?', 'Can you think of an argument against your view?', 'What is your evidence?' and 'Is there another argument for what you believe?' Machi and McEvoy (2009) identify two types of arguments in literature reviews: the argument of discovery and the argument of advocacy. The argument of discovery involves critical discussion on the current knowledge and understandings in the core area of research, providing a historical and/or current overview of the area and issues, and identifying patterns in the evidence from literature. The argument of advocacy is supported by, and leads on from, the argument of discovery. It involves the critique of literature, using that literature to support new arguments and to answer the research questions.

Hart (1998) believes that researchers should try to be reflexive in their writing and examine their own bias so that their objectivity is very clear. The literature review should critically evaluate the texts read. A critical evaluation should assess the relevance and quality within an explicit structure of the relation between the texts and the questions being investigated. This is easier said than done, since the evaluation often influences the relevance and quality! A critical evaluation is an intellectual process, rather than an end. During this process, the review is constructed, and then deconstructed through reflection, and then reconstructed through an iterative process. In principle, this should be repeated until the writer is completely satisfied, but in practice it stops when the writer has used up the allocated time! The writing can be made more persuasive by using rather than describing what has been read – that is, by being analytical, evaluative and critical. It is easier to be analytical and persuasive if the reading is managed, so that the information that the review produces is filed in a systematic way.

Making the writing clear, systematic and coherent will help the reader make sense of and enjoy the literature review. Hart (1998) also identifies some things to avoid. These include the omission of seminal texts, which also need to be accurately referenced; some texts will discuss theories of education and mention the name of the theorist, but not reference their work. Adopting this style is not scholarly and indicates that the ideas from theory have been acquired by 'folklore' or handed down orally. It is much better to read the original work, so that an accurate and objective view of the theory can be acquired. It is also tempting to use the 'jargon' of other authors' work, as this can appear to be more scholarly, whereas in reality it exposes weaknesses of understanding.

Plagiarism

Plagiarism is the unacknowledged incorporation in written work of material derived from the work, published or unpublished, of another. Plagiarism might include:

- the inclusion in work of more than a single phrase from another person's work without the use of quotation marks and acknowledgement of the sources
- the summarising of another person's work by simply changing a few words or altering the order of presentation, without acknowledgement
- the use of the ideas of another person without acknowledgement of the source
- copying the work of another researcher, with or without their knowledge or agreement.

Plagiarism can be avoided by ensuring that any quotations from published and unpublished sources are indicated and acknowledged, as are sources of illustrations, photographs, maps and statistics. Web-based materials should not be directly downloaded and used and should be referenced fully. Care needs to be taken when paraphrasing material from others; it is better to use reading by engaging in a discussion of the ideas of the author, rather than describe what the author says in quotations and it is also important that all sources of referencing be acknowledged.

Using reading to inform reflection and analysis

Reading should be analysed and used in the literature review to support critical discussion and arguments being developed. Analysis of reading involves reading to fully understanding the issues being raised by the authors. This is why it is necessary to read for understanding and recognise the objectivity or bias of the literature and its author; as Hart (1998) suggests, you should not accept everything you read as truthful or believe everything you read. A good analysis of reading will attempt to understand the context and perspective of the author and identify and illuminate meanings and agendas. This will be an iterative process, so you will revisit texts and ideas, uncovering different meanings or interpretations as you become more knowledgeable in the area being researched. In this way the literature review needs to be revisited at different points in time during the research process and modified accordingly. It is certainly not something that can be written at the start of the research and then left while the primary data are collected and analysed and the final parts of the research are written.

Machi and McEvoy (2009, p. 111) identify nine patterns of argument that a literature review may follow.

- **Cause and effect** – The review of the literature may indicate that certain results follow certain actions. However, there is a need to be tentative and it is very difficult in educational research to 'prove' cause and effect.
- **Effect to cause** – The review of literature may indicate effects where the cause can be tracked back.
- **Sign** – The review of literature may indicate that certain effects are indicated by signs or symbols.
- **Sample-to-population** – Generalisations can be made from the sample population to the population as a whole, based on the research findings reviewed.
- **Population-to-sample** – Arguments can be made that the findings for a large group are also applicable to a small specific group within that larger one.
- **Parallel case** – An argument is made, where there are two similar groups, that what is found out about one will be the same for the other.
- **Analogy** – Assumptions are made that two similar cases will have the same results or conclusions.
- **Authority** – An argument is made that because more than one author writes about an issue, the claim is more valid.
- **Ends–means** – The literature indicates that the results are directly attributed to a specific action.

Writing the literature review

Writing is not something that happens at the end of the research process, but importantly is an integral part of the process itself. Writing should accompany each step in the process and should begin at the earliest opportunity. It is important that reading, and collecting reading, does not become an excuse to avoid writing. Writing and reorganising writing helps to clarify thinking, makes writing less difficult and thus supports the research process. As writing progresses a logical structure emerges. Most important in the writing process is to keep very accurate references of reading to avoid wasting time, effort and useful material, which cannot then be used in the review because it cannot be located. Note: Remember to ensure that page numbers are noted for quotes from the outset and to check when redrafting in order to save hours later.

The structure of the literature review can be in three parts: introduction, main body and conclusion. The introduction should introduce the area, maybe providing an overview and key issues, and set the context for the review. This may involve a historical overview of events in the area leading up to the current day. The main body of the review will include key pointers in the development of major concepts, influential studies and analysis of past research. If the area is well researched, there can be some sorting of research for relevance, narrowing the focus to studies closest to the research area being undertaken. It is helpful to state those sources that are not included – for example, those not in English. If the area is under-researched, there may be a need to make links between the current problems and research in similar areas or with different age groups. Having too much or too little research in the area are both problematic, but both can lead to a good and critical review. In this way the gap in the research and how the current research fills that gap can be identified.

Box 3 Reflective task to assess your review-writing skills.

In writing the review, consider what readers will judge it by.

One important criterion will be the selection of the literature and whether it matches the scope and purpose of the review. The literature selected should be a balanced coverage of the available texts and include the most recent and relevant research studies. All literature needs to be well referenced.

Another criterion will be the critique of the literature and whether the order, themes and ideas are logically sorted and deeply critiqued. The reader will also consider to what extent the review moves seamlessly from the general to the specific, identifying the place of the current research in the area.

A third criterion will be the ability to summarise and interpret the literature, so that the review provides a justification for current research questions posed.

Look at some writing you are engaged in and consider the following questions.

- How well does your work summarise and interpret the literature?
- How well does your writing address the research questions?
- How well does your work make links between policy, practice and research?
- Have you provided a deep and analytical critique of literature? How?
- How accurate are your references? Check, as there are always some errors in every piece of writing.

Machi and McEvoy (2009) provide two stages in writing a literature review: writing to understand and writing to be understood. Writing to understand involves taking ownership over the focus area and using it effectively. Writing to be understood involves the ability to tell the story and engage the reader. In this way, the literature review should emphasise the writer's understanding of the area being reviewed and be coherent and express this understanding to the reader.

A literature review does not have to be written in the academic language register but does need to be clear and thorough, with no colloquialisms.

Sources of literature evidence

Sources provide different levels of rigour in their publishing criteria. Sometimes they are clear about this, but often it remains implicit. Journals carry with them a reputation based on the quality of their peer review and their acceptance rates. Reputable journals carry a statement about their publishing requirements, and the best adopt a process of anonymised reviews by those who are active in the field and have a body of accepted publications in such journals. So, the *International Journal of Science Education* has an editorial board chosen from the international community of those whose work has already been published previously. It is usual for more than one reviewer to work on each paper. This anonymous 'internal scrutiny' checks for relevance to issues of the day, significance of the research topic, the rigour of the literature review, transparency and rigour of data collection, and the validity of analysis and interpretation. The final decision about whether to publish or not rests with the editor.

There are some flaws in this process, but it is the best one we have, and is called peer review. The papers are written for peers – that is, those who are active in the research field – and not primarily for teachers. This is so for every research discipline, not just education. The editor does exert his or her own influence on the kinds of articles that are eventually published, so different international journals will be suitable for their particular area or methodology. Other journals, such as the ASE's *School Science Review*, or *Primary Science*, have articles that reflect their readership, with fewer research articles and more pieces related to the teacher's everyday activity. Their refereeing process is less focused on research rigour, and more on readability or providing some examples of pedagogy.

Just as journals have different standards of refereeing, so do books. In general, books are considered to be scholarship – that is, a reinterpretation of primary and secondary literature to produce a review for its audience. In the case of books published by a publishing house, that publisher exercises a similar refereeing process to that described for journals. Some publishers, such as Routledge, Sage and the Open University Press, have established an international reputation for a rigorous reviewing process that decides whether to publish or not. At the other extreme are small books that are self-published, where the quality is unknown. Generally, international publishers, such as those named above, can be trusted to publish accurate and reliable material, whereas self-published books must be checked more carefully.

Websites have the same hierarchy of quality. Those from organisations such as the BBC, and learned scientific societies, are checked for rigour by external referees, or internally by those with accepted expertise. Nevertheless, live websites are unlikely to be as accurate as books and research papers, simply because of the time element.

There is a collection of valuable documents that inform the literature review, even though they are not research or scholarship in the commonly accepted view. These include government websites, sites for think-tanks, and sites for reputable organisations. They will include personal articles, opinion articles, and reviews that are strongly influenced by the writer or organisation. Sometimes, the website declares its interest but they must be subject to scrutiny by comparison with more trusted sources if they are quoted as authoritative. Wiki sites, such as Wikipedia, deserve a special mention, as well as receiving strong views from academics. Wikipedia is a communal resource, not an authoritative academic source in the traditional sense. It can be incomplete, have errors, and may lack stability with some topics. Of course, even written articles or books can be incomplete or have errors, so it is always good practice to check your source as far as possible, but this is especially good advice for Wikipedia references. Wikipedia may be a good starting point, but caution is essential. Wikipedia itself has an extensive article on its own reliability, where it admits to some errors and quotes accusations about liberal bias. Note: The literature review may be added to at a later date as new reading is uncovered, but when this section is completed it is not the end of critical reading which should be used throughout the research writing.

References

Golden-Biddle, K. and Locke, K. (1997) *Composing Qualitative Research.* Thousand Oaks, California: Sage.

Hart, C. (1998) *Doing a Literature Review: Releasing the social science research imagination.* London: Sage.

Machi, L.A. and McEvoy, B.T. (2009) *The Literature Review.* Thousand Oaks, California: Corwin Press.

Osborne, J., Erduran, S. and Simon, S. (2004) *Ideas, Evidence and Argument in Science. In-service training pack, resource pack and video.* London: Nuffield Foundation.

Petty, G. (2008) *Evidence-based Teaching – A practical approach.* Cheltenham: Nelson Thornes.

Thody, A. (2006) *Writing and Presenting Research.* London: Sage.

Toulmin, S. (1958) *The Uses of Argument.* Cambridge: Cambridge University Press.

Chapter 21

Deciding paradigms and methodology

Jane Johnston

Paradigms

Box 1 Reflective task to help you situate yourself and your research.

Consider the definitions of each of the three main paradigms and consider which aspects of each:

- you feel most comfortable with
- fit your research questions
- match your professional context.

Consider the following:

- How do you address the challenges/dilemmas associated with research in one paradigm/mixed paradigms?
- How does knowledge of your philosophical stance help you in researching?

Positivism

The positivist paradigm is historically associated with the philosophy of Auguste Comte (1798–1857) and is based on scientific principles of research, generating knowledge through observation and experiment (Comte, 1856). Positivism limits research to what truths can be researched, or the *'clearest possible ideal of knowledge'* (Cohen, Manion and Morrison 2000, p. 9). It is, however, less successful in social contexts and research involving the understanding of human behaviour (Cohen *et al.* 2000). Positive research often involves quantitative data (see Table 1).

Interpretive

Interpretive research is based on phenomenology (a theoretical viewpoint believing that individual behaviour is determined by experience), ethnomethodology (the view that reality is socially constructed) and symbolic interactionism (concerned with understanding and interpreting social interactions).

The interpretative paradigm aims to understand and interpret human behaviour and social phenomena and is thus qualitative in nature.

Critical theory
Critical theory grew out of a perceived mismatch between reality and existing paradigms. It is characterised by three types of interest, which generate three types of knowledge (Habermas, 1970):

- technical interest or control of the physical environment, which generates empirical and analytical knowledge
- practical interest or understanding the meanings of situations, which generates interpretative and historical knowledge
- emancipating interest or provision for growth and advancement, which generates critical knowledge and is concerned with exposing conditions of constraints and domination.

A research paradigm is the philosophy or set of beliefs that are the first structural layer of any research. The word 'paradigm' comes from the Greek *paradeiknyai*, which means 'to show side by side'. The beliefs that characterise a paradigm are not ones that can be proven, as with all philosophical stances, but they do form a basic framework within which the research sits, and define what the research 'looks like' (Guba and Lincoln, 1995).

Guba and Lincoln (1995) state that the basic beliefs that define a particular research paradigm may be summarised by the responses given to three fundamental questions:

1 **the ontological question** – 'What is the form and nature of reality?'
2 **the epistemological question** – 'What is the basic belief about knowledge?' (That is, 'What can be known?')
3 **the methodological question** – 'How can the researcher go about finding out whatever he or she believes can be known?'

Hammersley (2007) identifies that '*some classifications of methodological approaches in social and educational research are quite abstract, distinguishing between just two or three competing alternatives*' – quantitative/positivist (numerical data that quantifies/pursuit of knowledge as truth) and qualitative/anti-positivist/interpretive (explanatory data such as words or pictures that attempts to understand issues)– although some identify a third as being a mixed paradigm (Tashakkori and Teddlie, 2003), which is not a helpful category and poses as many philosophical problems as solutions. This is mainly because it is easy to resort to this as a default position without the reflection necessary in deciding what paradigm fits your philosophical beliefs and the research you are undertaking. Guba and Lincoln (2005) have identified three sub-categories of qualitative or post-modern paradigms – critical theory, constructivism, and participatory research – and also that the boundaries between paradigms are indistinct. In this section we identify three main paradigms, positivism, interpretive and critical theory (see Box 1 for definitions of these).

There are other researchers who have attempted to provide other sub-categories of educational research, but Hammersley (2007) considers that:

'there is no single, all-purpose way of drawing distinctions among the various approaches that can now be found within the field of educational research. Rather, different typologies, operating at different levels of abstraction and focusing on various lines of distinction, will need to be adopted on different occasions for different purposes. Furthermore, great care needs to be exercised in thinking about different types of work in the field, not only to avoid mis-description and significant omission but also the danger of presenting the differences as clearer and more fixed than they actually are.'

Hammersley (2007 www.bera.ac.uk/methodological-paradigms-in-educational-research (accessed 15 July 2011).)

Science education research is situated in the cross section between the three main paradigms, drawing upon the positivist by courtesy of its scientific background, the interpretative by courtesy of its place in social and educational research, and critical theory because of the need to situate the research in the historical context of science education.

Methodologies

Methodology is the type of research and is the second structural layer for research. It is a much more concrete layer than the paradigm, and structures the whole research from the outset. The choice of methodology leads from the choice of paradigm, and is influenced by the focus of the research and the research questions. The methodology then determines the choice of research methods (ways to collect data), the analytical structures and the structure of the research report. In this way, the choice of methodology is central and crucial to the research.

Table 1 looks at the connection between research paradigms, general research approaches and methodologies, and illustrates how some methodologies fit some paradigms more appropriately than others. For example, positivist paradigms lead to the collection of quantitative data through surveys and quasi-experiments, whereas interpretive paradigms lead to qualitative data through evaluations, narrative and case studies, and critical theory as a paradigm will engage in critique of policy and research and action research methodologies.

Table 1 Paradigms and methodologies for educational research (adapted from Dash, 2010).

Research paradigm	Main research approach	Research methodologies
positivist	quantitative	correlational quasi-experimental *ex post facto* research surveys
interpretive	qualitative	evaluation biographical/narrative case study
critical theory	critical and action-orientated	ideology critique action research

Doing research

Dash (2010) identifies that the choice of methodology is determined by:

- the social/educational phenomena being investigated
- the level of objectivity/subjectivity of the phenomena
- the existing knowledge and social reality in the research area and the constraints these pose on data collection and dissemination
- the relationship of the researcher to the research.

The different methodologies have their own individual characteristics and you, as researcher, need to understand them in order to make a decision about which type best describes your planned research.

Correlational research

Correlational research examines interrelationships between two or more variables involved in the research. It attempts to ask questions about whether there is a relationship, what direction any relationship follows and the extent or magnitude of the relationship (Cohen *et al.* 2000). The National Foundation for Educational Research (NFER) website identifies correlational research – for example, research by Kirkup *et al.* (2008) looks at the relationships between SAT scores and UK A level results and shows a high correlation. The validity of correlational research is increased with larger samples, so that relationships cannot just be explained by chance. You may start with a hypothesis that there is a positive or a negative correlation and this can then be tested. Computer programs can support the calculation of correlations and aid analysis; retesting can even increase reliability. However, correlation cannot identify the cause of a relationship, or provide any understanding of why there is an apparent relationship.

Quasi-experimental

Educational research cannot undertake true experiments, as it is not possible to control variables in social and educational contexts. The closest you can get to an experiment is a quasi-experiment, where experimental and control groups are used.

Schagen (2009, p. 36) believes there is a good place for quasi-experimental research to replace government-initiated research that is *'based not on research but on politically based assumptions about what "must work", and put in place without a proper pilot or a clear plan for evaluation'*. Schagen suggests that randomised control trials (RCTs) are desirable for educational-based initiatives to ensure that they *'actually made a difference to desired outcomes before being implemented nationally'*. This may eliminate some of the problems Tooley and Darby (1998) identify as associated with qualitative research methodologies. Quasi-experimental research tends to be larger scale and needs to use groups that match as closely as possible to make the research more valid. If the experimental and control groups are very different, then the results are less valid. An example of quasi-experimental research may be having one experimental class or school engaged in a new approach to teaching and learning and a closely matching class or school that is using a traditional approach, with test scores of each being collected. In small-scale research, attempts to be quasi-experimental by the same teacher teaching two classes, one in one way and one in another, are usually confounded by the teacher preferring one method over another. Although it may occasionally be possible to find two comparable classes, they may well not be at the same time on the same days, providing yet another variable.

Ex post facto research

Ex post facto (after the fact) research is retrospective research, which investigates possible cause-and-effect relationships and refers to an activity in which the researcher does not control the variables but examines the effect of a naturally occurring treatment after it has occurred. In other words, it is a study that attempts to discover the pre-existing causal conditions between groups, and this can be a dilemma for the researcher as there can be no control over the similarities between the groups being studied (Ary *et al.* 2010).

Ex post facto research is carried out by observing an existing condition or state of affairs and searching back in time for plausible causal factors. Ary *et al.* (2010) identify two types of *ex post facto* research. The first is proactive, or co-relational research, which involves starting with the independent variable and testing the dependent variable to determine the relationship between them. The second is retroactive, or causal research, which seeks to find causal relationships by starting with the dependant variable (Cohen *et al.* 2000). Care needs to be taken to ensure that conclusions are not drawn regarding cause and effect, just because two factors correlate. The disadvantage of this research is that only partial control is possible. Steps to successful *ex post facto* research involve:

- statement of the problem
- choosing the sample groups to be investigated, ensuring that they differ with regard to the variable
- making groups equal by pairing off
- identifying statistical analysis techniques
- choosing independent and dependent variables
- collecting and analysing data
- confirming or rejecting the hypothesis.

Surveys

A survey is a non-experimental, descriptive research method. It can be useful when, as part of your research, you want to collect data on phenomena that cannot be directly observed or when you want to collect data from a large number of participants. A survey can be quantitative (asking closed questions) and/or qualitative (asking open-ended questions), collecting data on opinions, ideas or issues. Data are usually collected through questionnaires and interviews (see Chapter 22). There are different types of surveys, as described below (Babbie, 1973).

- **Cross-sectional surveys** gather data from individuals or groups at a single point in time. For example, a survey could ask students to evaluate a lesson, or teachers to identify their opinions of a new strategy.
- **Longitudinal surveys** collect data over a period of time, so that changes over time can be described and explained. Longitudinal surveys can include trend studies, cohort studies, and panel studies. Trend studies focus on a particular group and changes and differences over time can be seen. For example, trend studies may look at combining data on boys' behaviour and academic achievement during compulsory schooling. They are typically not composed of the same people and don't need to be conducted by just one researcher or research project, so data from separate research

studies of the same population may be combined in order to show a trend. Cohort studies also focus on a particular population, but survey the same cohort every time – so, for example, boys' behaviour and academic achievement in year 7 could be surveyed in a cohort study.

- **Panel studies** attempt to find out why changes in the population are occurring, since they use the same sample of people (the panel). An example could be that a group of newly qualified teachers are asked how initial teacher education has prepared them to teach, at the start and at the end of their induction year, and then at regular intervals they are asked how continuing professional development is supporting their ability to teach. Panel studies tend to be expensive and time-consuming, and have a high attrition (drop out) rates.

Cresswell (2009) identifies decisions that need to be made when considering using surveys. These include identifying the purpose of the survey research, why a survey is the best methodology and what type of survey is most appropriate. These are decisions that need to be made in designing any research, but it is easy to turn to a more familiar methodology, rather than choosing one that is the best fit for the research being planned.

The advent of technology, especially online interactive websites, makes some surveys easier to conduct. SurveyMonkey (www.surveymonkey.com) is one of these and offers a selection of question types, some with drop down menus:

- multiple choice
- matrix of choices
- rating scale
- text boxes
- demographics.

Ethics statements can be written as an introduction, leaving respondents to accept these by voluntary participation. Multiple entries by single respondents require careful methods to detect and treat. Data entry can be validated online, for instance by checking the format of number or date entry, or email addresses, or restricting text length. Data collection can be synchronous – by printing out the form for handwritten responses in a class, for example – or asynchronous, where the survey can be taken any time, anywhere. The electronic nature of the survey means that sample sizes can be large, although response rates may be low. The data can be analysed in real time, and at the survey end. Free response text entry avoids the need for transcription of handwritten responses. Data can be analysed automatically, producing statistical information and graphs as required, or downloaded to be analysed by the researcher, using SPSS, for example (SPSS: Statistical Package for the Social Sciences – a computer package used to support qualitative data analysis). Electronic survey methods also facilitate access to groups such as parents, employers and the general public to elicit opinions – for example, about a move towards a different teaching method. Electronic survey methods are only as good as the questions used.

Evaluation

Educational evaluation involves the appraisal of an educational programme or an aspect or aspects of the educational process. Large-scale evaluation may be used to provide information on effectiveness, as a measure of performance for those funding programmes and other stakeholders. Smaller-scale evaluation may involve individual professionals in reflective practice (Schön, 1983), both 'reflection-in-action' (while doing something) and 'reflection-on-action' (after you have done it). Parlett and Hamilton (1972) introduced 'illuminative evaluation' as a qualitative evaluation methodology, which studies an innovative programme by illuminating a range of qualitative questions. In this way, evaluation can not only identify the worth of an educational initiative, but also attempt to understand how and why it is successful and what impact this has on participants: students, teachers, parents, schools and so on. Parlett and Hamilton recognise the criticisms of objectivity that can be associated with this more qualitative type of evaluation, but identify how triangulation (cross-checking in data collection or analysis) can overcome this. Other types of evaluation include:

- **appreciative inquiry**, which was designed as an organisational tool and focuses on positive aspects for evaluation (Cooperrider and Srivastva, 1987; Reed, 2007), through a cycle that aims to discover what is good, imagine new goals and work out how to reach these collaboratively
- **layered evaluation**, which involves layers of reacting to those involved in a programme, learning from the analysis, changing behaviour and evaluating results.

Research papers on educational evaluation can be found in *Studies in Educational Evaluation* published by Elsevier (www.elsevier.com).

Biographical/Narrative

Accounts or narratives are types of interpretive research, with ethnographic elements, where situations are considered from the participants' perspectives. Clough (2002) identifies that narrative can be a useful approach in education as it has the capacity to uncover data that may be of importance in understanding the symbolism of educational issues. Narrative can include fictional stories, which can be analysed to identify underlying symbolisms. Narrative can be life stories (Goodson and Sikes, 2001) illustrating patterns in people's lives and can include analysis of critical incidents or critical events (Wragg, 1994), which have shaped their professional lives (such as good/bad teachers) or led them to a particular personal stance (for example, subject choices or attitudes to science). Narratives can also be historical accounts (McCulloch and Richardson, 2000), maybe looking at historical journals (such as Leonardo da Vinci's notebooks or Galileo's drawings and observational notes). Narratives have the advantage of being a flexible methodology, collecting data from the narrator's perspective and may identify rare events that might be missed by other methodologies. The disadvantages are that the reported narrative is constructed by the narrator and can be biased, or focus on memorable and negative incidents, rather than more common, unmemorable ones.

Case study

Case study research examines a phenomenon within its real-life context. It can involve either single or multiple case studies, and can provide quantitative and qualitative evidence to enable the researcher to understand the phenomenon (Bassey, 1999). So case study research can involve an in-depth, longitudinal examination of a single instance or event that illustrates the bigger picture, or provides understanding of why an event occurred. Single case studies may also have embedded cases or fields (Yin, 1984). Cases are not normally randomly selected, but chosen to test a certain theory (theoretical sampling) or chosen by information-oriented sampling, as opposed to random sampling. Yin (1984) also identifies three types of case study:

- **exploratory**, which may be a pilot study in preparation for future research
- **descriptive**, which may provide narrative accounts
- **explanatory**, which may test theories and hypotheses.

Strengths of case study as a methodology include its being strong in realism, so that it recognises the tensions and ambiguities in social truth, and that it allows tentative generalisations about the case, or from the case to wider education. A disadvantage is that case study can be seen as a default methodology by researchers who are attempting to identify suitable methodologies, but without any real understanding of why their research is a case study or how a case study looks. Other disadvantages are that the results may not be easily generalisable and researcher bias can be a real issue.

Ideology critique

Ideology critique asks questions that may be considered too self-evident to be put into question, encouraging critical engagement with ideological claims. It attempts to look beneath the obvious and self-evident in order to examine contradictions and counter arguments and claims (Adorno, 1981). Reflecting on ideologies and behaviours in action can help analysis of reality and 'truth' and previously assumed normal practices are revealed to be part of socially constructed realities. Ideology critique can entail critical incident analysis, involving description of the incident and attribution of meaning and significance to it, exploration of inconsistencies, paradoxes, contradictions and omissions, and assignation of explanations to explain anomalies and discrepancies. It may involve analysing discourse, situations and inter-reactions according to a Marxist or feminist perspective.

The initial steps for ideology critique, which help to elicit 'critical' or 'emancipatory' knowledge (Friesen, 2008) are:

1   identifying ideas or claims that are presented as obvious, inevitable or matter-of-fact in dominant bodies or sources of knowledge
2   scrutinising these ideas or claims in the context provided in other more marginal knowledge forms or sources
3   revealing through this scrutiny that behind dominant claims and ideas lie one or more politically charged and often contradictory ways of understanding the issue or phenomenon in question
4   using this underlying conflict as the basis for developing alternative forms of understanding and pointing to concrete possibilities for action.

Action research

Action research is a methodology in which the professional attempts to improve or develop practice in a cyclic way, by planning the next step of action or development as a result of analysis of the previous action or development (Elliot, 1991; McNiff with Whitehead, 2002). Action research thus involves reflective practice (Schön, 1983), and is distinct from many other forms of research in that the professional looks at his or her own practice (a form of practitioner research) and develops an aspect of it, rather than producing new knowledge (Elliott, 1991). Since action research is an inquiry conducted by the self into the self, questions are asked as to why you are doing something and how you can improve your practice. In this way, action research is an open-ended cycle of reflection, with no fixed hypothesis, but the idea that there is something to develop.

The action research cycle starts with a problem or dilemma and a plan to solve the problem or develop practice. The plan is made up of action steps and, after each one, the evidence produced is analysed and used to inform the planning of the next action step (hence the open-ended, flexible characteristics and the 'fuzziness' of the data). In this way action research involves a spiral or cycle of planning, action, monitoring and reflection. This is significantly different from other research methodologies and it needs to be analysed as the data are collected and written up in a particular way. The steps can become blurred and the researcher may find the action and reflection become synonymous.

Box 2 Reflective task on choosing the right methodology.

This task is designed to help you choose the correct methodology for you, and to match the research questions. It may also be an opportunity for you to explore the use of less familiar methodologies and broaden your research skills and understandings.

- What research methodology do you feel most comfortable with and why?
- What research methodology do you feel less comfortable with and why?
- Which research methodology best matches your research questions?

You may need to change your methodology, or your questions, to ensure there is a good match/coherence between them.

Methodological problems

One problem with deciding on methodology is a lack of understanding of what the different methodologies are capable of doing, and what they are not capable of doing. For example, there is a need to understand that positivist methodologies use quantitative data that tells you what, when, who etc. rather than qualitative data that tells you how and why. This quantitative data is analysed in order to prove or disprove a theory and does not look at underlying ideas, assumptions in the data or explain ambiguities in the data. Methodologies that use qualitative data involve inductive thought, which begins with observation or examination of events and uses these to make more general statements.

It is easy to decide a methodology with little thought as to what it actually says about the research being undertaken and how it should structure that research from planning to report. Often inexperienced practitioner researchers will default to methodologies that they feel comfortable with, so that any research that is involved in development in the classroom becomes action research and any research that occurs in a school becomes a case study. When you have chosen your methodology and questions, you need to read and reflect on that methodology so you can see what it looks like in action and plan accordingly.

Tooley and Darby (1998) found when examining research articles in four British journals that there were methodological problems associated with qualitative research. In particular, the case study journals tended to be studies of individual teachers, students, groups of teachers or students, and individual institutions. The problems are associated with the subjectivity of the methodology, sample bias and lack of triangulation, so that researchers often interpret data as they would like to see it (Wragg, 1994). This is a problem for many professionals engaged in partisan research (Tooley and Darby, 1998) as, without support, it is easy to analyse data to fit the assumptions they already have.

Bassey (1998, 1999) identified that much research, especially case study research, and educational and social research, produces 'fuzzy' generalisations. This can be considered as an excuse for bias. Hammersley (2001) argues that what Bassey (1999) has identified is not a distinct type of generalisation but a way of processing data. For the professional engaged in research these discussions can be confusing as well as encouraging – confusing because professionals like to believe that researchers agree, and encouraging for those that are at the level of development that enables them to engage in the debate.

References

Adorno, T. (1981) *Minima Moralia: Reflections from a damaged life*. London: Verso.

Ary, D., Cheser, L., Razavieh, A. and Sorenson, C. (2010) *Introduction to Research in Education*. Eighth edition. Belmont, California: Wadsworth Cengage Learning.

Babbie, E.R. (1973) *Survey Research Methods*. Belmont, California: Wadsworth Pub. Co.

Bassey, M. (1998) *Fuzzy Generalisation: An approach to building educational theory*. Paper presented at the British Educational Research Association annual conference, The Queen's University of Belfast, Northern Ireland, 27–30 August 1998. Available at: www.leeds.ac.uk/educol/documents/000000801.htm (accessed 15 July 2011).

Bassey, M. (1999) *Case Study Research in Educational Settings*. Buckingham: Open University Press.

Clough, P. (2002) *Narratives and Fictions in Educational Research*. Buckingham: Open University Press.

Cohen, L., Manion, L. and Morrison, K. (2000) *Research Methods in Education*. Fifth edition. London: Routledge Falmer.

Comte, A. (1856) *A General View of Positivism (Discours sur l'Esprit Positif,* 1844). New York: Cambridge University Press (2009). Available online via Google Books.

Cooperrider, D.L. and Srivastva, S. (1987) Appreciative inquiry in organisational life. *Research in Organisational Change and Development* 1, 129–169.

Cresswell, J.W. (2009) *Research Design. Qualitative, quantitative and mixed methods approaches 3rd edition*. London: Sage

Dash, N.K. (2010) Selection of the research paradigm and methodology. *Online Research Methods Resource for Teachers and Trainers*. Available at: www.celt.mmu.ac.uk/research methods/Modules/Selection_of_methodology/index.php (accessed 15 July 2011).

Elliott, J. (1991) *Action Research for Educational Change*. Buckingham: Open University Press.

Friesen, N. (2008) Critical theory: Ideology critique and the myths of e-learning. *Ubiquity* **9**(22) (3–9 June, 2008) http://ubiquity.acm.org/article.cfm?id=1386860 (accessed 15 July 2011).

Guba, E.G. and Lincoln, Y.S. (1995) Competing paradigms in qualitative research. In Denzin, N.K. and Lincoln, Y.S. (eds) *Handbook of Qualitative Research*. Thousand Oaks, California: Sage.

Goodson, I. and Sikes, P. (2001) *Life History Research in Educational Settings. Learning from lives*. Buckingham: Open University Press.

Habermas, J. (1970) *Knowledge and Human Interests* (Shapiro, J., translator). London: Heinemann.

Hammersley, M. (2001) On Michael Bassey's concept of the fuzzy generalisation. *Oxford Review of Education* (June 2001) 219–225.

Hammersley, M. (2007) *Methodological Paradigms in Educational Research*. London: TLRP. Available at: www.bera.ac.uk/methodological-paradigms-in-educational-research (accessed 15 July 2011).

Kirkup, C., Morrison, J. and Whetton, C. (2008) *Relationships Between A level Grades and SAT Scores in a Sample of UK Students*. National Foundation for Educational Research. Available at: www.nfer.ac.uk/nfer/publications/44412/44412.pdf (accessed 15 July 2011).

McCulloch, G. and Richardson, W. (2000) *Historical Research in Educational Settings*. Maidenhead: Open University Press.

McNiff, J. with Whitehead, J. (2002) *Action Research. Principles and practice*. Second edition. London: Routledge.

Parlett, M. and Hamilton, D. (1972) Evaluation as illumination: a new approach to the study of innovatory programmes. Reprinted in Parlett, M. and Dearden, G. (eds) (1977) *Introduction to Illuminative Evaluation: studies in higher education*. Cardiff-by-the-Sea, California, USA: Pacific Soundings Press. Guildford, UK: Society for Research into Higher Education.

Reed, J. (2007) *Appreciative Inquiry. Research for change*. London: Sage.

Schagen, A. (2009) A simple guide to voodoo statistics. *Education Journal* 112, 33–36. Available at: www.nfer.ac.uk/nfer/publications/55501/55501.pdf (accessed 15 July 2011).

Schön, D. (1983) *The Reflective Practitioner*. San Francisco: Jossey-Bass.

Tashakkori, A. and Teddlie, C. (eds) (2003) *Handbook of Mixed Methods in Social and Behavioral Research*. Thousand Oaks, California: Sage.

Tooley, J. and Darby, D. (1998) *Educational Research: a critique*. London: Ofsted.

Wragg, E.C. (1994) *An Introduction to Classroom Observation*. London: Routledge.

Yin, R.K. (1984) *Case Study Research: Design and methods*. Beverley Hills: Sage.

Websites

ASE (Association for Science Education)   www.ase.org.uk
Elsevier (publications)   www.elsevier.com
NFER (National Foundation for Educational Research)   www.nfer.ac.uk
TLRP (Teaching and Learning Research Programme)   www.tlrp.org

Useful books

McNiff, J. and Whitehead, J. (2011) *All You Need to Know about Action Research*. Second edition. London: Sage.

Thomas, C. (2011) *How to do Your Case Study. A guide for students and researchers*. London: Sage.

Chapter 22

Research methods

Jane Johnston and Rob Toplis

Research methods are the ways in which data are collected (often referred to as research instruments or tools). Most methods can be used in any research methodology, but some methods are more applicable and useful to particular types of research. For example, surveys are likely to involve questioning in the form of interviews or questionnaires, while action research may be more likely to use observation and analysis of results or work.

When deciding which methods to use in a particular piece of research it is important to ensure that they match or complement the philosophy underpinning the methodology, so that there is coherence in the approach of the research. Each method used should be critiqued so that its value in the specific research is clearly justified. The critique should consider:

- how the research questions can be answered through the methods
- the reliability of the methods used – that is, whether the method can be replicated with the same results
- the validity of the methods used – that is, whether the method collects truthful data
- how the researcher can ensure objectivity in employing the method and analysing the data
- how triangulation of methods (using more than one method to collect the same data) can enhance the data collected and increase validity.

Before choosing the methods to collect data, the researcher needs to decide who the research participants are. Sampling can be random, that is representative of the group, or theoretical chosen to test out a theory (see Chapter 19).

Questionnaires

Questionnaires can be a very useful way to collect quantitative data from a large sample and are therefore useful in surveys and evaluations (Gillham, 2007). There are a number of different types of questionnaires, such as:

- Likert-style questionnaires (Likert, 1932), which can measure attitudes by asking participants to identify statements with which they 'strongly agree', 'agree', 'disagree' or 'strongly disagree' (with sometimes a middle category of 'neither agree nor disagree' and/or 'not applicable')

- semantic differential questionnaires (Osgood, Suci and Tannenbaum, 1957), in which respondents choose along a scale between two bipolar adjectives (such as 'happy–sad', 'fun–boring', and so on)
- rating scales, in which respondents choose along a scale of 0 (low) to 10 (high)
- questionnaires with closed questions such as 'yes/no' or multiple-choice questions
- questionnaires with open-ended questions – these can be completely unstructured, involve word association, sentence completion, matching, identification or explanation of pictures; examples include the thematic apperception tests used in psychology and psychiatry (Cramer, 2004).

Questionnaires need to be carefully constructed to ensure that they are not misleading and that they collect the required data. For this reason, Cohen, Manion and Morrison (2000) recommend piloting questions. This can be done with a focus group who can give advice on the different interpretations of the questions. Alternately, pre-validated questionnaires can be used provided the necessary permissions are obtained from the researchers who originally constructed them.

Designing and administering your questionnaire to achieve the maximum return rate requires preparation that anticipates when, where and how respondents will most positively respond. The return rate of questionnaires can be low and decrease the validity, as respondents may be those who have particular issues to raise or may not answer truthfully. In addition, the sample size and number of respondents can affect both reliability and validity. Verification of data collected from questionnaires can be assisted by following up a sample of those completing the questionnaires and can lead to generation of theory. These follow-up interviews can help to illuminate the reasons behind answers and support analysis.

Interviews

Interviews have a number of advantages in terms of the data they can provide. When compared with, for example, survey methods their big advantage is the high quality of the data. Drever (1995) highlights this by pointing out the flexibility and completeness of the interview method when compared with questionnaires. Yin (1989) notes that:

'One of the most important sources of case study information is the interview.'

Yin (1989, p. 88)

There are several reasons for the use of interviews. Firstly, interviews are a method of exploring what people think about something and therefore provide data about how *they* see things and what *their* perceptions are (Woods, 1999). Interviews are therefore a method of reporting on human affairs through the eyes of specific interviewees (Yin, 1989). The interview becomes a probe and could be:

'... *potentially the most powerful and direct method of assessing a student's understanding.*'

Abdullah and Scaife (1997, p. 79)

Secondly, interviews can provide a way of 'making things happen' and 'stimulating the flow of data' (Woods, 1999, p. 62). This can be an important feature in encouraging some students to 'open up' and provide information that may not be forthcoming using other methods such as questionnaires. Finally, interview methods can provide a way of corroborating evidence obtained from other sources, allowing triangulation.

There are potential ethical problems with interview recording and transcription. Students' and teachers' names are likely to be used and heard on tape recordings; interview notes may contain names for later reference; the researcher may wish to remember certain personalities for later follow-up; research reports may be read years later. How are the informants to remain anonymous? It becomes the responsibility of the researcher to ensure anonymity and to make this clear to informants. Smith (1990, p. 262), in his classroom research in a Washington school, believed strongly that *every proper name in the story would be coded for anonymity'*. Should these codes be initials? Could these be recognised? Should they be code letters or numbers? The use of pseudonyms may have advantages of being more personal and realistic for the reader as well as being easier for the researcher to attach a personality to and remember. However, the use of pseudonyms brings the added responsibility of reflecting the ethnic and gender origins of the informants and to use names appropriate for the setting (time and place). This is not to highlight differences between the informants or the data they provide but to maintain the *'textual character'* (Delamont and Atkinson, 1995, p. 71) to ensure the credibility of the work.

Types of interview

The choice here seems to be between structured, semi-structured and open or unstructured interview methods.

The first of these, structured interviews, are likely to be narrow and inflexible and do not allow the opportunity to follow up interviewee responses, probe further or seek explanations by exploring individual viewpoints (Drever, 1995). Their very structure and the need to obtain answers to specific questions may even intimidate some individuals: they do not lend themselves to student–teacher rapport. The more tightly constrained approach may result in the gathering of data that strongly reflects the researcher's views or perspectives.

At first sight, open or unstructured interviews may appear to be a very promising approach; it is a method favoured by ethnographic researchers where the aim is to see the world through the other person's eyes (Drever, 1995). Woods (1999) notes that 'interview' is a rather inappropriate term, preferring to regard them as conversations or discussions, especially when views, thoughts, opinions or perspectives are openly sought. This then points to one of the two main problems with open-ended approaches – they take a great deal of time. Not only initial interviews are involved but also subsequent interviews to obtain more targeted information and to fill the gaps left by earlier interviews (Stake, 1998). In addition, a good deal of time can be spent handling the resulting data (Hegarty, 1985). The second problem concerns the very fact that the interviewer is trying to find out the interviewee's frame of reference rather than working within agreed and shared frames of reference in a single businesslike dialogue (Drever, 1995). One criticism of this latter view may be that a shared and agreed frame of reference is really too much to assume.

Semi-structured interviews can provide the best compromise. They have the advantages of being sufficiently structured to allow direction for specific questions to be answered, there is flexibility for those questions to be closed or more open-ended and there is sufficient interviewer control to allow further probing and exploration of answers (Drever, 1995). From the interviewee's standpoint, there is a fair degree of freedom of talk and expression and the opportunity to question the interviewer where necessary. The semi-structured interview can combine with other methods to produce data that are rich in content but more efficient in collection and analysis time.

Cohen *et al.* (2000) report a more detailed view of the focused interview where the distinctive feature is that there is prior analysis of the situation in which the subjects have been involved and this directs the interview.

We should also note, in passing, elite interviewing, which aims to collect data from those who have pre-eminent positions in their profession. Apart from the difficulties of gaining access, elite interviewees are strong characters who can easily dominate the interview to their own advantage, disrupting the data collection process.

Interview problems and approaches

Literature on the problems of the interview method indicate there are three main issues: interviewee reticence, interviewee bias and interviewer bias.

Interviewee reticence

The purpose of conducting interviews is to obtain information. This is impossible if, for various reasons, the subject is unable or unwilling to provide it. A degree of rapport must be established, as there is no point interviewing a resentful, indifferent or frightened student (White and Gunstone, 1992). Firstly, the environment must be suitable; a noisy area with the possibility of disturbance or distraction is far from conducive. This aspect may almost be taken for granted, but schools can be busy places with shouts, laughter and even normal conversations echoing along corridors and through hallways. Some preparation may be needed in order to find a place without these disturbances and without the possibility of interruption. Secondly, seating arrangements must be suitable. Walker (1985, p. 108) reports that Lawrence Stenhouse advocated sitting side-by-side instead of face-to-face in order to avoid any idea of confrontation. (Lawrence Stenhouse (1926–1982) was an educational thinker who promoted practitioner research. He worked at the Centre for Applied Research in Education (CARE) at the University of East Anglia). Sitting side-by-side may make eye contact difficult but any relaxed seating arrangement may help reduce reticence from the interviewee. An interview is, after all, a form of discussion and not an interrogation. In the study reported by Stenhouse a seating arrangement around a table was used. Thirdly, the personal attitudes and approaches of the interviewer can build rapport. Interviewees must feel as comfortable and secure as possible and in order to make this so a number of approaches are important.

The first step combines a very brief explanation of what the research is about with an ethical discussion in which permission must be gained to interview the subject. As part of this, assurances must be made concerning anonymity – apart from the ethical standpoint, this simple courtesy may help the interviewee to see the importance of the research and draw them into the process.

As a second step it is important to make the subjects aware that the questions are in no way a test, they will not be marked and nobody will be informed about their performance (White and Gunstone, 1992).

A third aspect to reducing reticence is the personal approach taken by the interviewer. This is a problem for teachers in their own school where their different roles as teacher, researcher and interviewer may impinge on and interact with one another (Powney and Watts, 1987). With the assurances from the second step about questions not being related to tests or marks, it should be possible to reduce the conflict of roles between the student and teacher. However, this can only happen if the teacher is fully aware of these roles and can take the sometimes difficult steps to change their behaviour. White and Gunstone summarise this conflict:

> 'Interviewers must not be judgmental, lest they inhibit the responses. It is not easy for a teacher to refrain from comment when a student says something either perceptive or misguided. The teacher needs to follow interviewer's practice of neutral comments such as "Uh-huh" and "Can you tell me more about that?", and restrain from common classroom responses such as "good", "correct" and "no, that's wrong".'

White and Gunstone (1992, pp. 68–69)

Group interviews (sometimes referred to as focus groups) may be a useful approach to reducing reticence from individual subjects. Although this may have the disadvantage of one or two individuals dominating the conversation while others take a more passive role (Drever, 1995; Wellington, 1996), confidence is likely to be much greater. In this situation, audio recording *and* note taking are important methods for capturing all contributions to the discussion although interviewee reticence may again become apparent with the use of audio recorders. Audio recording can provide a full and accurate record but many people find it intrusive and cumbersome (Walker, 1985). Woods (1999) recognises the benefit of audio recording but suggests that where people are dubious about its use there may be some negotiation, such as the interviewee's ownership of the recorded data being made clear. It is essential to request subjects' permission to record interviews. Concerns can be overcome if students are allowed to listen to themselves after the recording: this can be a motivating strategy (Abdullah and Scaife (1997) and also helps to verify interpretations.

On a purely practical level, audio recording has the disadvantage of recording all the unwanted sound as well as what is wanted. This can be reduced by careful selection of rooms, using a pad between the table and recorder and careful positioning of the microphone.

One disadvantage of recording detailed and accurate data means that there is likely to be a great deal of time spent transcribing it. This can be reduced somewhat by selecting certain, illustrative quotes and using narrative where appropriate. However, critics of this approach would suggest that one of the advantages of audio recording, objectivity, has now been diminished by the researcher's subjective interpretation of the dialogue. Woods (1999, p. 82) suggests a possible solution to this problem, involving two stages. The first involves listening to the whole recording, making an index and any notes on its contents and then, during the second stage, selecting those sections for transcribing.

The final method of reducing reticence in interviewees is the selection of those individuals who will provide the most valuable data: the key informants. A good informant is more than just an interview 'subject' as he or she has the knowledge and experience, is articulate and has the time to be interviewed (Stake, 1998); good informants *are often critical to the success of the case study* (Yin, 1989, p. 89).

Interviewee bias

Interview data are based on verbal reports and therefore on the observations and perceptions of the interviewees. Because of their interpretative nature, the data are prone to varying degrees of bias and steps must be taken to become aware of the sources of bias and take these into account when dealing with the design and validity of interviews. Woods (1999) mentions a number of influences such as ulterior motives, values and traumatic incidents that may effect the information. In their discussion based on the question 'How do you know the informant is telling the truth?' (although there are discussions in the research community about what is 'truth'), Dean and Whyte (1969) categorise interviewee's statements into two main groups: their reports on subjective data and their reporting of objective data (Dean and Whyte use the term 'informant' to mean any interviewee rather than the idea of a 'key informant' as mentioned above). When discussing informants' feelings or subjective reporting they refer to a number of factors such as ulterior motives, bars to spontaneity, a desire to please the interviewer, and idiosyncratic factors that may change views from one interview to another. Major sources of distortion in reports of objective data include the lack of direct observation or recollection of the observation, inaccurate observation due to selective perception, and conscious or unconscious modification of the facts.

Interviewer bias

The whole point of the interview method is to:

> '... secure what is within the minds of the interviewees, uncoloured and unaffected by the interviewer.'

> Woods (1999, p. 6)

Although this was quoted in the context of unstructured interviews, it applies equally to semi-structured approaches where the bias of the interviewer must be minimised. This takes a great deal of awareness as some bias may be almost unconscious or taken for granted. Interviewers may have values, judgments or backgrounds that are not shared by, or may be in direct conflict with, the interviewee. The interviewer must adopt a position of complete neutrality. Wellington (1996, p. 32) provides examples of three types of questions to avoid:

- double-barrelled questions containing two questions in one
- two-in-one questions where two opposites are combined, such as 'What are the advantages and disadvantages of ...'
- loaded questions that are emotionally charged.

Another important and avoidable source of interviewer bias in questioning is the use of prompts rather than probes. Drever (1995) mentions that prompts are used to encourage interviewees to answer and to ensure that they say as much as they can or wish to. However, in his examples they are innocuous questions such as 'Anything else?' or quotations from published material that could be regarded as stimuli. It is the use of prompts that provide suggestions or 'put words into the mouths' of interviewees that must be avoided at all costs – otherwise that section of the interview becomes invalid and must be ignored. The example, 'Apart from your results, measuring and temperatures, what else did you talk about? Did you have a general chit-chat some of the time?' demonstrates not only the 'putting words into the mouth' problem but also indicates a certain amount of impatience on the part of the interviewer to obtain data, and this itself brings in bias. Probes, on the other hand, can be used to expand detail and understanding and are valuable in open-ended questioning (Wellington, 1996).

The final source of interviewer bias is the desire to teach. If there is a less than satisfactory response there is 'a temptation to put the student right, to explain, to inform' (White and Gunstone, 1992, p. 69). After years of teaching, this is an understandable, almost unconscious, habit but one that introduces bias and diminishes the involvement of the interviewee.

Discussions

Discussions are less formal than interviews and can help to verify and illuminate data collected in other ways. Discussions may be fluid in nature to allow for unplanned lines of thought and unexpected data arising from these. Alternatively, a discussion might be structured to ensure that answers to particular questions are obtained, or be an open forum involving focus groups in some active participation or negotiation.

The use of focus groups (Morgan, 1997) can be helpful in gaining different perspectives about the same issue. In addition, as already noted, focus groups can help to boost the participants' confidence and reduce reticence, but they are not the best context in which to elicit individual responses. Indeed, there is a danger that a dominant character could skew the information gathered by preventing others from fully expressing their own views.

The focus group can provide an insight into and data about the interactions between participants and draws the group's attitudes, feelings, beliefs, experiences and reactions. This kind of data, about relationships, interactions and influence, cannot be collected using other methods. Focus group discussions can be particularly useful when there are power differences between groups, when the interactions of the groups and the language they use are analysed and opinions on an issue are being elicited (Morgan and Kreuger, 1993).

The moderator of the group (who is not necessarily the researcher) has a difficult role and requires good interpersonal and leadership skills. A problem of discussions is that if the moderator does not use such skills, he or she can inadvertently lead the participants and this will affect the validity of results.

A discussion can be used at the start of a research project, or during it, or even at the end. It can help to evaluate or triangulate data collected using different methods. Data can be captured on video, stored as audio files or summarised in a notebook, and transcripts of audio and video recordings can support self-evaluation and help to identify overlooked interactions and ideas. As noted in the previous section (page 204), recording may affect the quality of the data as, for example, some group members may not disclose data if it is obviously being recorded.

Observation

Observation can help the researcher to understand processes, events and development. Observation as a research method can develop from reflective practice and support learning and teaching (Pollard, 2005; Gillham, 2008). Observation is more than just looking. It involves watching closely, critical listening, discussing or questioning, analysing work/answers/observations. Observations can be focused, so that the observer is looking for something specific. or they can be unfocused, thus not excluding interesting but unexpected events, and can support generation of theory.

The observer can be inside the observations (participant observation) or outside the observations (non-participant observation) – for example, the observer may be the classroom teacher involved in the teaching or learning, or an independent observer 'looking on'. Participant observation can involve an element of ethnographic (naturalistic) research, but this only really happens if the researcher is part of the research group being studied – for example, if students are used as researchers. Non-participant observations are more objective and less open to problems of external validity, but the observer can affect the data collected as the observed may not behave in normal ways. All observations need to be analysed and discussed with others for verification, to ensure the observer does not assign meaning to the data that is not valid.

Analysis of textual data

Products, outcomes or documents can be collected and analysed to help answer research questions. These may include test results, students' work, or diaries/journals. Collecting data from children has the same problems as for any assessment, as different meanings can be assigned to the outcome and this can affect validity. This can be overcome in part by triangulation – using other methods to collect similar data, or questioning children about their outcomes. Evidence collected from children can be a powerful way to find out about them and, in action research, helps the researcher to make decisions to continue to support them in the next cycle of research. Other methods to support triangulation and add validity to the research include observation and narratives.

Other products, outcomes and documents that can be collected are teacher evaluation or appraisal documents, school policies or minutes of meetings. They can be useful in historical or comparative research and enable such aspects as value, learning and efficiency to be considered.

Images

Photographs provide a snapshot of action in context. They can provide evidence of actions, teaching and learning, and be valuable evidence in research. They are usually used in qualitative approaches and can help to validate data collected using other methods.

Photographs and videos can be taken overtly or covertly, the advantage of the latter approach being that it may not affect the behaviour of those being photographed. Since the ethics of using images for research purposes necessitates permissions from parents and students, completely covert photography may not be possible – but once permissions have been received, covert photographs or videos can be taken. Prosser and Schwartz (1998) identify that photography is a threatening method, although it can be less threatening if the researched participants are involved in the capture of images, with, for example, students as researchers (Schratz and Steiner-Löffler, 1998; Thomson, 2008).

All images need to be able to tell a story and can be a rich source of qualitative evidence. Video recordings can also provide rich data in the form of actions, talk, body language and context. Apart from ethical issues, validity can be problematic with images. However, this can be improved by triangulation; allowing the participants to tell the story behind the image.

Images can also be used for stimulated recall, to promote the interviewee providing a richer description or explanation of an event or part of a lesson (Calderhead, 1981). There is a danger that the post-event account may not tally with what the interviewee had in mind at the time, and this is difficult to investigate. It is open to reflective justification.

Narratives

Narratives can use the participants' own voices as data. Narrative can enable unexpected data to be collected (perhaps through a reflective journal) and help illumination and understanding of data and analysis. Narratives can be more than anecdotes and provide powerful insights into situations. They can be in the form of case study exemplars of practice or research, or identification of critical incidents in the participant's life. Sometimes the narrative is supported by images, such as photographs or drawings (Leitch, 2008). The story can be told by different participants, triangulating data and providing a more vivid and comprehensive picture of the action, event or situation being described or focused upon. A story told from different perspectives allows layers of data to be analysed and a more valid (truthful) picture begins to be revealed.

Recent innovations in technology have provided improvement in clarity of audio recording, less obtrusive recording instruments, increased storage potential, and access to digital enhancement, all of which aid capture and utilisation of the exact words of a narrative (for example, Fernandes and Griffiths, 2007; Murthy, 2008).

Box 1 Reflective task on the reliability, validity and objectivity of research methods.

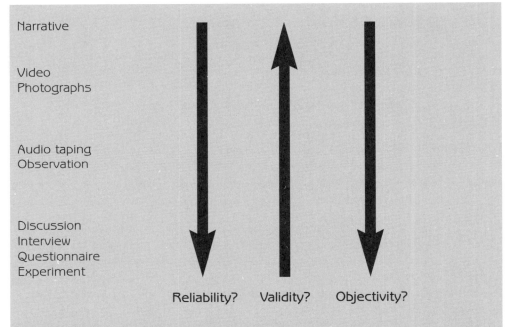

Narrative

Video
Photographs

Audio taping
Observation

Discussion
Interview
Questionnaire
Experiment

Reliability?   Validity?   Objectivity?

Figure 1 Reliability, validity and objectivity of research methods

Look at the figure. Review each research method. Consider whether you have used it and how reliable you think it is.

Consider the reliability/validity/objectivity arrows. Do you agree that the more valid the method, the more unreliable it is? Or the more reliable, the less valid? Or the greater the validity, the greater the problems with objectivity?

Which methods could you use in your research? Choose a method with greater validity and consider how you could use it in your research. How would you ensure reliability, validity and objectivity?

References

Abdullah, A. and Scaife, J. (1997) Using interviews to assess children's understanding of science concepts. *School Science Review* **78**(285) 79–84.

Calderhead, J. (1981) Stimulated recall: a method for research on teaching. *British Journal of Educational Psychology* **51**(2) 211–217.

Cohen, L., Manion, L. and Morrison, K. (2000) *Research Methods in Education*. Fifth edition. London: Routledge Falmer.

Cramer, P. (2004) *Storytelling, Narrative, and the Thematic Apperception Test*. New York: Guilford Press.

Dean, J.P. and Whyte, W.F. (1969) How do you know the informant is telling the truth? In McCall, G.J. and Simmons, J.L. (eds) *Issues in Participant Observation: A text and reader* (pp. 105–115). Reading, Massachusetts: Addison-Wesley.

Delamont, S. and Atkinson, P. (1995) A green hill far away? Pseudonyms in educational ethnography. In Delamont, S. and Atkinson, P. (eds) *Fighting Familiarity* (pp. 71–84). Cresskill, New Jersey: Hampton Press.

Drever, R. (1995) *Using Semi-Structured Interviews in Small-Scale Research*. Edinburgh: The Scottish Council for Research in Education.

Fernandes, R.S. and Griffiths, S. (2007) Portable MP3 players: innovative devices for recording qualitative interviews. *Nurse Research* **15**(1) 7–15.

Gillham, B. (2007) *Developing a Questionnaire*. Second edition. London: Continuum.

Gillham, B. (2008) *Observation Techniques. Structured to unstructured.* London: Continuum.

Hegarty, S. (1985) Introduction. In Hegarty, S. and Evans, P. (eds) *Research and Evaluation Methods in Special Education* (pp. 109–113). Windsor: NFER-Nelson.

Leitch, R. (2008) Creatively researching children's narratives through images and drawings. In Thomson, P. (ed) *Doing Visual Research with Children and Young People*. London: Routledge Falmer.

Likert, R. (1932) *A Technique for the Measurement of Attitudes*. New York: Columbia University Press.

Morgan D.L. (1997) *Focus Groups as Qualitative Research*. Second edition. London: Sage.

Morgan D.L. and Kreuger R.A. (1993) When to use focus groups and why. In Morgan, D.L. (ed) *Successful Focus Groups*. London: Sage.

Murthy D (2008) Digital ethnography. An examination of new technologies for social research. *Sociology* **42**(5) 837–855.

Osgood, C.E., Suci, G. and Tannenbaum, P. (1957) *The Measurement of Meaning*. University of Illinois: University of Illinois Press.

Pollard, A. (2005) *Reflective Teaching: Evidence-informed professional practice*. Second edition. London: Continuum.

Powney, J. and Watts, M. (1987) *Interviewing in Educational Research*. London: Routledge and Kegan Paul.

Prosser, J. and Schwartz, D. (1998) Photographs within the sociological research process. In Prosser, J. (ed) *Image-Based Research. A sourcebook for qualitative researchers*. London: Routledge Falmer.

Schratz, M. and Steiner-Löffler, U. (1998) Pupils using photographs in school self-evaluation. In Prosser, J. (ed) *Image-Based Research. A sourcebook for qualitative researchers.* London: Routledge Falmer.

Smith, L. (1990) Ethics in qualitative field research: an individual perspective. In Eisner, E.W. and Peshkin, A. (eds) *Qualitative Inquiry in Education* (pp. 258–276). New York: Teachers College Press.

Stake, R.E. (1998) Case studies. In Denzin, N.K. and Lincoln, Y.S. (eds) *Strategies of Qualitative Inquiry* (pp. 86–109). Thousand Oaks, California: Sage.

Thomson, P. (2008) (ed) *Doing Visual Research with Children and Young People.* London: Routledge Falmer.

Walker, R. (1985) *Doing Research. A handbook for teachers.* London: Methuen.

Wellington, J. (1996) *Methods and Issues in Educational Research.* Sheffield: University of Sheffield Division of Education, Papers in Education.

White, R. and Gunstone, R. (1992) *Probing Understanding.* London: Falmer Press.

Woods, P. (1999) *Successful Writing for Qualitative Research.* London: Routledge.

Yin, R. (1989) *Case Study Research. Design and methods.* Revised edition. Newbury Park, California: Sage.

Chapter 23

Analysing data

Jane Johnston

Once data have been collected using a variety of methods (Chapter 22), they need to be presented in the thesis. Raw data presented in the research report can be unfathomable to the reader and so it needs to be sorted and analysed. The purpose of the Outcomes and Analysis section of any piece of research is to present and analyse data.

What is analysis?

Analysis involves the researcher in attempting to understand, clarify or illuminate. Quantitative data can be analysed to identify 'what' and 'how many'; when there is a qualitative element to the data, the analysis can be extended to answer some 'why' and 'how' questions. The analysis should show understanding of the underlying assumptions, tensions and ambiguities in the data. It should identify clarity in pinpointing the issues or factors underpinning situations. Qualitative data should illuminate the meaning of data, such as revealing why something has happened, or why there is a particular response. Wolcott (1994) identifies distinctions between description, analysis and interpretation, with analysis being the examination of data using systematic and standardised measures and interpretation involving understanding of the data using careful reflection and intuition. This makes a distinction between quantitative and qualitative analysis, which may be unhelpful, as it appears to reduce qualitative analysis to a lesser status.

Box 1 Reflective task on analysis skills.

How good are you at analysing? Consider the following questions and use the answers to reflect on your analytical ability.

- Do you accept what you see and hear, or do you question evidence?
- How do you find out the meanings behind evidence?
- Why do you think it is important to understand hidden meanings?
- How does understanding, as opposed to knowledge, help you in your professional work?
- How do you ensure objectivity when analysing evidence?
- How do you verify ideas from analysis?

Look at the section 'What is analysis?' above and identify which aspects you need to develop.

Come back to this reflective task when you have read the chapter and review your position. Identify what you need to do to develop your analytical skills.

Analysing quantitative data

If the researcher has collected quantitative data, it is important to understand what statistical analysis techniques are best used to help make sense of the data (see, for example, Lewis, 1967; Pell and Fogelman, 2007). If the data are in the form of questionnaire results perhaps using a single sample and a Likert scale (Likert, 1932), a Wilcoxon Sign Test could clarify the results (Wilcoxon, 1945). The Wilcoxon signed-rank test is a paired different (non-parametric statistical) hypothesis test which can be used when comparing two related samples or repeated measurements on a single sample to ascertain differences. The Likert scale is commonly used in questionnaires to ascertain the participants' level of agreement with statements (completely agree, agree, disagree, completely disagree).

If there is data from two surveys or tests and the significant difference between the two is to be analysed, a Mann-Whitney rank test would be appropriate. A chi-squared test could be used to compare two groups, or a correlation test employed to see how two sets of data are linked.

There are many statistical forms of analysis, with many potential pitfalls, that cannot be dealt with here. The reader who wishes to delve into these further should read, for example, Diamond and Jefferies (2000) in their publication on beginning statistics for social science researchers.

Analysing observations

When analysing data from observation, the researcher attempts to understand what is happening, why individuals react in certain ways and in certain situations. The researcher looks underneath the obvious and reveals why something happens. They may use the analysis to resolve problems and clarify purposes and intentions. Through analysis, the researcher may identify the main factors affecting the practice being researched, or the issues emerging from the data collected, or the components involved in the actions being researched. This will help the researcher to understand the data.

Videoed or photographed observations can be analysed using analytical software, or viewed and the main actions noted and categorised. The analytical framework should be decided at the research design stage when decisions are made about what observations or photographs to take, or an observational schedule is prepared. However, sometimes grounded theory (Glaser and Strauss, 1967) may be used and the analytical framework may emerge from the data after initial analysis. Triangulation of analysis can be achieved by comparing observations with a co-researcher or critical friend, or asking observed participants to verify analysis. Both observations and photographs may be analysed and validated during the course of the data collection process (Prosser and Schwartz, 1998), so that decisions on further data collection can be made. Photographs should be looked at holistically before micro-analysis occurs. In research where students were also co-researchers (Schratz and Steiner-Löffler, 1998; Haw, 2008), choice of photographs was used as part of the analysis, so the students chose the analytical framework in this way.

Analysing narratives

Danto (1985) argues that the basic structure of knowledge is narrative. Narrative provides a way of organising the complex forms of experience so that they can be told, recounted and hence made predictable. It is by being able to tell a story again and again that a sense of stability, identity, recognisability and hence action and learning becomes possible. Despite the flux and the change that takes place, a story points to recurrent features and essential structures and processes.

Analysis of narrative can help to understand why something has happened or why an idea is held, provide alternative explanations for events or ideas, and help the researcher to look at a situation from other perspectives. Bassey (1999) presented interview data from various sources as a series of letters from a fictional trainee teacher. He ensured the trustworthiness of the interpretation through triangulation of the analysis, by asking the interviewees for comment. Bassey proposes several advantages to the use of fiction as a technique in research writing – for example:

- it provides a coherent and readable interpretation of different data sources
- incidents remain vivid and powerfully expressed, but are not traceable to any one source.

Stronach and MacLure (1997) offer a different interpretation of the same interview data to illustrate the 'struggle' between researchers and their subject. The contrast between the portraits is fascinating in itself. The meta-analysis of the methods raises important questions about the roles of research and researchers. Handy's (1989) study uses anecdotes as vehicles for conveying considerable amounts of information and also for facilitating understanding, persuading and learning. The anecdotes are not used in any rigorous manner, but are still effective because they can be used in relation to other experiences.

Narrative analyses involve the identification of sequential data (a timeline of an event) and contexts (the situation, people involved and so on). Sequences may be of different kinds, such as cause–effect sequences where a particular stimulus or input is associated with a particular response or output. There may also be several possible outputs associated with a particular input. In addition, the relationship may be merely a correlation without necessarily having any causal connection. The context is of two kinds: symbolic and material. A symbolic context involves all the values, norms, beliefs, and linguistic and cultural forms of a given society or group. A material context refers to the resources, and the nature of the physical environment, including the built environment of housing, roads and so on. The material context can, of course, have symbolic import just as the symbolic context can have a material form. In analysing narrative, the researcher explores the main characters, their beliefs, values and the ways in which the narrative relates experience and relationships. Consideration of narrative from different participants – for example, students, teachers and parents – may provide valuable insights into the different views they hold about themselves, their roles in the context and the relationships between them. Gender or power relationships may be explored – for example, the relationship between teachers and the boys and girls they teach may be analysed.

The end result of a narrative is essentially a case study (Bassey, 1999), providing a rich data base which can be analysed in a number of different ways, and – importantly – a holistic view, rather than a *'fragmented approach of statistical strategies'* (Schostak, 2010).

Analysing interviews

In analysing narrative or answers to questions, the researcher will have to scratch beneath the surface of what is being said, to analyse the words and understand the explicit and implicit meanings. One way to ensure that interview data are rich for analysis is to ask analytical questions ('how?' and 'why?' and 'so what?') as opposed to descriptive questions ('when?' and 'where?' and 'what?').

Wysocki and Lynch (2007) identify the difficulty of transcribing taped interviews accurately. The spoken word is less articulate than the written word and contains many contractions, changes of direction, hesitations and inconsistencies that make sense in dialogue but not in written form. When these have been removed in the transcript and some sense made of the words, the end result is very different from the social encounter of the actual interview (Cohen, Manion and Morrison, 2000) and will contain much of the researcher's understanding. This makes it even more important to ask the interviewees for verification of meanings.

The data from interviews can be collated and categorised, maybe according to predefined categories relating to the actual questions, or according to themes arising from the analysis. These may include the occurrence of themes or words in the interview, or patterns in the themes. It may include behaviours observed during the interview, or relationships between interviewees, their answers and behaviours. Even though the data can be categorised, it is likely that much of the analysis will be interpretative (Cohen *et al.* 2000; Wolcott, 2009), or have an interpretative element, and this poses analytical difficulties, but has the advantage of leading to different levels of interpretation and validity.

Analysis in action research

In action research methodology (Chapter 21), the research cycle demands that analysis occurs during and after each action research step and informs the next cycle of research. Data can be collected using a variety of methods (Chapter 22) in order to answer the research questions. As the data are analysed new issues, themes or questions may be revealed and these can be used to inform the researcher on both the success of the action research development and new avenues for research uncovered (Elliott, 1991). If the analysis is not an on-going part of the process and does not inform each step of the research, then the research is not action research.

Deepening analysis

In order to be deeply analytic, the researcher should look more deeply at events, situations and evidence, and begin to identify different layers of analysis. This may involve:

- mining the data to different depths
- unwrapping the layers of the data to uncover different and maybe hidden meanings
- sorting data in different ways
- exploring chronology or history of events
- viewing data from a number of different perspectives
- identifying patterns in the data.

In this way, deep analysis may lead to more profound understanding of the whole data set in context, of individual pieces of data, and of the way the individual parts interact and make a whole. In addition, deep qualitative analysis should *'confound issues, revealing them in their complexity, rather than reducing them to simple explanation'* (Wolcott, 2009, p. 32). It should explore tensions, expose anomalies and ambiguities, and develop argument (see Chapter 20 for more about the development of persuasive arguments). Wolcott (2009) conceptualises qualitative research as a 'tree', with:

> *'… the major research activities as roots penetrating deep into the events of everyday life through the three ways of gathering data: examining, enquiring, and experiencing. Firmly anchored in, and drawing nourishment through, these three roots is a solid 'trunk' that represents the dominant core activity of qualitative research: participant observation. Emanating from the trunk are sturdy limbs that represent major variations of qualitative research. These limbs require varying degrees of personal involvement of the researcher at interviewing or observing. Each of these branches in turn has smaller branches that collectively comprise every possible strategy available from that branch.'*

Wolcott (2009, p. 82)

These different branches (methods) can be a way to deepen analysis, by exploring the similarities and differences in the data acquired using different methods. Similarities can be the closest you can get, in qualitative data analysis, to the truth and exploration of the reasons for differences can also support validity.

Concept (mind) mapping can be a way to organise and represent relationships between concepts or knowledge (Novak and Gowan, 1984). The difference between a concept map and a brainstorm is that on a concept map the relationships between the concepts are identified with words or phrases along the linking arrows. The researcher can create a concept map using the data collected and analyse it by identifying links, patterns and gaps in the data. The research participants can also be asked to sort the data and create individual or group concept maps and in this way support the analysis and provide a form of triangulation. Alternatively, the researcher can create a concept map from the data collected and then this analysis can be discussed with the research participants to increase validity.

The use of Ishikawa diagrams (fishbone diagram Fgure 1) can also be a way to help sort data for analysis. Ishikawa diagrams were created in Japan by Kaoru Ishikawa to identify cause and effect in product design. They are called fishbone diagrams because of their shape. In this analysis, causes are placed along each 'bone' and may include categories such as people, methods, machines, materials, measurements and environment.

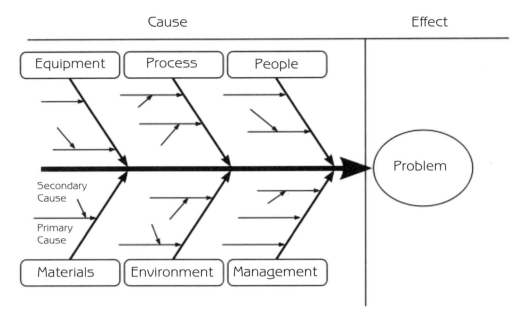

Figure 1 Fishbone diagram.

Ishikawa diagrams have been used in education to identify and list all the factors that are conditioning a problem or issue to be researched. They are also a group problem analysis technique that can be used with research participants as a way to collect and analyse data at hand. Steps in using the Ishikawa diagram are:

1   identification of a problem, which is written in a box on one side of the diagram (the 'fish head'), with a line drawn across the page
2   identification of the major factors influencing the problem (people, policies, practices, resources, external factors and so on) – each factor can be placed along a 'fishbone'
3   identification of possible causes for each factor by research participants, shown as smaller lines coming off the 'bones' of the fish; complex factors can be broken up into even smaller parts to aid analysis
4   analysis of the resulting diagram to identify all the causes of the problem.

Another way to identify and analyse factors affecting areas or problems is to use 'force field analysis', which, like an Ishikawa diagram, can provide a framework for analysing factors in social situations, and was designed specifically for this purpose by Lewin (1943). It recognises the dynamic nature of social situations and allows for this. Force field analysis involves identifying the current context and situation and also the desired situation or development. Then the factors supporting change and movement towards the desired situation are identified, as well as the factors inhibiting the development. These can be mapped diagrammatically so that an individual or group analysis can identify the 'field' and the motives, values, needs, moods, goals, anxieties and ideals associated with the change or development.

Current State

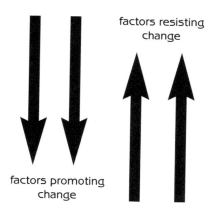

factors resisting
change

factors promoting
change

Desired State

Figure 2 Force field analysis

Meta-analysis, or the analysis of other analyses, has the advantage of making good use of small-scale research that on its own may be of limited value in extending knowledge in the area (Fitz-Gibbon, 1985). Cooper (2010) and Fitz-Gibbon (1985) identify steps to meta-analysis, which include:

1 identifying the research questions
2 finding the quality studies that can inform the meta-analysis
3 analysing the data from the studies and correlating findings, or grouping evidence/ primary analyses
4 interpreting from the newly sorted and analysed evidence.

Box 2 Reflective task on choosing analytical techniques.

> The analytical structure can be decided at the planning stage of the research process (see Chapter 19), although it may be adapted later at the analysis stage, or it may not be decided until the later stages, as theory emerges from the research.
>
> • What type of analysis do you feel most comfortable with?
> • Why do you feel more comfortable with this type of analysis?
>
> Consider the data you are collecting in your current research.
>
> • How could other analytical techniques add to the research and increase validity?
> • How can you develop your analytical skills?
> • Why would this development aid your ability as a researcher?

References

Bassey, M. (1999) *Case Study Research in Educational Settings.* Buckingham: Open University Press.

Cohen, L., Manion, L. and Morrison, K. (2000) *Research Methods in Education.* Fifth edition. London: Routledge Falmer.

Cooper, H. (2010) *Research Synthesis and Meta-Analysis. A step by step approach.* Fourth edition. Thousand Oaks, California: Sage.

Danto, A.C. (1985) *Narration and Knowledge.* New York: Columbia University Press.

Diamond, I. and Jefferies, J. (2000) *Beginning Statistics. An introduction for social scientists.* Thousand Oaks, California: Sage.

Elliott, J. (1991) *Action Research for Educational Change.* Buckingham: Open University Press.

Fitz-Gibbon, C.T. (1985) The implications of meta-analysis for educational research. *British Educational Research Journal,* **11**(1) 45–49.

Glaser, B.G. and Strauss, A. (1967) *Discovery of Grounded Theory. Strategies for qualitative research.* Mill Valley, California: Sociology Press.

Handy, C. (1989) *The Age of Unreason.* Arrow Books.

Haw, K. (2008) 'Voice' and video. Seen, heard and listened to? In Thomson, P. (ed) *Doing Visual Research with Children and Young People.* London: Routledge Falmer.

Lewin, K. (1943) Defining the field at a given time. *Psychological Review* **50**, 292–310.

Lewis, D. (1967) *Statistical Methods in Education.* London: University of London Press.

Likert, R. (1932) *A Technique for the Measurement of Attitudes.* New York: Columbia University Press.

Novak, J. and Gowan, D.B. (1984) *Learning How to Learn.* Cambridge: Cambridge University Press.

Pell, A. and Fogelman, K. (2007) Analysing quantitative data. In Briggs, A. and Coleman, M. (eds) *Research Methods in Educational Leadership and Management.* London: Sage.

Prosser, J. and Schwartz, D. (1998) Photographs within the sociological research process. In Prosser, J. (ed) *Image-Based Research. A sourcebook for qualitative researchers.* London: Routledge Falmer.

Schostak, J.F. (2010) *Narrative as a Vehicle for Research.* Inquiry Learning Unit. Available at: www.enquirylearning.net/ELU/Issues/Research/Res3.html (accessed 15 July 2011).

Schratz, M. and Steiner-Löffler, U. (1998) Pupils using photographs in school self-evaluation. In Prosser, J. (ed) *Image-Based Research. A sourcebook for qualitative researchers.* London: Routledge Falmer.

Stronach, I. and MacLure, B. (1997) *Educational Research Undone: The postmodern embrace.* Buckingham: Open University Press.

Wilcoxon, F. (1945) Individual comparisons by ranking methods. *Biometrics* **1**, 80–83.

Wolcott, H.F. (1994) *Transforming Qualitative Data: Description, analysis and interpretation.* Thousand Oaks, California: Sage.

Wolcott, H.F. (2009) *Writing Up Qualitative Research.* Third edition. Thousand Oaks, California: Sage

Wysocki, A.F. and Lynch, D.A. (2007) *Compose, Design, Advocate.* Harlow: Pearsons.

Chapter 24

Synthesis of ideas

Jane Johnston

What is synthesis?

Synthesis is a very important skill that enables the researcher to draw upon a wide range of primary and secondary analysis, assemble and connect it together, in order to make sense of and discuss the research findings. Synthesis may involve drawing together analysis from different studies, although it should not be mistaken for the meta-analysis described in Chapter 23, in which research findings from a range of studies are analysed to answer new questions or provide new insights into the area (Cooper, 2010). Neither should it be mistaken for the synthesis that occurs in reviewing the literature in the area (see Chapter 20). Synthesis in this context (in individual research projects) involves combining the analysis of literature and the analysis of primary data, and critical discussion of the implications arising out of them. It attempts to make sense of the analysis from primary data and secondary data (literature), drawing inferences from the findings. In synthesising data, the researcher may produce new ideas or models and make tentative generalisations. In qualitative research, this may be the fuzzy generalisations advocated by Bassey (1998, 1999), but importantly in any small-scale practitioner research, this is likely to be very tentative and focused on the researcher's practice and context. We must always acknowledge the danger of researcher bias that can happen, and the use of critical friends to mitigate this. In larger-scale research, generalisations still need to be tentative, but applicability to other similar contexts is more certain.

Gardner (2007) identifies that the ability to synthesise is an intellectual skill of increasing importance in modern society. He argues that in modern society where sources of information are rapidly increasing it is important to be able to:

- survey a wide range of sources or experiences
- make decisions about what is important or not
- combine information in a meaningful way
- communicate that information in an understandable way.

This is because in many professions, including teaching, and careers in science and communication, those involved need to be able to synthesise huge amounts of information. A synthesising mind will have an area of expertise (a discipline), know the trusted sources of information within the discipline, be able to keep an overview of the area being considered (the big picture), and consider the details. A synthesising mind can be both a searchlight, having a broad overview, seeing and making use of the links between disciplines or areas and monitoring changes in the area, and also be a laser beam, having in-depth knowledge within the area.

According to Gardner (2007) there are different types of synthesis:

- **fictional and non-fictional narratives**, where information from different sources is combined into a coherent whole – the types of narratives described in Chapter 23, which synthesise analysis of evidence from different participants into a fictional narrative (see also Bassey, 1998), are examples of this type of synthesis
- **taxonomies**, in which information is sorted and ordered
- **complex concepts**, in which new ideas are synthesised from a range of evidence
- **rules and aphorisms**, such as common phrases and folklore
- **powerful metaphors**, images and themes
- **embodiments without words**, such as can be encompassed within a piece of art, or a model
- **theories**, developed from a synthesis of ideas
- **meta-theories**, or overarching theories or paradigms that replace previous theories or encompass a number of different theories.

Critical discussion of findings

Synthesising involves breadth and depth of understanding, making links between different analyses and engaging in a deep and critical discussion of ideas, implications or models of thinking that have emerged from the analysis. Most importantly, it does not repeat the analysis, but moves forward from it to greater clarity, sophistication of ideas and understanding. It is sometimes tempting to repeat analysis or deviate into discussions that are very important to the researcher, but not grounded in the research evidence. In order to synthesise effectively, it may be sensible to identify clearly what will be achieved through the synthesis and how it builds on the research analysis (Gardner, 2007).

The 'Discussion of findings' section of a research report may start with a brief summary of the findings and then identify the main implications for further discussion. It is important to limit the discussion to the main implications so that the discussion can be deep and critical, rather than superficial. Each issue should be grounded in the research findings and have an implication for the researcher's practice and provision, and maybe some tentative implications for wider practice and provision.

Yates (2004) identifies three claims made of good research: that it should contribute to learning, have applications for teachers, and be scientifically based. The first two have implications for the researcher when discussing findings and this author would argue that the third is inappropriate in most interpretative educational research. Contribution to learning is a debatable area (Yates, 2004) and can take a number of forms; learning can be personal to the researcher or applicable to the wider educational community. Personal learning would be evident in the discussion, with the more sophisticated conceptual understandings that the research has developed being discussed. Learning for the wider educational community is often more appropriate for doctorates but most research adds to the wider learning in the area. Educational research should have some applications – that is, it should or could:

- be accessible to a wide range of professional practitioners and be written in an accessible way
- have an impact on practice and provision in the researcher's own context
- have some tentative applications to wider educational practice.

The discussion of each issue should consider (but not repeat) the analysis from the literature review and the primary data analysis, and then discuss them critically. Care needs to be taken to ensure that relationships between data are not over or under-emphasised, leading to incorrect results. Cooper (2010) believes in a systematic research synthesis using scientific guidelines, arguing that this does not necessarily inhibit innovative thinking, but poses challenges in collecting, evaluating and analysing data representing an original contribution to the area of research. Roberts (2007) identifies that:

'The process of interpretation is not a simple "mechanical" exercise, but involves "imagination" – connections, choices, insights'.

Roberts (2007, p. 72)

Presenting and analysing data are not enough, and the researcher needs to engage in a deep discussion, making connections between ideas, identifying relationships and extrapolating from the evidence in an innovative, creative, but not fictitious way. In this way, the skill of argumentation (Toulmin, 1958) should be exercised (Chapter 20).

Critical discussion will involve making links between policy, practice and research, recognising the tensions that exist between them, and noting the ambiguities and inconsistencies between the theory and the evidence from the research. The discussion will use reading from the literature review but also, where appropriate, new reading to reflect the issues being discussed. This is because the issues may be extensions of the ideas raised earlier in the research, or be new avenues that start in the data but extend beyond the original ideas or deviate from them. The discussion will explore the conceptual understanding in the area and extend this, demonstrating that the researcher has extended his or her personal understanding, and showing the contribution to the shared knowledge in the area. Roberts (2007) identifies the importance of remembering that the researcher interprets and theorises and does not just collect and state evidence. Rather, they compare and contrast ideas, juxtapose issues and think deeply about consequences. In this way, while this discussion is challenging and can be arduous it is also 'exciting, stimulating and rewarding' (Roberts, 2007, p. 75).

Gardner (2007) identifies components of synthesis: to have a goal, a starting point, a strategy and to draft and redraft. He believes that a goal should identify what the researcher hopes the synthesis will achieve and the starting point is the initial building block for the synthesis, so that the research can develop from this. The strategy can involve decisions about the type of synthesis to be employed (see above) and include the scientific guidelines as identified by Cooper (2010).

Box I Reflective task on critical discussion.

Review the quality of your discussion and check for coherence, continuity and compelling arguments. Be ruthlessly honest about your writing style – you are aiming for a style that is consistent, fluent and vivid, yet not overstated. As you do this, consider the following questions.

- Are research questions explicitly addressed?
- Is evidence from personal research used thoroughly?
- Is new evidence introduced without justification?
- Is evidence from reading integrated within the argument?
- Is the argument cogent and compelling or is it overstated, simplistic or over-generalised at times?

Conclusions

The conclusions to research are like an effective plenary, in that they should not simply repeat what has already been stated but drive the implications forward and identify how the research questions have been answered. They should sum up the implications as discussed in the 'Discussion of findings' and identify the meaning of the research, for the researcher and for the wider educational community, being careful not to overstate the generalisability of the results. One of Denscombe's (2002, p. 140) ten ground rules for research is that *'research should produce findings from which generalisations can be made'*. This rule is based on the premise that social research involves identification of how far the findings are replicated in, or representative of, others: students, teachers, parents, classes, schools, areas and so on. These may be 'fuzzy' generalisations as identified by Bassey (1998, 1999) where the research has looked at a sample of the whole population (see also Chapter 21) or more certain generalisations where the sample is representative of, and in proportion to, the population (Denscombe, 2002). In drawing conclusions, the researcher needs to be clear on the difference between generalising from the findings and assuming that the research is completely transferable. Transferring ideas from one piece of research to another context implies inferences that may not exist, although this may be the innovative aspect of the research (Denscombe, 2002; Roberts, 2007).

The conclusion, for Masters and Doctoral-level work, should also reflect on the impact of the research process on the personal and professional development of the researcher and evaluate the research undertaken. In evaluating the research, it is important to be objective and to be clear how the research could be improved. This may mean identifying how appropriate the research questions were, and whether they needed adapting during the research process. It may be that there was an inconsistency between the research questions and the data collected, which meant that the questions required adaptation, for example. In this way, research should not be seen as a completely predefined process, but rather an iterative and developmental process. If the methodology is later found to be less appropriate than another methodology, this should be recognised and discussed. If the methods were not ones that supported the collection of rich data, or other methods would have enhanced the research, this too should be acknowledged. It should be hoped that the researcher has developed his or her research skills through the process of researching and that, if the research were to be undertaken again, he or she would do it differently. This too should be acknowledged and the reasons discussed. In this way, the researcher should identify his or her personal and professional development.

Box 2 Reflective task on the quality of conclusions.

Review the quality of your conclusions by asking yourself the following questions.

- Is there an actual conclusion, rather than just a summary?
- Is the conclusion convincing, yet duly tentative?
- Has the research an apparent or potential impact on the educational setting?
- Does the conclusion justly claim to enhance our knowledge and understanding in some specific area?
- Do you reflect on your personal and professional learning through undertaking this research?

Box 3 Reflective task on coherence in the research report.

Use a table like the one shown to help you ensure that there is coherence between your 'Discussion of findings' and 'Conclusion', and the rest of the research report. Read through your research starting from the 'Conclusion' and working back to the 'Discussion of findings', and then eventually to the start. After each section, use the table to identify the main themes emerging. At the end, look to see if the themes are consistent across the sections.

Literature review	Analysis and outcomes	Discussion of findings (synthesis, discussion, summary)		Conclusions	
Data		Relationship to research questions	Issues emerging	Implications for future practice specifically and education generally (tentatively)	Further research

References

Bassey, M. (1998) *Fuzzy Generalisation: An approach to building educational theory*. Paper presented at the British Educational Research Association annual conference, The Queen's University of Belfast, Northern Ireland, 27–30 August 1998. Available at: www.leeds.ac.uk/educol/documents/000000801.htm (accessed 15 July 2011).

Bassey, M. (1999) *Case Study Research in Educational Settings*. Buckingham: Open University Press.

Cooper, H. (2010) *Research Synthesis and Meta-Analysis. A step by step approach*. Fourth edition. Thousand Oaks, California: Sage.

Denscombe, M. (2002) *Ground Rules for Good Research. A ten-point guide for social researchers*. Maidenhead: Open University Press.

Gardner, H. (2007) *Five Minds for the Future*. Harvard: Harvard Business School.

Roberts, B. (2007) *Getting the Most out of the Research Experience. What every researcher needs to know*. London: Sage.

Toulmin, S. (1958) *The Uses of Argument*. Cambridge: Cambridge University Press.

Yates, L. (2004) *What Does Good Education Research Look Like?* Maidenhead: Open University Press.

Chapter 25

Presenting the research and findings and offering recommendations

Jane Johnston

When the research has been completed, it needs to be presented. There is a question, though, of what exactly needs to be presented, and to whom. The whole research, if it is for an award, has its readership, the examination system, as a form of rigorous scrutiny. Making an award at Masters or Doctoral level is recognition of the value of the whole piece of work. There are, though, other audiences. The research can be rewritten in the form of a book or monograph that is made available commercially. Any reinterpretation for this audience is determined by the author and publisher – perhaps it will focus on the methodology as a service to other researchers, or on the literature search, as a review of up-to-date literature to a research community. Sometimes, and this happens often in science education, the book is written for discerning practising teachers, to share in a readable form the process and significant outcomes for these educators. One or more research papers may be written, drawing on the same research, with some focusing on issues of methodology such as validity and reliability, and others on analytical processes, while others may focus on new knowledge claims, providing sufficient but not comprehensive data to substantiate those claims. Some researchers reconstruct their research, or parts of it, for practising teachers through professional journals such as *School Science Review* and *Primary Science*, although this seems not to be so common these days. More commonly, nowadays, researchers attend professional conferences to provide oral or poster presentations to support reflective discussion. These usually focus on specific findings rather than the literature survey or methodology, and data are often aggregated for simplicity. Researchers may also reconstruct their research as professional development activities, conducted by themselves or CPD providers. Sometimes, researchers also contribute to textbook writing, for school-aged students, or for teachers on teacher education courses. Output is often in traditional written form, but may involve other forms of activity, such as card sorts, debates, poster production and concept maps. The ASE provides a number of opportunities to present practitioner research findings, through the Annual Conference, regional symposia and regional conferences and through publications such as *Education in Science*, the *Journal of Emergent Science*, *Primary Science* and *School Science Review*. More information can be found on the ASE website www.ase.org.uk

Writing up research

Writing is an iterative process. It should begin at the earliest stages of the research and continue throughout the research proposal, research journal and drafts of sections or chapters. It is important not to leave the writing until the end of the research, as this can lead to a lack of coherence between the research design, analysis and synthesis (and in fact the writing process helps to clarify and connect intent, approach and findings). Writing is also an essential tool for researchers who are being assessed through the presentation of ideas in short written assignments, longer dissertations, or in peer-reviewed journals. Excellent research can fall down at this last hurdle if the written word does not convey clearly the aim(s), outcomes and excellence of the research, and this emphasises the importance of the writing process.

The structure for the final report is often dictated by the guidelines given to the researcher by the awarding body (in the case of a thesis) or by the journal. However, decisions about structure need to be taken with the research methodology in mind as well as the audience. Different methodologies may need to written up in different ways, so a report of a piece of action research that tells the story of actions, and analysis of those actions (Elliott, 1991), will look very different from the case study research that synthesises ideas into a piece of narrative (Bassey, 1999; Clough, 2002), and different again from a piece of empirical research. When you decide your methodology (Chapter 22) you need to consider what the study will look like in its final written form and keep this in mind throughout the data collection and analytical processes, ensuring that the relevant primary data are collected and written up in a form that is appropriate to the type of research.

Table 1 provides a basic structure for the written aspect. Each researcher needs to provide his or her own structure for the written work, which best shows his or her understanding of both research and the subject being researched.

Table 1 Writing models for different methodologies.

Survey, Comparative, Historical, Case study					Narrative, Story		Action research	
Introduction					Introduction		Introduction	
Review of literature	Methodology and research methods				Methodology and reseach methods	Review of literature	Review of literature	Methodology and research methods
Methodology and research methods	Review of literature				Review of literature	Methodology and research methods	Methodology and research methods	Review of literature
Analysis and outcomes					Analysis and outcomes		Analysis of Action Step 1	
Method 1	Then	Case study 1	Issue 1	Question 1	Complete story, narrative	Narrative 1	Analysis of Action Step 2	
Method 2	Now	Case study 2	Issue 2	Question 2		Narrative 2	Analysis of Action Step 3	
Method 3		Case study 3 etc.	Issue 3 etc.	Question 3 etc.		Narrative 3	Analysis of Action Step 4 etc.	
Discussion of findings Question 1 Question 2 Question 3 etc.				Discussion of findings	Discussion of findings Question 1 Question 2 Question 3		Discussion of findings Question 1 Question 2 Question 3	
Conclusion including evaluation of research and professional development					Conclusion including evaluation of research and professional development		Conclusion including evaluation of research and professional development	

Box 1 Reflective task on report structure.

Look at Table 1 and decide what methodology fits your research focus. Think how your research will be set out in the final report, from the guidelines. This is the structure you need to work towards.

- How does the structure allow you to be innovative?
- What are the constraints that the structure imposes on your research?
- How can you overcome the constraints?

Writing for a Masters award

The final Masters dissertation is designed to enable you to examine, in some depth, aspects of practice of particular relevance to your own educational setting. Research and reflection on your practice will form an essential part of your work, but the discussion should be structured to set the particular investigation(s) you undertake in a wider context and to evaluate it in the light of current research and contemporary educational debate. The organisation of your written report should aim to clarify the relationship between these different elements. A possible structure could be as set out in the following sections.

Preliminaries

i   title page
ii   table of contents listing each chapter of the dissertation in sequence, with page numbers
iii list of tables and/or figures included in the text – one clear way of doing this is to number them within the chapter (for example, in Chapter 3 find 3.1, 3.2, and so on); each table or figure requires a clear explanatory title, followed by a list of acronyms, if appropriate
iv   acknowledgements, if any, should be on a separate page following the table of contents – however, there is a need to respect the right to anonymity of both individuals and institutions that form the subjects of the research
v   signed ethical declaration
vi   an abstract – that is, a short summary (the number of words will be identified by the awarding institution); the abstract should be written in the past tense and identify:

- the focus and context of the study
- the particular research question(s) raised
- the methodology and research techniques used
- any conclusions reached and recommendations offered for others.

Introduction

When writing the introduction to the research, it is helpful if the researcher addresses questions such as:

- 'Why is the study relevant?'
- 'How does it add to understanding of the area?'
- 'What is the expected professional value of the findings?
- 'What are the exact questions that you seek to answer?'

The introduction should identify and describe the focus of the research and the rationale for the research. It should identify the context in which the research takes place, the participants involved and situate the researcher into the research. It should arrest and engage the reader and ensure both empathy and interest in the research quest.

Review of the literature

A more extensive discussion of the literature review can be found in Chapter 20. The review of literature provides the theoretical framework for empirical aspects of the research and further exploration and discussion of educational issues. The researcher needs to demonstrate, through the review of literature, awareness of the ideas, issues and research that have preceded this project, so that an informed argument can be developed that includes analytical critique and theoretical models. This may involve:

- an outline of the history and development of theories, policies and practices in the area of interest
- a survey of recent research into the area considering the methods used as well as the conclusions reached
- a reflection of tensions, disagreements, omissions and ambiguities in the literature
- an identification of how the projected research will contribute to understanding in the area.

Methodology and research methods

Details of this section can be found in Chapters 21 and 22. This section of the research dissertation should provide a clear rationale for the research methodology, detail of the context in which the work was undertaken, and description, development and justification of the research methods used to acquire and analyse information. It should also include a statement of ethical considerations. In this section the researcher needs to convince the reader of his or her awareness of the strengths and limitations of the research design, including the reliability and validity of both the data collection and the strategies to be used for analysis of data.

Analysis and outcomes

The structure of this section is crucial to enable the reader to understand how and what data were collected and share in the understanding of the analysis. Decisions about how to subdivide this section of the report depend on the methodology, which helps to structure the writing (see Table 1). The most common way to divide the section is to focus on each research instrument in turn, so that the data collected using it is analysed systematically. However, the structure for action research will be different, where the outcomes are often recorded as a chronological sequence of action steps reflecting on findings and how these influenced plans. For case study and narrative, the structure may again be chronological, with the chronology being the narrative sequence or focus on separate case studies.

The evidence on which the discussion is based should be incorporated in the text (graphs, interviews, photographs and so on) so that there is coherence and the reader does not have to frequently look in the appendices. Indeed, stating 'as you can see from the appendix' can be very frustrating for the reader, who is effectively being expected to undertake the analysis for themselves, rather than have the analysis explained for them by the researcher. Longer extracts, from which the data are taken (such as transcripts, or detailed numerical data) may be included as an appendix and quoted in the text, and this helps the reader see the full context of the data. Other data, such as questionnaires, video footage and so on, do not need to be in the appendices, but can be kept in a separate archive.

This section simply presents relevant outcomes clearly and succinctly. It is essential that the researcher analyses the findings and does not simply describe them.

Discussion of findings

In this section, the researcher needs to synthesise and succinctly summarise data (Chapter 24). The synthesis considers what the research contributes to each of the research questions, reflects on the literature review and how to further develop the arguments begun in that section. The empirical research is likely to prompt the researcher to suggest further research, extend reading and introduce new texts and arguments at this point. The researcher should consider alternative interpretations and state findings accordingly, probably quite tentatively. This part of the dissertation is likely to be one of the longest, and the most interesting part to write, as well as being the most challenging.

Conclusions and issues for further research

Like an effective plenary, the conclusion should not simply repeat material already stated but drive the implications forward. It is important not to overstate the generalisability of the research results but, on the other hand, implications for both the site of the research and for the wider educational community should be considered. The conclusion should also reflect on the impact of the research process on the personal and professional development of the author and participants involved in the research.

Appendices

The appendices follow the main text and conclusions and in most dissertations are not included in the word count. They should include supporting material (for example, the research tools used, transcripts of discussions, students' work, teachers' plans, extracts from recordings, tables of results, and so on) or any other evidence which, if included in the main text, would interrupt the flow. However, only material that is directly referred to in the text should be included (and it should be referred to in chronological order). The rest of the evidence you simply store in an archive because it may be of further use in subsequent writing and research activities. Some awarding bodies require the appendices to include a signed ethical declaration confirming that you have read and adhered to research ethics guidance.

References

A bibliographical list of references is always the last item in the written report. It must include every published work referred to in the text in such a way that the reader could easily locate the full text. There may be an additional list of further background reading that is not directly referred to.

Box 2 Reflective task on questions to consider when writing a dissertation.

Look at the questions in below, which are designed to help you write the different sections of your dissertation.

Abstract
Does the abstract clearly state the context, the questions, the research project and the conclusions?

Title
Is the title clear and to the point?

Style

Is there an overuse of exclamations and rhetorical questions?

Is there an overuse of the passive tense?

Are gendered pronouns used inappropriately?

Are sentences too long and complex?

Are paragraphs fragmented and under-developed?

Does analysis and synthesis outweigh description?

Is there a consistent and attractive personal writing style?

Is there a clear flow between chapters?

Presentation

Are conventions followed consistently? For example:

- order of headings
- use of capital letters e.g. key stage or Key Stage?
- use of Harvard referencing system (author date: page)

Is punctuation in bibliography and references consistent?

Are pages clear and uncluttered?

Are all figures and diagrams explicitly titled and listed in the contents?

Is anonymity meticulously observed for individuals and institutions?

Are commas and apostrophes used accurately?

Are there any repetitions that can be cut?

Atherton (2005) notes the importance of addressing the module outcomes in the written dissertation, but also that this does not mean they have to be addressed directly. The evidence for the outcomes may be implicit rather than explicit, but they must be evident to any reader, so that a dissertation *'imbued with similar understanding, and no contrary evidence of ignoring the ethical dimension, would amply demonstrate the achievement of the outcome'* (Atherton, 2005).

Writing for a journal article or book

Writing for a research journal is an exact and particular skill and the final product needs to be accurate. Each journal will have information on the scope of the journal, guidance on types of papers and written style and criteria to review the article. It is important to look at these to ensure the research fits with the journal and can be written in the journal style. Criteria for peer review are likely to include:

- relevance to the journal's aims and scope
- contribution to the knowledge base
- quality of research
- quality of written communication.

Doing research

A monograph is likely to be a longer piece of academic writing and can therefore expand on the ideas and discuss issues more fully. Some publishers specialise in monographs and they would also advertise review criteria and support the writing process. They will have a commissioning editor who will talk through a proposal and send it to review before the full text is written. The advice given by reviewers can be quite contradictory, but this does not have to be so if the publisher/editor has chosen reviewers carefully and given them clear guidance about the purpose of the review and the criteria by which the work is to be reviewed. Wolcott (2009) identifies the value of a good editor, who can give constructive advice and support the writing process. The researcher may seek support from a critical friend, a senior academic (many higher education institutions have an academic whose role is to support practitioner research, writing and publication), or a journal editor. A good editor will provide constructive advice but not attempt to reconstruct the written work so that the researcher's voice is lost.

Empirical research articles and research monographs should provide information about the research in a similar way to the dissertation but in a more succinct way:

- abstract
- background/knowledge base
- methodology and methods
- results
- discussion of findings
- references

Writing for the professional audience involves a different writing technique (Henn, Weinstein and Foard, 2006) and the challenge here is to make the research accessible without 'dumbing' down. Articles are likely to be very short and should engage the reader, make the research understandable and focus on the implications and relevance of the research for practice and provision.

The audience for professional texts is not just different, it is also potentially larger and so this can be a way of communicating the research to a larger group of academics and professionals. Research can also be written into chapters of edited books or longer professional books. Edited books contain chapters written by different authors collated by a book editor and will involve a commissioning and publishing editor as well. Editors come in a variety of forms and it is useful for the researcher to find out who they are writing for as this will make the process easier. Most editors are sympathetic to the academic and professional context and are very aware of the publication issues. It is important to ensure that the integrity of the research is not impaired by a desire for consistency of style or content and the researcher may have to negotiate the content with an editor to ensure that what they want to communicate remains intact.

The longer professional book can spend significant time considering the practical implications for teachers and look more explicitly at research into practice. In this type of publication, the author has more freedom to present their research in a way that they feel best conveys the messages.

Writing tips

Each researcher will have the ideal environment or time of day for writing (Henn *et al.* 2006). Some will require quiet and comfortable environments and others will listen to music or the radio while writing. Most will write directly using a computer but a few will prefer to write by hand and type up later. There is not one way of writing or one environment suitable for all.

Henn *et al.* (2006) and Trafford and Lesham (2008) recognise the importance of writing for an audience and being very clear what type of research is being written. Indeed, Trafford and Lesham consider that the researcher should bear in mind from the outset what the final outputs of the research are. This will enable the researcher to improve the quality of the output.

Thody (2006) identifies that beginnings and endings of written work are important. The beginning captures the reader and the end leaves them with a sense of the worth of the research. Thody provides some objectives for abstracts, executive summaries, key points and prefaces in published work. These include *'outlines that guide'*, *'invitations that attract'* and *'summaries that grab'* (Thody, 2006, p. 162). Continuing to write in an engaging style will help the reader remain with the text, rather than drift off.

The accuracy of the text is also important. Being literate is essential for all publication of written work and this means that the work should be proofread to eradicate as far as possible all spelling and typographical errors, grammatical errors, misuses of words and *'academic obscurantism'* (Atherton, 2005). Accuracy of referencing helps to avoid plagiarism. Neville (2007, p. 7) identifies five principles of referencing:

1 the principle of intellectual property, thus avoiding plagiarism
2 the principle of access, providing references that can be easily accessed and checked by the reader
3 the principle of economy, summarising evidence from referencing in a succinct way
4 the principle of standardisation, using a standard system of referencing (usually the name, date or Harvard system)
5 the principle of transparency – that is, avoiding ambiguities, and making meanings clear.

Criticality is an important feature of good academic writing (see also Chapter 24). This does not mean being critical or criticising (Atherton, 2005) but comparing and contrasting, seeking out and exploring ambiguities and challenging assumptions and assertions. Criticality involves use of evidence to support arguments, exploring the values implicit in the research and making them explicit. Criticality also involves recognition and deep discussion of tensions between policy and practice and research, persuasive arguments and the use of evidence strategically as part of a deep analysis or discussion.

One problem in writing that adversely affects criticality can be that there is irrelevant data used in the final report. This may occur when the researcher has collected a great deal of data, much of it relevant to the area of research and informing his or her conceptual understanding, but some being not directly relevant to the study and not answering the research questions. For this reason, it is advisable for the researcher to sift through the data and not use irrelevant material. This material is not wasted as it has informed ideas and can be used on other occasions. The urge to sneak it into the work by adding it in the discussion of findings or putting it in an appendix may be strong, but it will just detract, and not enhance.

Doing research

Another pitfall to avoid is assigning meanings to the research findings without evidence, and over-inflating the application of the research findings. The researcher who is desperately seeking significance can only be disappointed. If the data are not as conclusive as the researcher would like, it can be tempting to try to persuade the reader that they are more significant than they really are. The researcher needs to be honest and remember that with small-scale qualitative research it is less likely that findings will be of huge significance. It is more important to look at the data more deeply and try to understand it; to see if there is more to it, if one looks carefully. The researcher should remember too that sometimes things that do not turn out the way one expects prove more interesting than those that do!

Providing coherence in the text will help to make a better piece of writing. This means that the researcher should provide explanations and make things clear for the reader; there is nothing worse than reading a piece of work that frustrates or is unfathomable. For example, research questions are decided early in the research process, but may change as the research progresses. They help structure the work and so need to be constantly referred to and, if changed, the changes need to be consistent throughout the written work to ensure its focus and coherence. In speaking, we often tend to repeat statements in different words to reinforce points. In writing, subtly different terms can create ambiguities for the reader and prevent coherence. In writing it is therefore important to make clear whether two words or phrases mean exactly the same thing or not (for example, midday assistants and midday supervisors; children and students; oracy and talk). If the two terms do in fact have the same meaning in your context, it is probably best to use only one to avoid suggesting otherwise. Writing can also be made more coherent by structuring the work using sub-headings related to the methodology, so that the final written report clearly reflects the methodology used in the research. Finally, greater coherence is achieved when the researcher expresses the meaning of others' work by expressing it in his or her own words, rather than quoting large sections of the original publication. The researcher should try to tell a clear story without repetition of issues and themes.

Clarity of the written word is an important part of communication. The use of words (sometimes called 'weasel' words) that do not really say anything detracts from this. Words, such as 'basically' and 'generally' may pad out the work, but don't really add anything significant. Other examples include:

'It has long been known ...' or 'I did not look up the reference'

'It is evident ...' or '**someone** might believe me'

'It is believed that ...' or 'I think'

'Typically ...' or 'I have not got a clue'

'Nevertheless ...' or 'I am going to keep going'.

PsyPAG (2005, pp. 48–49)

Research should be written in plain English and clarify meanings.

Most scientific reports are written in the passive tense but this does not have to be the case for educational research. It is more important that the researcher 'owns' the inquiry, so the use of active verbs in the first person ('I found ...', 'we developed ...' and so on) can be appropriate and professional. It is important, however, not to move from one style to another and to maintain consistency of writing style.

Box 3 Reflective task on writing.

Use the writing tips provided in this section to check work in progress or finished work.

Presenting research

Oral presentations can be good ways to communicate research findings but also can help to articulate understandings and ultimately help with written communication. A researcher who seeks out opportunities to speak out and articulate ideas is likely to advantage their personal and professional development. Critical friends groups, action learning sets and informal presentations as part of research programmes can provide opportunities for small and larger group discussions and help clarify ideas.

Formally presenting research at conferences and in assessed presentations also helps the researcher to articulate ideas coherently, although, of course, the audience is different and so the presentation style needs to be adapted to take this into account (Thody, 2006; Gray, 2009). Oral presentation requires the researcher to engage with the audience and it is better to have eye contact, referring to notes rather than reading from them, or using notes only as a prompt. An excellent visual and oral presentation would motivate and engage the audience and have a clear sense of purpose. It is easy to spend considerable time making presentations visually striking and even engaging, but failing to have a clear objective and not engaging the reader orally, and so the presentation fails in its purpose. The structure of the presentation needs to be carefully considered. It is better to have main bullet points that are expanded upon, rather than a huge amount of data that the audience cannot fully comprehend. Gray (2009) considers that it is best to present two or three key messages clearly than overload the audience with dense slides of data than cannot possibly be explored deeply in a short space of time. They also identify that engagement is enhanced through the use of personal stories or metaphors. The use of multimedia enables quality visual cues to engage, but the resource fails if:

- there are too many slides
- slides are too densely packed
- slides are written in small writing that cannot be read from a distance
- the researcher reads from the slides
- the researcher is looking at the screen and not the audience.

Poster presentations can use the available technology to create a poster that conveys the research findings succinctly and visually. They can be particularly useful if the data collected includes images, diagrams or simple tables. They can be less useful if the research has complex data and analysis that cannot be succinctly and clearly displayed visually. As with oral presentations that use visual resources, poster presentations cannot contain everything the researcher has done; indeed the worst posters are simply a written paper stuck on a wall. They need to convey the message in an A1 format, using pictures, diagrams and a few words. Occasionally a separate paper is presented with the poster, but this does not mean that the researcher can or should spend less time on the poster or be less concerned in conveying the message succinctly. Poster presentations also involve an element of oral presentation, as – depending on the conference – the researcher will either formally present their research in a few words or a few minutes, or informally discuss their poster and the research with others. In the former situation, the posters may be presented in a timed slot, but in the latter they may be set out and left for a longer period of time so that a wider audience can view them. This actually can enable the researcher to communicate their research to a wider audience.

Box 4 Reflective task on oral and poster presentations.

You can use published criteria from conferences to review your own oral or poster presentation synopsis before submitting it to a conference. Consider the following.

- Have you addressed the conference aims?
- Is the rationale for the research clear?
- Are the methodology and methods clearly linked to the research questions?
- Is the analytical framework clear?
- Have you identified the main implications of the research?
- Can the implications be tracked to the analysis?

You can also present your research to some critical friends and ask them to provide guidance for improvement. You may ask them to consider whether or not:

- you clearly articulate the research orally and visually
- you engage the audience
- the research design, analysis and findings are clear.

They can also identify questions that a more formal audience may ask and so help you to prepare more effectively for your presentation.

References

Atherton, J.S. (2005) *Academic Practice: Writing at master's level.* Available at: www.doceo.co.uk /academic/m_writing.htm (accessed 15 July 2011).

Bassey, M. (1999) *Case Study Research in Educational Settings.* Buckingham: Open University Press.

Clough, P. (2002) *Narratives and Fictions in Educational Research.* Buckingham: Open University Press.

Elliott, J. (1991) *Action Research for Educational Change.* Buckingham: Open University Press.

Gray, D.E. (2009) *Doing Research in the Real World.* Second edition. London: Sage.

Henn, M., Weinstein, M. and Foard, N. (2006) *A Critical Introduction to Social Research.* Second edition. London: Sage.

Neville, C. (2007) *The Complete Guide to Referencing and Avoiding Plagiarism.* Maidenhead: Open University Press.

PsyPAG Quarterly June 2005: 48–49.

Thody, A. (2006) *Writing and Presenting Research.* London: Sage.

Trafford, V. and Lesham, S. (2008) *Stepping Stones to Achieving Your Doctorate by Focusing on your Viva from the Start.* Maidenhead: Open University Press.

Wolcott, H.F. (2009) *Writing Up Qualitative Research.* Third edition. Thousand Oaks, California: Sage.

Glossary

Action research   Action research is a cyclic methodology whereby researchers attempt to develop and research an area of practice through a reflective cycle of planning, doing and reviewing, with each cycle of research and development being planned as a result of the analysis of the previous cycle's actions.

Analysis   A research skill involving breaking down ideas, reading or observations to understand them and their constituent parts.

Argument   An informed or evidence-based assertion or opinion. The skill of argument involves using evidence to support declarative statements and analyse counter arguments.

Case study   A research methodology that involves the collection and presentation of detailed information about a particular participant or small group, frequently including the accounts of subjects themselves.

Correlation   1 A common statistical analysis, usually abbreviated as r, which measures the degree of relationship between pairs of interval variables in a sample. The range of correlation is from -1.00 to zero to +1.00.

2 A relationship between two sets of variables, though a correlation does not necessarily indicate a causal relationship.

Covariate   A product of the correlation of two related variables times their standard deviations. Used in true experiments to measure the difference of treatment between them.

Critical listening   A practitioner research skill that involves the ability not only to pay attention to what is heard, but to question the information and ask for clarification.

Deductive   A form of reasoning in which conclusions are formulated about particulars from general or universal premises.

Dependability   Being able to account for changes in the design of the study and the changing conditions surrounding what was studied.

Design flexibility   A quality of an observational study allowing researchers to pursue inquiries on new topics or questions that emerge from initial research.

Deviation   The distance between the mean and a particular data point in a given distribution.

Discussion   A research method involving informal questioning and/or listening to conversations or dialogue.

Glossary

Empirical research	'The process of developing systematised knowledge gained from observations that are formulated to support insights and generalisations about the phenomena under study.' Lauer, J. M. and Asher, J. W. (1988). *Composition Research: Empirical Designs.* Oxford: Oxford University Press
Epistemology	The study of, or theory of, knowledge.
Ethics	Moral principles or values. The conduct of research to protect the individual, group, institution or educational integrity.
Ethnography	A methodology involving the study of groups and/or cultures over a period of time. The goal of this type of research is to comprehend the particular group/culture through observer immersion into the culture or group (see also *naturalistic inquiry*).
Experiment	A research methodology that creates an environment in which to observe and interpret the results of a research question. A key element in experimental research is that participants in a study are randomly assigned to groups. In an attempt to create a causal model (that is, to discover the causal origin of a particular phenomenon), groups are treated differently and measurements are conducted to determine if different treatments appear to lead to different effects.
Factor analysis	A statistical test that explores relationships among data. The test explores which variables in a data set are most related to each other. In a carefully constructed survey, for example, factor analysis can yield information on patterns of responses, not simply data on a single response. Larger tendencies may then be interpreted, indicating behaviour trends rather than simply responses to specific questions.
Generalisability	The extent to which research findings and conclusions from a study conducted on a sample population can be applied to the population at large.
Grounded theory	Practice of developing theories from research. Theories are grounded in research, but researchers add their own insight into why those experiences exist.
Hypothesis	A tentative explanation based on theory to predict a causal relationship between variables.
Illuminative evaluation	A research methodology involving evaluation that attempts to understand and assess against success criteria.
Inductive analysis	A form of analysis based on inductive reasoning; a researcher using inductive analysis starts with answers, but forms questions throughout the research process.
Interview	A research tool in which a researcher asks questions of participants; interviews may be audio- or video-recorded for later transcription and analysis.

Narrative inquiry	A qualitative research methodology based on a researcher's narrative account of the investigation, not to be confused with a narrative examined by the researcher as data (which is a method).
Naturalistic inquiry	Observational research of a group in its natural setting.
Ontology	The study of the nature of being, existence or reality in general, as well as of the basic categories of being and their relations.
Paradigm	A philosophical or theoretical framework.
Phenomenology	A qualitative research approach concerned with understanding certain group behaviours from that group's point of view.
Positivism	Positivism takes the approach that a 'scientific method' based on empirical evidence and subject to positive verification from evidence related to the senses, including measurement, is the only valid way to discover true knowledge.
Practitioner research	A research methodology undertaken by practitioners into their own practice.
Qualitative research	A research paradigm in which the researcher explores relationships using textual or pictorial, rather than quantitative (numerical), data. Case study, action research and ethnography are considered forms of qualitative research. Results are not usually considered fully generalisable, but are often transferable.
Quantitative research	A research paradigm in which the researcher explores relationships using numerical data. Survey can (in some cases) involve quantitative research. Results can often be generalised, though this is not always the case.
Quasi-experiment	A research methodology, similar to true experiments, but which uses non-randomised groups. It incorporates interpretation and transferability in order to compensate for lack of control of variables.
Random sampling	The process used in research to draw a sample of a population strictly by chance, yielding no discernible pattern beyond chance. Random sampling can be accomplished by first numbering the population, then selecting the sample according to a table of random numbers or using a random-number computer generator. The sample is said to be random because there is no regular or discernible pattern or order. Random sample selection is used under the assumption that sufficiently large samples assigned randomly will exhibit a distribution comparable to that of the population from which the sample is drawn.
Reflection-in-action	Reflection during the course of an action (while doing something).
Reflection-on-action	Reflection after an action (after you have done it).
Reflective journal	A journal that notes all ideas, reading, observations and analyses and is used to develop reflective practice or research practice.

Glossary

Survey
A research method that includes at least one question, which is either open-ended or closed, and employs an oral or written method for asking these questions. The goal of a survey is to gain specific information about either a specific group or a representative sample of a particular group. Results are typically used to understand the attitudes, beliefs or knowledge of a particular group.

Synthesis
To take analyses from a wide range of primary and secondary evidence and put them back together in order to draw conclusions, make sense of the whole, draw inferences, produce new ideas or models and identify implications.

Validity
The degree to which a study accurately reflects or assesses the specific concept that the researcher is attempting to measure. A method can be reliable, consistently measuring the same thing, but not valid.

Index

Index

Index

Index